Treatise on Nature and Grace

TREATISE ON NATURE AND GRACE

NICOLAS MALEBRANCHE

Translated with an introduction and notes by
PATRICK RILEY

CLARENDON PRESS · OXFORD
1992

Oxford University Press, Walton Street, Oxford OX2 6DP
Oxford New York Toronto
Delhi Bombay Calcutta Madras Karachi
Petaling Jaya Singapore Hong Kong Tokyo
Nairobi Dar es Salaam Cape Town
Melbourne Auckland
and associated companies in
Berlin Ibadan

Oxford is a trade mark of Oxford University Press

Published in the United States
by Oxford University Press, New York

British Library Cataloguing in Publication Data
Data available

Library of Congress Cataloging in Publication Data
Malebranche, Nicolas, 1638–1715.
[Traité de la nature et de la grace. English]
Treatise on nature and grace / Nicolas Malebranche; translated,
with an introduction and notes by Patrick Riley.
Translation of: Traité de la nature et de la grace.
Includes bibliographical references and index.
1. Nature—Religious aspects—Christianity—Early works to 1800.
2. Grace (Theology)—Early works to 1800. 3. God—Will—Early works
to 1800. I. Riley, Patrick, 1941– . II. Title.
BT695.5.M3513   1992   234—dc20   92–9612
ISBN 0–19–824832–6

Typeset by Hope Services (Abingdon) Ltd
Printed in Great Britain
by Biddles Ltd.
Guildford and King's Lynn

In Memoriam
MICHAEL OAKESHOTT
1901–1990

Acknowledgements

It is a pleasure to be able to acknowledge the kindness of those who have made possible the first English version of Malebranche's *Treatise of Nature and Grace* to appear since 1695. First and foremost, Mrs Angela Blackburn of Oxford University Press deserves thanks for countless, thoughtful helps which sustained me during the two years' labour which went into the volume. Encouraging notes—usually granting extra time!—made the whole enterprise possible.

It is also satisfying to be able to thank Princeton University Press for its generous permission to reuse some parts of my *The General Will before Rousseau* (1986) in the Introduction; without that permission I would have had to rewrite passages which (I thought) were already as adequate as I could make them. And I would not have had enough free time to produce this edition at all, had not the National Endowment for the Humanities awarded me a timely research grant which liberated me—a grant fleshed out by the Research Committee of the University of Wisconsin (Madison), which has treated me with unfailing generosity for twenty years.

Various libraries in France and England also offered me much-appreciated help. The Bibliothèque Nationale, Paris, kindly furnished the portrait of Malebranche which appears on the dust-jacket; and at Oxford University both the Philosophy Library and the Maison Française cheerfully placed needed volumes at my disposal.

The whole project would have come to nothing without the constant support of my wife, Joan A. Riley, who generously typed the whole manuscript, and who pulled me out of errors and absurdities which her fine Catholic education made visible to her. It is she who makes my whole scholarly life possible—and the rest of my life as well.

I dedicate this edition of *Nature and Grace* to the memory of Michael Oakeshott, who died in December 1990 in his ninetieth year. It is to Oakeshott that I owe my whole intellectual life: my reading of his introduction to Hobbes's *Leviathan* when I was 17 was so inspiring that I determined to take up moral and political philosophy for my life's work. Later he was my tutor at the London School of Economics—he taught me much of what I know, and the memory of his elegant, graceful lectures is unforgettable.

After his retirement he was able to reread all of his favourite works—not least those in theology (which had been the subject of his earliest published essays in the late 1920s). At our last meeting, in May 1990, he generously encouraged my work on Malebranche, and gave me helpful advice about seventeenth-century French theology. And in his last long letter to me he said that

during the last couple of years since I came to live here [in Dorset], spending much of my time re-reading all the books which I first read 50 or 60 years ago, I have gone back to 'theology'—or rather, to reflection upon religion. And I would like, more than anything else, to extend those brief pages in *On Human Conduct* into an essay (you know how I admire and value this literary form) on religion, and particularly on the Christian religion. This ambition came to me, partly, from my re-reading all that St Augustine wrote—St Augustine and Montaigne, the two most remarkable men who have ever lived.

Had Oakeshott lived, he would surely have discussed the Malebranche who synthesized Augustinian theology and modern French thought; now that work will never appear, and we are permanently the poorer for it.

P.R.

Oxford
June 1991

Contents

Biographical Note		xi
A Note on the Text		xiv
Biographical Sketches		xvii
Introduction		I
Treatise on Nature and Grace by Nicolas Malebranche		105
Excerpt of a Letter		107
Notice		110
Discourse I	On the Necessity of General Laws of Nature and of Grace	112
Discourse II	On the Laws of Grace in Particular, and on the Occasional Causes Which Govern Them and Which Determine Their Efficacy	138
Discourse III	On Grace. On the Way in Which It Acts in Us	169
Illustration	What It Is to Act by General Wills, and by Particular Wills	195
Selected Critical Bibliography		217
Index		221

Biographical Note

Nicolas Malebranche, whose birth and death dates correspond exactly to those of Louis XIV (1638–1715), was born in Paris, the son of a secretary to Louis XIII and of a mother whose brother had been Viceroy of Canada. Owing to poor health (including curvature of the spine), Malebranche was privately educated; only at the age of 16 did he become a student at the Collège de la Marche, and this was followed by theological studies at the Sorbonne (1656–9). The Scholastic education which he received at the Sorbonne was 'distasteful' to him; he prepared for, but did not receive, a *baccalauréat* in theology. He was received into the Oratoire (founded by Cardinal Bérulle) in 1660 and, after further studies in ecclesiastical history, linguistics, and the Bible, was ordained a priest in 1664.

Nothing in Malebranche's life up to this point gave the slightest hint that he would become 'the greatest French metaphysician' after Descartes; his theology teachers, indeed, had judged him 'mediocre'. But in 1664 Malebranche stumbled across Descartes's posthumously published *De l'homme*; and, in André's celebrated account (*Vie du R. P. Malebranche*), he was so 'ecstatic' that he experienced 'such violent palpitations of the heart that he was obliged to leave his book at frequent intervals, and to interrupt his reading of it in order to breathe more easily'. Thereafter Malebranche conceived his life's work as the conciliation of Cartesianism and of Augustinianism; certainly he read each in the light of the other.

The first fruit of this synthetic operation was the treatise *De la recherche de la vérité* (1674–5), which urged that human beings will grasp 'clear and distinct' ideas provided by reason only when the passions are 'silent'—only when they have been delivered 'little by little from the illusions of our senses, from the visions of our imagination, and from the impression which the imagination of other men makes upon our mind' (*Recherche* II. 3). The *Search after Truth* was widely admired, even by Jansenists such as Antoine Arnauld; and the volume of *Éclaircissements* which Malebranche added to the *Recherche* in the 1678 edition brought about no great controversy. The sixteenth 'Illustration', however, had intimated that God governs the realms of nature and of grace equally through simple, constant, uniform, general 'Cartesian' laws, not through *Providence particulière* and miracles; and when these thoughts were fully worked up into the *Traité de la nature et de la grâce* (published in 1680), Malebranche was engulfed by a wave of controversy which surrounded him for the rest of his philosophical life. Antoine Arnauld tried to suppress publication of *Nature et grâce*, actually borrowing the manuscript from the Dutch publisher; Bossuet attacked the treatise publicly during the funeral of the Queen of France (1683); Pierre Jurieu insisted that Malebranche's *recherche de la généralité* had 'ruined' divine providence. On the other side, Leibniz and Bayle pronounced *Nature et grâce* a work of genius— though both later had strong reservations.

Thrust into notorious prominence, Malebranche spent the 1680s defending himself against the assaults of Antoine Arnauld—his responses fill four volumes—and in writing the *Méditations chrétiennes et métaphysiques* (1683) and the *Traité de morale* (1684). By 1688 he managed to restate his theology in a more orthodox-appearing form, and the *Entretiens sur la métaphysique* gained the approval (or at least the silence) of Bossuet. In 1697, Malebranche entered the 'quietist' controversy over the 'disinterested love of God' which had destroyed all amity between Bossuet and Fénelon—by writing the *Traité de l'amour de Dieu*; in 1708 he published the brief *Entretien d'un philosophe chrétien et d'un philosophe chinois*, designed to show that all rational beings, always and everywhere, 'see' the same eternal verities—'in God', who is the ground but not the cause of those changeless truths. A final Jansenist attack led Malebranche to publish his last work, *Réflexions sur la prémotion physique*, in 1715; the *Réflexions* defended, against 'Calvinist' fatalism, the notion that human beings have the power to 'suspend' their consent to any particular motive while they seek after *le bien général*. This final work appeared in spring 1715; soon thereafter Malebranche began to decline; on 13 October 1715, he died at the age of 77.

At the time of his death, Malebranche was considered one of the three or four most important living European philosophers: Locke had troubled to write two large essays against him; Leibniz discussed him at great length in the *Theodicée*; Montesquieu called him one of the 'four great poets' (with Plato, Montaigne, and Shaftesbury); Rousseau was soon to rank him with Plato and Locke—his favourite ancient and modern thinkers. Even Kant would soon say that the 'fathers' of modern philosophy were Descartes, Leibniz, and Malebranche. To be sure, Malebranche's reputation finally declined outside France; but a recent revival of interest in his thought now makes possible the first English-language edition since 1695 of the *Traité de la nature et de la grâce*—the work which made *Malebranchisme* both famous and notorious.

A Note on the Text

Since Malebranche's *Traité de la nature et de la grâce* went through seven editions in his lifetime—the last in 1712, three years before his death—and since he enlarged and embroidered the work with each successive edition, it is by no means easy to decide which of the editions ought to be used as the basis of the first English translation since 1695. But a choice must be made, even if reasonable objections to that choice will continue to be put forward.

Despite those seven editions, it remains true that there is a *fundamental* difference between the first few editions (1680, 1681, 1683) and those which appeared after 1684. Beginning in that year, Malebranche interpolated into his text new sections called 'additions'; and these were mainly quotations from (or paraphrases of) patristic writings, designed to show that Malebranche had not treated 'the authority of tradition' (in Bossuet's phrase) with contempt, that he was not so radical a 'Cartesian' rationalist that he read the Bible and St Augustine negligently. As a defensive measure against traditionalist charges of 'novelty', then, Malebranche (beginning in 1684) 'scripturalized' his work, gave it the external trappings of greater orthodoxy—sometimes quoting two or three pages of Augustine, in Latin, between the sections of his original text. But Malebranche was always aware that this procedure damaged his book, even if it increased his safety. The forward 'movement' of the original text was severely impeded by the throwing up of these defensive bulwarks—which in any case did not save *Nature et grâce* from being condemned at Rome in 1690. (In response to the same traditionalist criticism, Malebranche also appended four 'Illustrations' to *Nature et grâce* between 1681 and 1684; since, however, these were not interpolated into the main text, they did no philosophical or literary damage. And the 'First Illustration' (1681) is an important amplification of Malebranche's view that God governs the realms of nature and grace through simple, constant, uniform 'general' laws.)

Commenting on the 'additions' which he had felt constrained to introduce in 1684, Malebranche insisted—in the later editions of *Nature et grâce*—that 'I think that I ought to give notice, that those who know well the principles which I have proven in *Recherche de la vérité* and elsewhere have no need of reading the *Additions* which follow'. But what is still more striking is the fact that Malebranche preserved, even in the final edition of 1712, a preface ('extrait d'une lettre') which clearly ruled out the interpolation of scriptural and patristic 'supports'. 'The individual character of the author', this preface asserts, 'is to speak clearly and with order, and to spread enlightenment in attentive minds: something he would not have been able to do, if he had been obliged to insert in his discourses a mass of passages, which often need to be explained, and which cause the sequence and the connection of his thoughts to be lost.' It is with good reason, then, that the eminent Malebranchist Henri Gouhier says that the original edition of *Nature et grâce* shows us the form that Malebranche 'wanted to give to it', while the post-1684 versions only reveal a transmogrified work 'which time imposed on him'.

No less a critic than Sainte-Beuve, in *Port-Royal*, described the losses that this transmogrification brought about.

The *Traité de la nature et de la grâce* is divided into three discourses . . . Each discourse, which itself has two parts, is composed of paragraphs which are more or less long, but always well proportioned, [which are] species of aphorisms, of metaphysical oracles, which move forward more or less like strophes . . . Now, if you like, the whole book has the beauty of a temple. In the later editions, the author caused each paragraph to be followed by additions or commentaries which damaged the original beauty [of the text] . . . One can imagine the annoyance of Malebranche in being obliged thus to upset the beauty of his architectural order to prop up its solidity. It is like an architect who, between every ornament and every column in a temple built by himself, should be obliged by his critics to insert wooden supports, on which would be posted the geometrical objections which are there exhibited.[1]

And, as Ginette Dreyfus has correctly added, 'the original plainness [*nudité*] of the *Traité* was in singular conformity to the spirit of the Malebranchist effort. The constant concern of Malebranche is that of making truth shine by consulting that universal reason with which the human mind is consubstantially united. By its presence alone, truth dissipates error.'[2] If one adds in Malebranche's conviction that Scripture is 'full of anthropologies',

---

[1] C. A. Sainte-Beuve, *Port-Royal*, VI. 6 (Paris: Hachette, 1922), p. 413.

[2] Ginette Dreyfus, 'Introduction' to Malebranche, *Traité de la nature et de la grâce*, in *Œuvres complètes de Malebranche* (Paris: Librairie Vrin, 1958), p. xvii.

and his claim that 'faith passes away, but reason subsists eternally', one will understand his reluctance to prop up his philosophy with 'authoritative' supports.

Given all of these considerations, but given also the fact that the 'First Illustration' from the 1681 edition is philosophically important and literarily harmless (since it is an appendix), the best course seems to be that of translating the 1680 original text—then grafting on the 'Éclaircissement' from the 1681 edition. This combination of the main text from the *editio princeps* and the 1681 'First Illustration' means that the present Oxford edition is *most* like the one designated as IIS by the editors of the Librairie Vrin critical edition of the *Œuvres complètes de Malebranche*; but edition IIS (Strasbourg 1681) omits two important sections of the 1680 text—sections which were known and commented on by Arnauld, Bayle, Leibniz, Fénelon, and Bossuet—and that suggests that fusing the 1680 and 1681 editions salvages everything worth having. (The remaining 'Illustrations', omitted here, are far less important; but some significant lines from them have been included in the editor's Introduction—thereby keeping what is important.)

That Introduction includes not just the important lines from the 'Illustrations'—and even a few from the 'additions', where these go beyond verbatim citation of Scripture or Augustine; above all it tries to fit *Nature et grâce* into the larger economy of *Malebranchisme* as a general doctrine. For some things merely hinted at, or sketchily treated, in *Nature et grâce*, are later fully developed in the *Traité de morale* (1684), in the *Entretiens sur la métaphysique* (1688), and in the *Prémotion physique* (1715). The constant aim of the Introduction is to integrate *Nature et grâce* into a general philosophical system produced by—in the words of Geneviève Rodis-Lewis—'the greatest French metaphysician'.[3]

[3] Geneviève Rodis-Lewis, 'Malebranche "moraliste"', in *Dix-septième siècle*, 159 (1988), 175.

Biographical Sketches

ANTOINE ARNAULD (1612–1694), the most intrepid defender of Jansenius and Jansenism (see below), finally expelled from the Sorbonne and driven into exile for his convictions. From 1680 to 1694, Arnauld and Malebranche engaged in an endless running polemic over *Nature et grâce*; much of Malebranche's later thought was developed in response to the Arnaldian critique.

PIERRE BAYLE (1647–1706), Calvinist theologian and man of letters, driven into exile in Rotterdam just before the revocation of the Edict of Nantes. An early defender of Malebranchian 'general' Providence in *Pensées diverses sur la comète* (1682), Bayle later, under the influence of Antoine Arnauld (see above), raised serious doubts about Malebranche's theodicy.

JACQUES-BÉNIGNE BOSSUET (1627–1704), Bishop of Meaux and tutor to the Dauphin, and the most important French ecclesiastic during the last quarter of the seventeenth century. He attacked Malebranche's notion of 'general' Providence during the funeral of the Queen of France (1683), and later produced a *Politics drawn from the Very Words of Holy Scripture* urging that God causes every earthly event through *Providence particulière*.

FRANÇOIS DE SALIGNAC DE LA MOTTE FÉNELON (1651–1715), disciple and then principal theological opponent of Bossuet. The Church condemned Fénelon's 'quietism' and 'disinterested love of God' as depriving Christians of legitimate hope of salvation. In *c*.1687–8, Fénelon produced a *Réfutation* of Malebranche, at the behest of Bossuet.

CORNELIUS JANSENIUS [JANSEN] (1585–1638), Flemish theologian, author of *Augustinus* (1640)—the book which gave rise to 'Jansenism'. Building on late works of St Augustine such as *De Natura et Gratia* and *De Correptione* which stressed the weakness of human will and the necessity of unmerited grace (together with the predestination of the elect), Jansenism was particularly attacked for casting doubt on St Paul's claim (1 Timothy) that 'God wills that all men be saved'. Jansenism found its greatest defenders in Antoine Arnauld and

Blaise Pascal (*Écrits sur la grâce* and *Pensées*); it was criticized as a form of demi-Calvinism by its detractors, and Malebranche often said that he wrote *Nature et grâce* to combat Jansenist errors.

PIERRE JURIEU (1637–1713), Calvinist minister and theologian, later exiled to Holland. He was the author of the *Letters to the Faithful of France who Groan under the Babylonian Captivity* (1686), and emerged as one of the great controversialists of the age—most often attacking his co-religionist and fellow-exile, Pierre Bayle.

Introduction

I

The original, governing, and radical idea of Malebranche's *Traité de la nature et de la grâce*—an idea that inspired Leibniz and the young Pierre Bayle, and scandalized Bossuet, Fénelon, and Antoine Arnauld—is that God governs the realms of nature and grace (equally) by simple, constant, uniform 'Cartesian' general laws and general wills (*volontés générales*), not through an *ad hoc* patchwork of capricious and changeable particular wills (*volontés particulières*).[1] *Nature et grâce* also contains many other, less radical, thoughts; but it was Malebranche's *recherche de la généralité*—which rules out *Providence particulière* and most miracles—that forcibly struck his contemporaries.

There was nothing at all unorthodox in writing a treatise called *Nature and Grace*: St Augustine himself, after all, had used that very title.[2] And, precisely after Augustine, a Christian could no longer treat nature *without* grace; the Aristotelian idea of nature as the realization of a *telos* which was always 'there' *in potentia* (as in an acorn's becoming an oak)[3] had now become criminal 'Pelagian' pride—the sinful conviction that one can reach one's natural 'end' without supernatural ('gracious') aid. (As Augustine himself asks in *De Natura et Gratia*, sect. LIX, 'Why did Pelagius want to defend nature alone, and why did he claim that man had been created in such a way that he could avoid all sin, if he had so willed? . . . If

---

[1] Malebranche, *Traité de la nature et de la grâce*, ed. Ginette Dreyfus, in *Œuvres complètes de Malebranche* (Paris: Vrin, 1958), 'Premier Discours' and 'Premier Éclaircissement'. For the best introduction to this work, see Malebranche, *Traité de la nature et de la grâce* [1680 text], ed. Ginette Dreyfus (Paris: Vrin, 1958). (In the *Œuvres complètes* the text used is the final one of 1712.) See also Judith N. Shklar, 'General Will', in *Dictionary of the History of Ideas*, ed. Philip Wiener (New York: Charles Scribner's Sons, 1973), ii. 275 ff. NB references to Malebranche's *Nature et grâce* in these footnotes begin with Discourse and section numbers from the original 1680 text (e.g. III, sect. I for Discourse III, sect. I); the page numbers then given refer to the 1958 Librairie Vrin edn.

[2] St Augustine, *De Natura et Gratia*, sects. LVIII–LIX. See also Augustine's letter to Hillary of Syracuse (*c.* AD 414).

[3] Aristotle, *Physics*, 256[b]; *Metaphysics*, 1015[a].

justice derives from our nature [alone], Christ died in vain.') And even Aquinas's demi-Aristotelianism, his claim that 'grace perfects nature, but does not destroy it,'[4] was not enough to rehabilitate 'mere' nature. What made Malebranche controversial was not the fact that he had written on 'nature and grace', but that he was suspected of doing violence to both nature and grace by seeing both as governed by 'Cartesian' *généralité*: at worst, he was suspected of letting 'physics' dominate metaphysics,[5] of permitting the Church to be converted into a laboratory.

To be sure, Malebranche tells us that if certain men (i.e. the Jansenists) had not *denied* God's 'general will to save all men', he would never have written *Nature et grâce*. 'If in this century men were not so obstinate in maintaining that God does not have a sincere will to save all men', Malebranche insists, 'it would not be so necessary to establish principles suitable to the destruction of this unfortunate opinion. But the necessity to combat errors reveals the principles which are appropriate to this effect. I protest before God that this has been the principle motive which pressed me to write [*Nature et grâce*].'[6] But *Nature et grâce* extends this *généralité* far beyond salvation: for in this work God governs the universe—physical and moral—through general laws and *volontés générales*. So in Malebranchism there is a fusion of 'Cartesian' physical *généralité* in the realm of nature and an 'Augustinian' salvific *volonté générale* in the realm of grace; that is why Henri Gouhier is so right to speak of an *Augustinisme cartésianisé* in Malebranche.[7] 1680, the publication year of *Nature et grâce*, offered a perfect chance to reaffirm, against Jansenism, the notion that God wills that all men be saved, and to celebrate a (more general) 'Cartesianism': the notion of 'general will' could defend early Augustine (affirming general salvation) against late, proto-Jansenist Augustine (stressing particular salvation of the elect), *and* show that a Cartesian 'reading' of a simple and uniform nature was correct. Of course it was not possible simply to lose Augustine and Descartes in each other: Augustine was a defender of

---

[4] St Thomas Aquinas, *Summa Theologica*, cited and well treated in A. P. d'Entrèves, *The Medieval Contribution to Political Thought* (Oxford: Clarendon Press, 1939), 20–1.

[5] Bossuet, letter to the Marquis d'Allemans (May 1687), in *Œuvres complètes de Malebranche*, xviii. 444 ff.

[6] Malebranche, *Lettres du P. Malebranche* (Paris, 1709), 189. Cited and treated in Dreyfus's introduction to Malebranche's *Nature et grâce* (1712 text), p. xliv.

[7] Henri Gouhier, *Fénelon philosophe* (Paris: Vrin, 1977), ch. 1.

the quasi-Platonic 'eternal verities' which Descartes ruled out in favour of divine creativity *ex nihilo*;[8] and on this point Malebranche (siding with Leibniz) aligned himself firmly with Plato.[9] But most of *Nature et grâce* flows from an effort to unite the figures whom Malebranche took to be the greatest representatives of antiquity and modernity, Christianity and science.

None the less one must remember that Malebranche would have had no occasion to represent divine *généralité* as governing 'Cartesian' nature and 'Augustinian' grace, had he not entered into a continuing debate—raging since at least the 1640s—over God's 'general will to save all men'.[10] One will never understand how ingeniously Malebranche extended and 'Cartesianized' this *volonté générale* until one knows what was said about such a divine will, in the half-century before *Nature et grâce*, by Jansenius, by Arnauld, by Pascal; a brief excursion into the doctrinal antecedents of Malebranchism is therefore as unavoidable as it is illuminating.

The Antecedents of Malebranche: Augustine, Aquinas, Arnauld

In the second quarter of the seventeenth century, the notion of *volonté générale* referred to the kind or type of will that God (supposedly) had in deciding who would be granted grace sufficient for salvation and who would be consigned to hell. The question at issue was: if 'God wills that all men be saved'—as St Paul asserts in a letter to his disciple Timothy[11]—does he have a *general will* which produces universal salvation? And if he does not, why does he will *particularly* that some men not be saved? There was a further question as well, namely whether God can justly save some and condemn others, particularly if (as St Augustine asserted) those whom God saves are rescued not through their own merit but through unmerited grace conferred by the will of God.[12] From the beginning, then, the notions of divine *volonté générale* and *volonté particulière* were parts of a larger question about the justice of God;

[8] Descartes, *Reply to the Six Objections*, trans. R. M. Eaton (New York: Charles Scribner's Sons, 1927), 264–6.

[9] Malebranche, *Réflexions sur la prémotion physique*, in *Œuvres complètes de Malebranche*, xvi. 93–104.

[10] See, *inter alia*, Alberto Postigliola, 'De Malebranche à Rousseau: Les Apories de la volonté générale', in *Annales de la Société Jean-Jacques Rousseau*, 39 (Geneva: Chez A. Jullien, 1980), 134 ff.

[11] 1 Timothy 2: 4.

[12] Or at least this is how many 17th-cent. Augustinians—such as Pascal— read St Augustine.

they were always 'legal' notions, in the largest possible sense of the
word 'legal'—in the sense that even theology is part of what Leibniz
called 'universal jurisprudence'.[13] The whole controversy over God's
'general will' to save 'all' men—and how this is to be reconciled with
the (equally scriptural) notion that 'many are called but few are
chosen'[14]—was very precisely summed up in a few words from the
last work (*Entretiens de Maxime et de Thémiste*, 1706) of Malebranche's
contemporary and correspondent, Pierre Bayle: 'The God of the
Christians wills that all men be saved; he has the power necessary to
save them all; he lacks neither power nor good will, and none the less
almost all men are damned.'[15] The effort to explain this state of
affairs led directly to the original theory of *volonté générale*.

The controversy about the nature of divine justice is nearly as old
as Christian philosophy itself; it was fully aired in the struggles
between St Augustine and the Pelagians, and resurfaced in
seventeenth-century disputes about grace between the Jansenists
and the Jesuits.[16] The actual terms 'general will' and 'particular
will', however, are not to be found in Augustine or Pelagius, or, for
that matter, in Jansenius' *Augustinus* or in the Jesuit Molina—
though Jansenius once uses the phrase *volonté particulière*, in
passing, in his last extant letter to Saint-Cyran.[17] Those terms, in
fact, are the modern successors to the Scholastic distinction between
the 'antecedent' and the 'consequent' will of God: according to this
doctrine, God willed 'antecedently' (or generally) that all men be
saved, but after the Fall of Adam he willed 'consequently' (or
particularly) that only some be saved.[18] The distinction between
'antecedent' and 'consequent' divine will is to be found in Scholastic

[13] Leibniz, *Opinion on the Principles of Pufendorf*, in *The Political Writings of Leibniz*, trans. and ed. Patrick Riley (Cambridge: Cambridge University Press, 1972), 3.
[14] Matthew 22: 14.
[15] Bayle, *Entretiens de Maxime et de Thémiste*, cited in E. Labrousse, *Pierre Bayle* (The Hague: Martinus Nijhoff, 1966), ii. 377.
[16] Nigel Abercrombie, *The Origins of Jansenism* (Oxford: Clarendon Press, 1936), 3–47, 93 ff. A mainly reliable work, though Abercrombie inclines towards Molinism and doubts the orthodox 'Augustinianism' of Jansenism.
[17] Jansénius, 172ᵉ Lettre à Saint-Cyran [23 Mar. 1635], in *Les Origines du Jansénisme I: Correspondance de Jansénius*, ed. Jean Orcibal (Paris: Vrin, 1947), 585. Complaining of the distractions that are keeping him from producing *Augustinus*, Jansenius none the less says that 'je crois que ces divertissemens mesmes me sont donnez par une volonté particulière de Dieu'.
[18] The Scholastic distinction between 'antecedent' and 'consequent' will was perfected by Leibniz in sect. 22–5 of his *Theodicée*.

philosophy as late as Suarez;[19] and even Leibniz used the terms 'general' and 'particular' will interchangeably with the older words,[20] as did writers such as Antoine Arnauld, the great Port-Royal logician.

So far as diligent enquiry will reveal, the first work of consequence to use the actual term 'general will' was Antoine Arnauld's *Première apologie pour M. Jansénius* (1644), which was written to refute a series of anti-Jansenist sermons that had been preached by the theologian Isaac Habert in the Cathedral of Notre-Dame (1642–3) at the express order of Cardinal Richelieu.[21]

Before Arnauld's *Première apologie*, certainly, one does not find the term *volonté générale* in the place or at the time that one might reasonably expect to find it. It does not appear, for example, in the protracted exchange of letters between Descartes's associate Father Mersenne and the Calvinist theologian André Rivet, though the most interesting of these letters date from 1640 (the very year of *Augustinus'* publication) and deal precisely with the universality or non-universality of salvation—Père Mersenne asserting that in order to avoid 'horror' and 'desperation', one must believe that 'God does not will the damnation of anyone, but [wills] that each be saved, if he wills to co-operate in his salvation',[22] Rivet replying that, since many are damned, Mersenne's alleged universal salvation imputes to God 'des désirs vains, et des volontés frustratoires' and tries to re-establish 'the paradise of Origen', in which even the devils are included.[23] But if the Mersenne–Rivet letter-exchange provided a perfect occasion to assert or deny a divine *volonté générale* to save 'all', the term did not actually appear; and this is probably an indication that before 1644 the expression was not current, even in the writings of a man like Mersenne who corresponded with every great figure of the age.[24]

---

[19] Suarez, *De Divina Substantia*, bk. III, ch. viii ('De Voluntate Antecedente et Consequente'), in *Opera Omnia* (Paris, 1856), i. 221 ff. Suarez treats antecedent and consequent will precisely in connection with St Paul's letter to Timothy.

[20] Leibniz, *Theodicy*, ed. A. Farrer (New Haven, Conn.: Yale University Press, 1952), 137: 'God wills antecedently the good [e.g. the general salvation of all men] and consequently the best [e.g. the particular salvation of some men].'

[21] J. Paquier, *Le Jansénisme* (Paris: Librairie Bloud, 1909), 159 ff.; A. Sedgwick, *Jansenism in Seventeenth-Century France* (Charlottesville, Va.: University Press of Virginia, 1977), 50 ff.

[22] *Correspondance du P[ère] Marin Mersenne*, ed. Cornelis de Waard (Paris: Éditions du Centre National de la Recerche Scientifique, 1967), x. 219.

[23] Ibid. 287.

[24] Including Descartes (above all) and Hobbes.

How 'Jansenism' should (or indeed can) be defined is beyond the scope of this work: whether it was an orthodox (though severe) 'Augustinianism', or a kind of heterodox 'semi-Calvinism', need not be settled here.[25] What does matter for present purposes is that it was the conflict between 'Jansenism' and its critics—Jesuit and otherwise—that served as the occasional cause of a revived dispute over the meaning of the scriptural assertion that 'God wills that all men be saved'. Whether justly or not, Jansenius' *Augustinus* was accused—first by Habert's Richelieu-inspired sermons, then by Nicolas Cornet, Syndic of the Sorbonne,[26] then by a letter to the Pope drafted by Habert using Cornet's charges,[27] finally by several papal bulls including *Cum Occasione* and (much later) *Unigenitus*—of having maintained 'five propositions' judged 'heretical' and 'scandalous';[28] and the last of the five propositions imputed to Jansenius asserted that 'it is a semi-Pelagian error to say that Jesus Christ died or spilled his blood for all men without exception'. Whether the five propositions were, in fact or in effect, contained in the *Augustinus* (as the Jesuits maintained), or were malicious fabrications of Cornet and Habert designed to ruin the reputation of St Augustine as *the* doctor of grace (as the Jansenists insisted), what is indisputable is that when Jansenists such as Arnauld and Pascal tried to defend Jansenius, they had to show that the Bishop of Ypres had correctly (that is, in the manner of St Augustine) understood the notion that *Deus vult omnes homines salvos fieri*: that a truly general will to save 'all' was fully reconcilable with the Jansenist notion that only the 'elect' (rather than 'all') actually enter the Kingdom of Heaven.[29] In short: had Jansenius and his principal apologists not tried to restrict, radically, the meaning of St Paul's letter to Timothy, the question of a justifiable 'general will' might never have become one of the great disputes of the seventeenth century. And

[25] For a brilliant restatement of the thesis—originally enunciated by Arnauld and Nicole—that Jansenism was in no sense a 'deviant sect', that it was simply what it claimed to be, a restoration of rightly understood Augustinianism, see Jean LaPorte, 'Le Jansénisme', in *Études d'histoire de la philosophie française au XVIIᵉ siècle* Paris: Vrin, 1951), 88 ff., esp. 105: 'Il n'y a plus de Jansénisme, parce qu'au fond il n'y en a jamais eu.'

[26] Sedgwick, *Jansenism in Seventeenth-Century France*, 50 ff.

[27] Ibid.

[28] Ibid. For an excellent study of the 'fifth Proposition', see Lucien Ceyssens, 'La Cinquième des propositions condamnés de Jansénius: Sa portée théologique', in *Jansénius et le Jansénisme dans les Pays-Bas*, ed. J. van Bavel (Louvain: Peeters, 1982).

[29] Paquier, *Le Jansénisme*, 150 ff.

then Malebranche, according to his own testimony, would have had no occasion to write *Nature et grâce*.

Antoine Arnauld, then, invented, or at least first made visible, the notion of 'general will'; but he did this, ironically enough, as part of a Jansenist effort to minimize (without annihilating) the notion that 'all' are saved, that salvation is 'general'. In Antoine Arnauld, the 'general' will is as little general as possible. In the *Première apologie pour M. Jansénius*, Arnauld acknowledges the nominal existence of a 'general will of God to save all men', but immediately narrows this 'generality' by insisting (with Jansenius) that it is 'semi-Pelagian' to construe St Paul's letter to Timothy *au pied de la lettre*, to understand divine *volonté générale* as requiring salvation 'generally for all men in particular, without excepting any of them'.[30] God's saving will is 'general', Arnauld argues, only in the sense that it applies 'to all sorts of conditions, ages, of sexes, of countries'; but it does not rescue every last single man *en particulier*.[31] Indeed he insists—and here Jansenist rigorism is at its clearest—that

It is certain that the source of all the errors of the semi-Pelagians is [their] not being able to endure the absolute and immutable decree of God, who . . . chose, from all eternity, without any regard for merit, a certain number of men, whom he destined for glory; leaving the others in the common mass of perdition, from which he is not obliged to pull them.[32]

Since God is 'not obliged' to pull all men from perdition, his 'general will' to save them all is attenuated, to put it mildly. And in slightly later works—such as his *Apologie pour les Saints Pères* (1651)—Arnauld carries this attenuation farther still. God's 'ante-cedent' will for 'the salvation of all men', he insists, 'is only a simple *velléité* and a simple wish, which involves no preparation of means' to effect this wish; his *volonté générale* 'is based only on a consideration of human nature in itself, which was created for salvation', but which, since the Fall, has richly deserved perdition.[33] Actually, Arnauld goes on, one could even say that God had a *volonté générale* to save 'the devils', who were once angels; but fallen angels, like fallen men, are now damned. All this is clearer, in Arnauld's view, if one sees that God's judgements, which are 'very just' though 'very secret', are like the decisions of an earthly judge, who

[30] Arnauld, *Œuvres de Messire Antoine Arnauld* (Brussels: Culture et Civilisation, 1967), xv–xvi. 184–5.
[31] Ibid.   [32] Ibid. 246.   [33] Ibid. xvii. 112.

condemns a thief or a murderer to death, but who none the less 'at the same time wills and wishes, by an antecedent will', that the life of this criminal, considered simply 'as a man and as a citizen', be 'saved'.[34] Obviously Arnauld tries to weaken the force of 'God wills that all men be saved' in two main ways: sometimes by diminishing the compass of 'all', sometimes by shrinking the meaning of 'will'. As Jean LaPorte has shown in his brilliant pro-Jansenist *La Doctrine de Port-Royal*, it is characteristic of St Augustine and the Augustinians (including, usually, the Jansenists) to attempt to pare down the term 'all', while it is typical of St Thomas and the Thomists to deflate divine 'will'.[35] St Augustine, in *De Correptione et Gratia* and in the *Enchiridion*, glosses 'all' to mean all *kinds* of persons (of all professions, ages, sexes, countries); and this equation of 'all' with 'some' (provided they are distributed over 'all' categories) is most often favoured by Arnauld. For the Augustinians, then, God wills to save not all men but all *sorts* of men; in the magnificent Latin of the *Enchiridion* (XXVII. 103), 'omnes homines omne genus hominum intelligamus per quascumque differentias distributum, reges, privatos, nobiles, ignobiles, sublimes, humiles, doctos, indoctos, integri corporis, debiles, ingeniosos, tardicordes, fatuos, divites, pauperes, mediocres, mares, feminas, infantes, pueros, adolescentes, juvenes, seniores, senes; in linguis omnibus, in moribus omnibus, in artibus omnibus, in professionibus omnibus.'[36] And on this point, at least, the claim that Jansenius was an orthodox Augustinian seems warranted: for in the section of *Augustinus* entitled 'De Gratia Christi Salvatoris', Jansenius urges that if one wants to avoid Pelagian and semi-Pelagian heresy in interpreting 'God wills that all men be saved', one must understand 'all' to refer, not to a divine salvific will 'for each and every single man' (*pro omnibus omnio singularibus hominibus*), but rather to a will for the salvation of every kind of man (*pro omni genere hominorum*)—Jews and Gentiles, servants and free men, public and private persons, wise and unwise.[37] One should add, however, that in his efforts to reduce 'all' men to the 'elect', Jansenius also relies on other patristic writings, and particularly on

[34] Arnauld, *Œuvres de Messire Antoine Arnauld* (Brussels: Culture et Civilisation, 1967), xvii. 112.
[35] *La Doctrine de Port-Royal: Les Vérités sur la grâce* (Paris: Vrin, 1923), 250–1.
[36] In *Œuvres de S. Augustin* (Paris: Desclée De Brouwer et Cie, 1947), ix. 290.
[37] *Augustinus* (Louvain, 1640), III. xx. 376.

St Prosper's argument that Christ died for 'all' men only in the sense that his sacrifice was sufficient to redeem all, but that the actual effect of his death was to redeem only a few—or, as Jansenius paraphrases St Prosper, 'Christum omnes redimisse sufficienter, non efficienter'.[38] None the less, Jansenius relies mainly on St Augustine, and on the notion that 'all' really means 'some'.

Aquinas's method—occasionally followed by Arnauld, as in the *Apologie pour les Saints Pères*—is very different. He preserves what one is tempted to call the natural meaning of 'all'—LaPorte calls it the 'unforced' meaning[39]—and makes 'will' the variable term, saying in *De Veritate* that 'God wills by an antecedent [or general] will that all men be saved, by reason of human nature, which he has made for salvation; but he wills by a consequent will that some be damned, because of the sins that are in them'.[40]

In view of Arnauld's diminishing of 'general will', whether by Augustinian or Thomistic means—a general will which he calls 'inefficacious' and a mere 'wish', and which he compares with earthly death-sentences for murder—it should come as no surprise that Arnauld particularly admired St Augustine's *De Correptione et Gratia*, the anti-Pelagian work which is hardest on the 'general' salvation of 'all' men. So much did Arnauld relish this work, indeed, that he published a French translation of it in 1644, to which he added a sombre and powerful Introduction. In this Introduction he warns Christians against falling into the 'criminal pride' of the 'Pelagians' and of 'the philosophers', who through 'unhappy presumption' treat man as independent;[41] and he once again minimizes the 'generality' of salvation, this time nearly to the vanishing point:

There are no mysteries which God hides so well from proud sages, as the mysteries of grace; for there are no others so opposed to the wise folly of the world, and to that spirit of pride which cannot suffer this sovereign Empire which God exercises over his creatures through his different judgements of pity and of justice—which can be secret, but which can only be very equitable, giving grace to some, because he is good, and not giving it to others, because he is just; and not doing wrong to anyone, because, all being guilty, he owes nothing to anyone, as St Augustine says so many times.[42]

---

[38] Ibid.   [39] Cited in LaPorte, *La Doctrine de Port-Royal*, 251.
[40] Ibid. 251–2.
[41] St Augustine, *De la correction et de la grâce*, trans. and intro. Antoine Arnauld (Paris, 1644), 4.   [42] Ibid. 7.

Here, of course, any 'general' will to save 'all' has (all but) disappeared. But even here what remains of *volonté générale* has 'legal' and moral implications: after all, it is 'just' and 'equitable' that God does not act on his original general 'wish' that all be saved, because all are 'guilty' and hence cannot rightly complain of not receiving the grace that would save them. In Arnauld, God's 'equitable' operation, his 'sovereign Empire', begins with general will, even if it rightfully ends with something radically different— though Arnauld would have felt no need to defend God's cause had he not feared that giving grace to some (only) *might* be viewed as an inequitable and arbitrary 'acceptation of persons'.[43] It is one of the great ironies of the history of ideas that *volonté générale* should be thrust into prominence by a thinker who thought that will very little 'general' indeed—as Malebranche was soon to point out in his various defences of the *Traité de la nature et de la grâce*.

The Antecedents of Malebranche: Pascal

But if it was Antoine Arnauld who (apparently) invented the terms *volonté générale* and *volonté particulière*, it was a far greater Jansenist—Blaise Pascal—who was the first to use the notions of *généralité* and of *particularité* in works (the *Pensées* and the *Écrits sur la grâce*) which are still read. (The works of Arnauld, in forty-five enormous volumes, are today almost unknown.[44]) And even in Pascal's *Écrits su la grâce* (c. 1656) the notion of *volonté générale* has 'legal' overtones, since he uses it in considering whether God can justly dispense sufficient grace for salvation only to those who merit, or whether by *volonté absolue* he can simply damn some and save others. The notion of an arbitrary *volonté absolue* he connects with Calvinism (which is, he says, 'injurious to God and insupportable to men'); while a notion of *volonté générale* he traces to 'the disciples of St Augustine', who, according to Pascal, believed that before the Fall of Adam 'God had a *volonté générale et conditionnelle* to save all men' (whereas after the Fall he willed, by a *volonté absolue* arising from pity, that some men still be saved though none merited it[45]). And Pascal plainly favours this version of 'Augustinianism': the

[43] This was to be Rousseau's argument against unequally conferred grace in *La Nouvelle Héloïse*; see part III of this Introduction.

[44] Except for the *Port-Royal Logic*, which has been repopularized by the efforts of Noam Chomsky.

[45] Pascal, *Écrits sur la grâce*, in *Œuvres de Blaise Pascal*, ed. L. Brunschvicg (Paris: Librairie Hachette, 1914), xi. 133–40.

Calvinists, by denying that God ever (even before the Fall) had a *volonté générale* to save all men, fall into an 'abominable opinion' which 'injures' common sense; the Pelagians, at the other extreme, by holding that 'God had a *volonté générale, égale et conditionnelle* to save all men' and that this *volonté générale* remained constant even after the Fall, so that God sent Christ into the world to help all men *merit* salvation, fall into an opposite excess by depriving God wholly of any *volonté absolue*, even after the sin of Adam.[46] Only Augustinianism, in combining a pre-Fall *volonté générale* with a post-Fall *volonté absolue*, Pascal says, strikes a proper balance between the polar errors of granting too much to God (Calvinism) or too much to men (Pelagianism).[47]

So anxious is Pascal to demonstrate the rightfulness of God's (Augustinian) operation—pre-lapsarian *volonté générale* followed by post-lapsarian *volonté absolue*—that he uses the word 'justice' (or its cognates) no fewer than six times in the central paragraphs of the *Première écrit sur la grâce*:

In the condition of innocence, God could not with justice damn a single man. God could not even refuse to men the graces sufficient for their salvation.

In the condition of corruption, God could with justice damn the entire mass; and those who are being born today without being rescued by baptism are damned and eternally deprived of the beatific vision, which is the greatest of evils.

Considering these two conditions [which are] so different, they [the Augustinians] have formed two different opinions concerning the will of God for the salvation of men.

They claim that, in connection with the state of innocence, God had a general and conditional will [*une volonté générale et conditionelle*] to save all men, provided that they willed it through free will, aided by sufficient graces which he gave them for their salvation, but which do not determine them infallibly to persevere in the good.

But that Adam, having through his free will misused this grace, and having revolted against God through a movement of his will and without the slightest impulsion from God (which would be detestable to imagine), has corrupted and infected the entire mass of men, such that humankind has become the just object of the anger and indignation of God. They understand that God has divided this mass, all equally guilty and wholly worthy of damnation; that he has willed to save a part [of the mass of men]

[46] Ibid. 134–52.   [47] Ibid. 135–40.

through an absolute will based on his pure and gratuitous pity, and that, leaving the other part in its damnation and in which he could with justice leave the entire mass, he previewed either the particular sins that each [person] would commit, or at least the original sin of which they are all guilty, and that, following this prevision, he willed to condemn them.[48]

'To this end', Pascal goes on, God 'sent Jesus Christ to save absolutely and by very efficacious means those whom he has chosen and predestined from this mass', so that it was only for the 'chosen' that Christ 'willed absolutely to merit salvation through his death'; he 'never had this same will for the salvation of the others who have not been delivered from this universal and just perdition'. The Augustinians further believe

that, none the less, some of those who are not predestined have been called for the good of the Elect, and thus to participate in the redemption by Jesus Christ. That it is the fault of these persons [who are 'called' but not predestined] that they do not persevere; that they could do so, if they willed, but that, since they are not of the number of the elect, God does not give them the efficacious graces without which they will never will it [salvation]. And thus there are three kinds of men: some who never come to the faith; others who come to it but who, not persevering, die in mortal sin: the last who come to the faith and who persevere in it with charity until death. Jesus Christ never had an absolute will that the first [group] receive the slightest grace through his death, since indeed they have received none.

He willed to redeem the second [group]; he gave them graces that would have led them to salvation, if they had used them well; but he did not will to give them that singular grace of perseverance, without which one cannot use [other graces] well.

But as for the final [group], Jesus Christ willed their salvation absolutely, and led them to it by certain and infallible means.[49]

That 'final group', evidently, is no longer 'all men' *en général*. Pascal, indeed, in accordance with his professed Augustinianism, follows the method of St Augustine's *Enchiridion* in reducing the salvation of all men to a smaller 'elected' number: 'the elect of God form a universality which is sometimes called *a world* because they

---

[48] Pascal, *Écrits sur la grâce*, in *Œuvres de Blaise Pascal*, ed. L. Brunschvicg (Paris: Librairie Hachette, 1914), xi. 135–7.

[49] Ibid. 148–9. The finest of all commentaries on the *Écrits sur la grâce* is that of Jan Miel in his invaluable *Pascal and Theology* (Baltimore: Johns Hopkins Press, 1969), 65 ff. For an exhaustive study of Pascal's Augustinianism, based on a minute reading of the writings of both figures, see Philippe Sellier, *Pascal et Saint Augustin* (Paris: A. Colin, 1970), *passim*.

are scattered throughout the world, sometimes *all*, because they make up a totality, sometimes *several*, because they are several between themselves, sometimes *few*, because they are few in proportion to the totality of the abandoned.'[50]

Despite the importance of Pascal's linking up of *généralité* with God's 'antecedent' will to save 'all men'—a will replaced (after the Fall) with an elect-electing particular will—it remains true that the fullest and best-known seventeenth-century exposition of the notions of 'general will' and 'particular will' was certainly Malebranche's *Traité de la nature et de la grâce* (1680). This work, which Leibniz called 'admirable',[51] was one of the most celebrated (and controversial) writings of its day: it was popularized and defended by Bayle in his journal, *Nouvelles de la République des Lettres*;[52] it was attacked by the long-lived and boundlessly productive Arnauld in his *Réflexions philosophiques et théologiques sur le nouveau système de la nature et de la grâce* (1685—forty years after the *Première apologie pour M. Jansénius*);[53] it was criticized by Fontenelle in his *Doutes sur le système physique des causes occasionnelles* (1686),[54] and (above all) by Bossuet in his *Oraison funèbre de Marie-Thérèse d' Autriche* (1683).[55] And if Fénelon's highly critical *Réfutation du système du Père Malebranche sur la nature et la grâce* (c.1687–8) remained unpublished until 1829, his opinion of Malebranchian *volonté générale* was tolerably clear in the fourth (1709) of his *Lettres sur la grâce et la prédestination*, written for François Lami.[56] Malebranche, for his part, defended his work in an endless running polemic with Arnauld (terminated only by the latter's death in 1694);[57] and as late as 1710

---

[50] Pascal, *Écrits sur la grâce*, 148–9.   [51] Leibniz, *Theodicy*, ed. Farrer, 254.

[52] May 1684, cited in Malebranche, *Œuvres complètes de Malebranche* (Vrin), viii–ix. 1152 ff.

[53] Cologne, 1685, *passim*.

[54] In *Œuvres complètes* (Paris, 1818), i. 627 ff.

[55] In *Œuvres de Bossuet*, ed. B. Vélat and Y. Champailler (Paris: Pléiade, 1961), 110. See Theodore Delmont, *Bossuet et les Saints Pères* (Geneva: Slatkine, 1970), 590 ff.

[56] Fénelon, *Réfutation du système du Père Malebranche sur la nature et la grâce*, in *Œuvres de Fénelon* (Paris: Chez Lefevre, 1835), ii. 232 ff. The fourth of the *Lettres sur la grâce* was published as early as 1718 in Fénelon, *Œuvres spirituelles* (Antwerp, 1718). A fine commentary on the *Réfutation* is to be found in Henri Gouhier, *Fénelon philosophe*, 33 ff. This book is also the best general introduction to French religious and moral thought in the 17th cent.; see the editor's review in *Philosophical Review*, 90: 2 (1981), 285–9.

[57] For a good brief account of this polemic, see Dreyfus's Introduction to Malebranche's *Nature et grâce* in *Œuvres complètes de Malebranche*, v, pp. xxxviii ff.

Leibniz devoted several large sections of his *Theodicée* to a spirited
defence of Malebranche's 'general will'.[58]

The Origins of Nature et grâce

The occasional cause of Malebranche's *Nature et grâce* was the
request of the theologian Michel Le Vassor—who had been
'converted' from Jansenism by Malebranche—for a short treatise on
grace usable in connection with his lectures on theology at a Paris
seminary.[59] Le Vassor's Malebranche-inspired lectures on grace
were popular enough to prompt an alarmed Arnauld to request a
meeting with Malebranche; and this meeting was attended not only
by Le Vassor, Malebranche, and Arnauld, but also by Arnauld's
discipline, the Oratorian Father Pasquier Quesnel, whose *Réflexions
morales* later occasioned an enormous conflict within the French
Church culminating in the condemnation of 101 'Jansenist' propositions in Pope Clement XI's *Unigenitus*.[60]

At this famous meeting, Arnauld's volubility denied Malebranche
much opportunity to clarify his views; the *Traité de la nature et de la
grâce* is a full working up—for Arnauld's benefit—of the shorter
treatise prepared for Le Vassor.[61] To be sure, that shorter treatise
was itself a working up of a few paragraphs on grace from the
sixteenth 'Éclaircissement' of the *Recherche de la vérité*, which
Malebranche had appended to the third edition in 1678. In this
'Éclaircissement' (which was scrapped in the final editions of the
Recherche), Malebranche argues that 'while God wills to save us all',
the fact that he operates through 'the simplest means'—through
uniform *volontés générales*, not through a multiplicity of *volontés
particulières*—means that some will *not* be saved.[62] Here, as is
evident, 'general will' is no longer a mere synonym for 'antecedent'
will: *volonté générale* is now associated with Cartesian constancy,
uniformity, and economy. This was to be elaborated in *Nature et
grâce*; but the sixteenth Éclaircissement' of the *Recherche* contains a

<hr />

[58] Leibniz, *Theodicy*, ed. Farrer, 254 ff. For a fuller view of the Malebranche–
Leibniz rapport, see André Robinet, *Malebranche et Leibniz: Relations personnelles*
(Paris: Vrin, 1955), esp. 403 ff. See also Gaston Grua, *Jurisprudence universelle et
théodicée selon Leibniz* (Paris: Presses Universitaires de France, 1953), 192 ff.
[59] For a good account of the composition and publication of *Nature et grâce*, see
Dreyfus's Introduction in *Œuvres complètes de Malebranche*, v, pp. xxii ff.
[60] Ibid.   [61] Ibid.
[62] Malebranche, *De la recherche de la vérité*, in *Œuvres complètes de Malebranche*, ii.
506.

defect which was not carried over into *Nature et grâce*, and which doubtless led to the final abandoning of this 'illustration'. Urging again that God acts 'always by the simplest means . . . in virtue of general wills', Malebranche observes that the Ten Commandments were written by the ancient Jews over their doorways, and argues that this 'spared God a particular will, if one can speak in this way, to inspire these thoughts in them'.[63] Now, obviously, a perfect being does not need to be 'spared' anything, even a *volonté particulière*, since the notion of need is meaningless for such a being; this is best pointed out, nearly a hundred years later, in the theological *Briefwechsel* between Julie de Wolmar and Saint-Preux which Rousseau inserts in Book VI of *La Nouvelle Héloïse*, where Julie mockingly points out to the Malebranchian Saint-Preux that only human beings need 'economy', that God does not need man to 'abridge his work' for him by following ready-made general rules.[64] (Saint-Preux responds that 'it is worthy of his wisdom to prefer the simplest means'.[65]) A thought roughly like this must have crossed Malebranche's mind—even in the sixteenth 'Éclaircissement' he says, 'if one can speak in this way'—and in *Nature et grâce* the 'simplicity' and generality of God's action is grounded not in any need for 'economy' or 'sparing' divine labour, but in the notion that simplicity and generality best *express* divine perfection.[66]

The Central Idea of Nature et grâce

In the 'Premier Éclaircissement' of the *Traité de la nature et de la grâce*, one sees at once that Malebranche is not going to treat divine *volonté générale* as something confined (particularly) to theology, to questions of grace and merit; one sees that he intends to treat 'general will' as something which is manifested in *all* of God's operations—as much in the realm of 'nature' as in the realm of 'grace'. Malebranche argues that 'God acts by *volontés générales* when he acts as a consequence of general laws which he has established';[67] and nature, he adds, 'is nothing but the general law which God has

---

[63] Ibid. 508. On the question how far Malebranche is an orthodox Cartesian, see Ferdinand Alquié, *Le Cartésianisme de Malebranche* (Paris: Vrin, 1974), 243 ff.

[64] Cited in Émile Bréhier, 'Les Lectures malebranchistes de J.-J. Rousseau', in *Revue internationale de philosophie*, 1 (1938–9), 113–14.

[65] Ibid.

[66] *Nature et grâce*, I, sect. XXXVII, 'addition', 47: God is obliged 'to act always in a way worthy of him, in simple, general, constant, and uniform ways'.

[67] Ibid., Illustration, sect. I, 147.

established in order to construct or to preserve his work by the simplest means, by an action which is always uniform, constant, perfectly worthy of an infinite wisdom and of a universal cause'.[68] God, on this view, 'does not act at all' by *volontés particulières*, by lawless *ad hoc* volitions, as do 'limited intelligences' whose thought is not 'infinite':[69] thus for Malebranche 'to establish general laws, and to choose the simplest ones which are at the same time the most fruitful, is a way of acting worthy of him whose wisdom has no limits'.[70] On the other hand, he insists, 'to act by *volontés particulières* shows a limited intelligence which cannot judge the consequences or the effects of less fruitful causes'.[71] And all of this is as true of grace as it is of nature: 'Since it is the same God who is the author of the order of grace and of that of nature, it is necessary that these two orders be in agreement. . . . Since God is a general cause whose wisdom has no limits, it is necessary . . . that in order of grace as well as in that of nature, he act as a general cause.'[72]

Now even at this point Malebranche's argument, though mainly a theological one, contains some points which could be read 'legally': the 'general will' manifests itself in general laws which are 'fruitful' and 'worthy' of infinite wisdom, whereas 'particular will' is 'limited', comparatively unintelligent, and lawless.

One need not jump to any premature conclusions, however, since Malebranche himself occasionally legalizes his argument—particularly in his effort to *justify* God's acting (exclusively) through *volontés générales*. If, he says, 'rain falls on certain lands, and if the sun roasts others . . . if a child comes into the world with a malformed and useless head . . . this is not at all because God wanted to produce those effects by *volontés particulières*; it is because he has established [general] laws for the communication of motion, whose effects are necessary consequences'.[73] Thus, according to Malebranche, 'one cannot say that God acts through caprice or ignorance' in permitting malformed children to be born or unripe fruit to fall: 'he has not established the laws of the communication of motion for the purpose of producing monsters, or of making fruits fall before their maturity'; he has willed these laws 'because of their fruitfulness, and not because of their sterility'.[74] Those who claim (says Malebranche)

---

[68] *Nature et grâce*, I, sect. XXXVII, 'addition', 47: God is obliged 'to act always in a way worthy of him, in simple, general, constant, and uniform ways'. Illustration, sect. III, 148.

[69] Ibid. I, sect. LVII, 63.   [70] Ibid., Illustration, XV, 166.

[71] Ibid.   [72] Ibid.   [73] Ibid. I, sect. XVIII 32.   [74] Ibid.

that God *ought*, through special, *ad hoc volontés particulières*, to suspend natural laws if their operation will harm the virtuous (or the innocent), or that he ought to confer grace only on those who will actually be saved by it, fail to understand that it is not worthy of an infinitely wise being to abandon general rules in order to find a suppositious perfect 'fit' between the particular case of each finite being and a *volonté particulière* suited to that case alone.[75]

By this point, evidently, the theological notion of *volonté générale* is becoming 'legalized': *volonté générale* originally manifested itself in general laws which were wise and fruitful; now that will, expressed in those laws, is just as well, and it is quite wrong to say that God ought to contrive a *volonté particulière* suited to each 'case' (even though the 'generality' of his will and of his laws will mean that grace will occasionally fall on a 'hardened' heart incapable of receiving it[76]). God, Malebranche urges, loves his wisdom more than he loves mankind ('c'est que Dieu aime davantage sa sagesse que son ouvrage'[77]): and his wisdom is expressed in general laws whose operation may have consequences (monstrous children, unripened fruit) which are not themselves willed and which cannot therefore give rise to charges of divine 'caprice' or 'ignorance'.

If Malebranche, in pleading the 'cause' of God (to use Leibniz's phrase), views divine *volonté générale* as issuing in wise and just laws, the *Traité de la nature et de la grâce* is further (and quite explicitly) legalized by an analogy which Malebranche himself draws between a well-governed earthly kingdom and a well-governed Creation. He begins with an argument about enlightened and unenlightened 'wills': 'The more enlightened an agent is, the more extensive are his *volontés*. A very limited mind undertakes new schemes at every moment; and when he wants to execute one of them, he uses several means, of which some are always useless.' But a 'broad and penetrating mind', he goes on, 'compares and weighs all things: he never forms plans except with the knowledge that he has the means to execute them'.[78] Malebranche then moves to his legislative analogy: 'A great number of laws in a state'—presumably a mere concatenation of many *volontés particulières*—'often shows little penetration and breadth of mind in those who have established

---

[75] Ibid. I, sect. LVII, 63–4, and Illustration, sect XV, 166 (*inter alia*).
[76] Ibid. I, sect. XLIV, 50–1.
[77] Ibid. I, sect. XXXIX, 'additions', 47.
[78] Ibid. I, sect. XXXVIII, 46.

them: it is often the mere experience of need, rather than wise foresight, which has ordained them.' God *qua* legislator has none of these defects, Malebranche claims: 'he need not multiply his *volontés*, which are the executive laws of his plans, any further than necessity obliges'. He must, Malebranche repeats, act through *volontés générales* 'and thus establish a constant and regulated order' by 'the simplest means': those who want God to act, not through '*les loix ou les volontés générales*' but through *volontés particulières*, simply 'imagine that God at every moment is performing miracles in their favour'. This partisanship for the particular, he says, 'flatters the self-love which relates everything to itself', and 'accommodates itself quite well' to 'ignorance'.[79]

Malebranche certainly believed that those who imagine a God thick with *volontés particulières* will use that alleged divine particularism to rationalize their own failure to embrace general principles. Indeed, he appeals to the notion of *particularisme* in attempting to explain the (lamentable) diversity of the world's moral opinions and practices. In the *Traité de morale* (1684), Malebranche argues that although 'universal reason is always the same' and 'order is immutable', none the less 'morality changes according to countries and according to the times'. Germans think it 'virtuous' to drink to excess; European nobles think it 'generous' to fight duels in defence of their honour.[80] Such people 'even imagine that God approves their conduct'; that, in the case of an aristocratic duel, he 'presides at the judgement and . . . awards 'the palm to him who is right'. To be sure, according to Malebranche, one can only imagine this if one thinks that 'God acts by *volontés particulières*'. And if even he is thought to operate particularly, why should not men as well? The man who imputes particular wills to God by 'letting himself be led by imagination, his enemy', will also have his own '*morale particulière*, his own devotion, his favourite virtue'.[81] What is essential is that one abandon *particularisme*, whether as something ascribed to God, or as something merely derived from human 'inclinations' and 'humours'. It is 'immutable order' which must serve as our 'inviolable and natural law', and 'imagination' which

---

[79] *Nature et grâce*, I, sect. XXXVII, 'addition', 47: God is obliged 'to act always in a way worthy of him, in simple, general, constant, and uniform ways'. Illustration, sect. XXXVIII, 46.

[80] *Traité de morale*, ed. M. Adam, in *Œuvres complètes de Malebranche*, xi. 31–2.

[81] Ibid. 32.

must be suppressed. For order is general, while imagination is all too particular.[82]

Malebranche's notion that those who believe that they are the beneficiaries of a miraculous *Providence particulière* are suffering from acute egomania is strongly reinforced in the 1683 *Méditations chrétiennes*, written concurrently with the fourth (and final) 'Éclaircissement' of the *Traité de la nature et de la grâce*. In the eighth *Méditation* Malebranche insists that 'the New Testament [*la nouvelle alliance*] is in perfect conformity with the simplicity of natural laws', even though those general laws 'cause so many evils in the world'. For the New Testament promises 'des biens éternels' to the just, as 'compensation' for their 'patience' in enduring monstrous children and unripened fruit; therefore it is 'not at all necessary that God perform miracles often' in order to deliver the just from their 'present evils'. To be sure, Malebranche concedes, under the Old Testament, miracles—or at least 'what are called miracles'—were more necessary; for the ancient Jews, who lacked Christ's salvific grace and who were 'un peu grossiers et charnels', needed, or at least asked for, exceptions in their favour from general and simple laws. And this, according to Malebranche, led God ('at least in appearance') to 'trouble the simplicity of the laws' in biblical times.[83] But Christians, Malebranche insists, should know better, and live with the simplicity of (occasionally ruinous) laws; he condemns those who, 'failing to respect the order of nature', imagine that 'on all occasions' God should 'protect them in a particular way [*d'une manière particulière*]'. Is some people's reliance on God, Malebranche asks rhetorically, a sign of 'the greatness of their faith', or rather a mark of 'a stupid and rash confidence' which makes them have contempt for 'human ways'? Malebranche does not doubt that the 'piety' of those who 'claim to be under *une protection de Dieu toute particulière*' can often be 'sincere'; but that sincerity is commonly 'neither wise nor enlightened'. That sincerity, indeed, he says, is usually 'filled with *amour-propre* and with secret pride'. Some people fancy, Malebranche adds, that God is only good in so far as he applies himself to making exceptions to 'the rules of wisdom'; but it should be remembered that 'God constantly follows the general laws

---

[82] Ibid. 32–3.
[83] Malebranche, *Méditations chrétiennes et métaphysiques*, in *Œuvres complètes de Malebranche*, x. 84.

which he has very wisely established'.[84] Here, then, *particularisme* is identified with self-love, rashness, stupidity, and making exceptions to general laws and wills.

So wise, constant, and just are God's *volontés générales*, in Malebranche's view, that it is a moral wrong (on the part of man) not to accept and respect these 'general wills' and to make them the measure of human conduct. In one of his numerous defences of *Nature et grâce*, Malebranche argues that 'if God did not act in consequence of general laws which he has established, no one would ever make any effort. Instead of descending a staircase step by step, one would rather throw oneself out of the windows, trusting himself to God.' But why, Malebranche asks, would it be 'sin' as well as 'folly' to 'hurl oneself' from a window? 'It would be sin,' he answers, 'because it would be tempting God: it would be claiming to obligate him to act in a manner unworthy of him, or through *volontés particulières*'; it would amount to telling God 'that his work is going to perish, if he himself does not trouble the simplicity of his ways'. And in addition to 'sin', of course, hurling oneself would be 'folly', for one must be 'mad' to imagine that 'God must regulate his action by our particular needs, and groundlessly change, out of love for us, the uniformity of his conduct'.[85]

The Reservations of Malebranche's Critics

For Malebranche's orthodox and conservative critics—most notably Bossuet, whose anti-Malebranchism will be treated shortly—perhaps the most distressing aspect of Malebranche's theory of divine *volonté générale* was the much-diminished weight and value given to (literally read) Scripture. In *Nature et grâce* Malebranche urges that 'those who claim that God has particular plans and wills for all the particular effects which are produced in consequence of general laws' ordinarily rely (not on philosophy but) on 'the authority of Scripture ' to 'shore up' their 'feeling'.[86] (The verb and noun are sufficiently revealing.) But, Malebranche argues, 'since Scripture was made for everybody, for the simple as well as for the learned, it is full of *anthropologies*'.

---

[84] Malebranche, *Méditations chrétiennes et métaphysiques*, in *Œuvres complètes de Malebranche*, x. 87–8.

[85] Malebranche, *Réponse au livre de Mr Arnau[l]d, Des vrais et des fausses idées*, in *Œuvres complètes de Malebranche*, vi–vii. 43.

[86] *Nature et grâce* I, sect. LVII, 61–6.

Scripture, he goes on, endows God with 'a body, a throne, a chariot, a retinue, the passions of joy, of sadness, of anger, of remorse, and the other movements of the soul'; it even goes beyond this and attributes to him 'ordinary human ways of acting, in order to speak to the simple in a more sensible way'. St Paul, Malebranche continues, in order to 'accommodate himself to everyone', speaks of 'sanctification' and predestination 'as if God acted ceaselessly' through *volontés particulières* to produce those particular effects; and even Christ himself, he adds, 'speaks of his Father as if he applied himself, through comparable *volontés*, to clothe the lilies of the field and to preserve the least hair on his disciples' heads'.[87] Despite all these 'anthropologies' and 'as ifs', introduced solely to make God 'lovable' to 'even the coarsest minds', Malebranche concludes, one must use the 'idea' of God (*qua* perfect being), coupled with those non-anthropological scriptural passages which are in 'conformity' to this idea, in order to correct the sense of some other passages which attribute 'parts' to God, or 'passions like our own'.[88] (To make his own non-reliance on Scripture quite plain, Malebranche omitted almost all reference to the Bible in the original (1680) edition of *Nature et grâce*. And when, later, out of prudence, he interpolated a number of scriptural passages, he took care to set them off from the 1680 text by labelling the new parts 'additions', and by having them set in a different typeface. Even in the Scripture-laden version of 1684, then, the 'authority of Scripture' is separated—physically separated—from the idea of an *être infiniment parfait*.[89])

The notion that Scripture 'represents' God as a 'man' who has 'passions of the soul' and *volontés particulières* merely to 'accommodate' the 'weakness' of 'even the coarsest minds', leads to a difficulty that an Augustinian (or at least a Jansenist) would find distressing. Pascal had argued that, in 'Augustinianism', God's pre-lapsarian *volonté générale* to save all men is replaced, after the Fall, by the election of a few for salvation through *miséricorde* or 'pity' (though none merited it);[90] Arnauld, in the preface to his translation of *De Correptione et Gratia*, had equally stressed an undeserved divine *miséricorde* which God might with perfect justice have withheld.[91] Now pity, of course,

[87] Ibid. 62.   [88] Ibid.

[89] If one examines the 1684 edition of *Nature et grâce* (Rotterdam: Chez Reinier Leers, 1684), one finds that all the additions to the 1680 text have been set in italic type.

[90] Pascal, *Écrits sur la grâce*, in *Œuvres*, ed. Brunschvicg, xi. 135–40.

[91] St Augustine, *De la correction et de la grâce*, trans. and intro. Arnauld, 7.

on a Malebranchian view, is a 'passion of the soul'; but it is only through 'weakness' and 'anthropomorphism' that we imagine these passions as animating God. If, for Malebranche, an *être parfait* does not 'really' have these passions, it cannot be the case that—as in Pascal—a *volonté générale* to save all is 'replaced' by a pitiful *volonté absolue* to save a few. Indeed while in Pascal *volonté générale* comes 'first', and gets replaced (by *miséricorde*), in Malebranche 'general will' governs the realms of nature and grace from the outset, once the world has been created by a *volonté particulière*.[92] (Even Malebranche treats the Creation as the product of *volonté particulière*, arguing in the 'Second Discourse' of *Nature et grâce* that until there are created things which can serve as the 'occasional' or 'second' causes of general laws, those general laws cannot operate;[93] and this 'occasionalism' will be treated later.)

Far from abandoning his position when he was accused of 'ruining' Providence—in a work such as Jurieu's *Esprit de M. Arnauld*[94]—Malebranche maintained it stoutly in the 'Dernier Éclaircissement' of *Nature et grâce*, which he added to the fourth edition in 1684, and which was provocatively entitled, 'The frequent miracles of the Old Testament do not show at all that God acts often by particular wills'. The 'proofs' which he has drawn 'from the idea of an infinitely perfect Being', Malebranche insists, make it clear that 'God executes his designs by general laws'. On the other hand it is 'not easy' to demonstrate that God operates ordinarily through *volontés particulières*, 'though Holy Scripture, which accommodates itself to our weakness, sometimes represents God as a man, and often has him act as men act'.[95] Here, as in the main text of *Nature et grâce*, the key notion is weakness: and any notion of divine *volonté particulière* simply accommodates that *faiblesse*. This is why Malebranche can maintain—this time in the 'Troisième Éclaircissement' of 1683—that 'there are ways of acting [which are] simple, fruitful, general, uniform, and constant', and which manifest 'wisdom, goodness, steadiness, [and] immutability in those who use them'; whereas there are ways which are 'complex, sterile, particular, lawless, and inconstant', and which reveal 'lack of intelligence,

---

[92] *Nature et grâce*, II, sect. III, 67.   [93] Ibid. 67–8.

[94] Pierre Jurieu, *L'Esprit de M. Arnau[l]d* (Deventer: Jean Columbius, 1684), 80 ff., esp. 80: 'Je ne scay si le P. Malebranche a eu un ami assez fidèle, pour luy apprendre qu'il n'y a jamais eu de livre plus generalement desapprouvé que' *Nature et grâce*.

[95] *Nature et grâce*, 204.

malignity, unsteadiness, [and] levity in those who use them'.[96] Thus a very effective heap of execrations is mounded around any *volonté particulière*, which turns out to be complex, sterile, lawless, inconstant, unintelligent, malignant, and frivolous.

Indeed, for Malebranche, it is precisely, *volonté particulière*, and not at all *volonté générale*, which 'ruins' Providence. In his *Réponse à une dissertation de M. Arnauld contre un éclaircissement de la nature et de la grâce* (1685), he argues that if Arnauld's insistence on miracles and constant divine *volontés particulières* does not 'overturn' Providence, it at least 'degrades it, humanizes it, and makes it either blind, or perverse'.[97]

Is there wisdom in creating monsters by *volontés particulières*? In making crops grow by rainfall, in order to ravage them by hail? In giving to men a thousand impulses of grace which misfortunes render useless? In making rain fall equally on sand and on cultivated ground? But all this is nothing. Is there wisdom and goodness in making impious princes reign, in suffering so great a number of heresies, in letting so many nations perish? Let M. Arnauld raise his head and discover all the evils which happen in the world, and let him justify Providence, on the supposition that God acts and must act through *volontés particulières*.[98]

It is Malebranche's view, in fact, that the classical 'theodicy problems'—reconciling a morally and physically imperfect world with God's 'power', 'goodness', and 'wisdom'—can *only* be solved by insisting that God wills generally. These problems Malebranche states starkly in *Nature et grâce*:

Holy Scripture teaches us on one hand that God wills that all men be saved, and that they come to a knowledge of the truth; and on the other, that he does everything that he wills: and none the less faith is not given to everyone; and the number of those that perish is much greater than that of the predestined. How can one reconcile this with his power?

God foresaw from all eternity both original sin, and the infinite number of persons that this sin would sweep into Hell. None the less he created the first man in a condition from which he knew he would fall; he even established between this man and his posterity relations which would communicate his sin to them, and render them all worthy of his aversion and his wrath. How can one reconcile this with his goodness?

God frequently diffuses graces, without having the effect for which his goodness obliges us to believe that he gives them. He increases piety in

---

[96] Ibid. 180.   [97] In *Œuvres complètes de Malebranche*, vi–vii. 591–2.
[98] Ibid. 592.

persons almost to the end of their life; and sin dominates them at death, and throws them into Hell. He makes the rain of grace fall on hardened hearts, as well as on prepared grounds: men resist it, and make it useless for their salvation. In a word, God undoes and re-does without cease: it seems that he wills, and no longer wills. How can one reconcile this with his wisdom?[99]

'Generality' and 'simplicity' of divine will, according to Malebranche, clears up these 'great difficulties', and explains how a being who loves order can permit disorder. 'God loves men, he wills to save them all,' Malebranche begins by saying, 'for order is his law.' None the less, Malebranche insists, God 'does not will to *do* what is necessary in order that all [men] know him and love him infallibly'. And this is simply because 'order does not permit that he have practical *volontés* proper to the execution of this design . . . He must not disturb the simplicity of his ways'.[100] Or, as Malebranche puts it in his *Réponse* to Arnauld's *Réflexions* on *Nature et grâce*,

The greater number of men are damned, and [yet] God wills to save them all. . . . Whence comes it, then, that sinners die in their sin? Is it better to maintain that God does *not* will to save them all, simply because it pleases him to act in that way, than to seek the general reason for it in what he owes to himself, to his wisdom, and to his other attributes? Is it not clear, or at least is it not a feeling in conformity with piety, that one must throw these unhappy effects back on to simplicity—in one word onto the divinity of his ways?[101]

And in his final work, published in the year of his death (1715), Malebranche reformulated this argument in an even stronger way—a way that Leibniz, among others, found excessive.

Infinity in all sorts of perfections is an attribute of the divinity, indeed his essential attribute, that which encloses all the others. Now between the finite and the infinite, the distance is infinite; the relation is nothing. The most excellent of creatures, compared to the divinity, is nothing; and God counts it as nothing in relation to himself. . . . It seems to me evident, that God conducts himself according to what he is, in remaining immobile, [even while] seeing the demon tempt, and man succumb to the temptation. . . .

[99] *Nature et grâce*, I, sects. XXXIX–XLI, 47–8.
[100] Cited in Ginette Dreyfus, *La Volonté selon Malebranche* (Paris: Vrin, 1958), 114. *Volonté selon Malebranche* (Paris: Vrin, 1958), 114.
[101] Malebranche, *Réponse au livre I des réflexions philosophiques*, in *Œuvres complètes de Malebranche*, viii–ix. 721. Cf. p. 722: 'S'il [Dieu] avoit une volonté absolue de sauver tous les hommes, sans avoir egard à la simplicité des moyens, il est certain qu'il les sauveroit tous.'

His immobility bears the character of his infinity . . . If God, in order to stop the Fall of Adam, had interrupted the ordinary course of his *providence générale*, that conduct would have expressed the false judgement that God had counted the worship that Adam rendered him as something, with respect to his infinite majesty. Now God must never trouble the simplicity of his ways, nor interrupt the wise, constant, and majestic course of his ordinary providence, by a particular and miraculous providence . . . God is infinitely wise, infinitely just, infinitely good, and he does men all the good he can—not absolutely, but acting according to what he is. . . .[102]

After this, it rings a little hollow when Malebranche adds that, none the less, 'God sincerely wills to save all men'. Small wonder that Leibniz, for all his general agreement with Malebranche, should complain that 'I do not know whether one should have recourse to the expedient [of saying] that God, by remaining immobile during the Fall of man . . . marks [in that way] that the most excellent creatures are nothing in relation to him'; that way of putting the matter, for Leibniz, can be 'abused', and even lead to 'the despotism of the supralapsarians'.[103] And perhaps the 'immobility' passage was the one that the Jesuit Rodolphe du Tertre had in mind when he published a three-volume attack on Malebranche even as the Oratorian lay on his death-bed: in the final volume of his *Réfutation d'un nouveau système de métaphysique proposé par le Père Malebranche*, du Tertre argues that

According to our author [Malebranche], God wills to save all men in this sense, that the ways . . . that he was indispensably obliged to follow in the execution of his work, will cause to enter into the future Church the most men that simplicity and generality will permit. [God] wills that all men be saved in this sense, that if there could be some other order of grace, equally worthy of him and more useful to men . . . he would have chosen it, or rather he would have been necessitated by his wisdom to choose it, in order not to contradict his attributes. There once again one sees what Father M[alebranche] calls God's true will that all men be saved—though at the same time he assures us that God cannot save more than he does save, without performing miracles that immutable order, which is his necessary law, does not permit him to perform . . .

This means that the new theologian judges it suitable, for good reasons, to give the name 'true and sincere will' to a chimerical *velléité* which it pleases him to imagine in God with respect to the salvation of men; such that,

---

[102] Malebranche, *Réflexions sur la prémotion physique*, 118.

[103] Leibniz, letter to Malebranche (Dec. 1711), cited in *Œuvres complètes de Malebranche*, xix. 815.

according to [Malebranche's] dictionary, to say that God truly wills that all men be saved is really to say that God would will this, if it could be, though it cannot be: that he would will it, supposing an impossible hypothesis, which would be that there is another way of acting [which is] more advantageous to men, and at the same time equally worthy of his attributes.[104]

Evidently, Malebranche was able to please neither the Jesuits, at one extreme, nor the Jansenists, at the other: for the Jesuits, Malebranche's God saves too few men, while for the Jansenists he saves too many (and would apparently save all if his generality and simplicity didn't forbid it). As Ginette Dreyfus has correctly said in her helpful *La Volonté selon Malebranche*, 'God wills to save all men, but wisdom forbids him to act in such a way that they would actually be saved' (p. 114). Generality, then, 'saves' God, though it fails to save all men.

The theodicy problems that 'generality' and 'simplicity' are meant to solve *must* have a resolution, according to Malebranche, because the radical imperfection and evil in the universe is all too real, not at all merely 'apparent'. If it were merely apparent, one could perhaps appeal to the notion of a mysterious *Dieu caché* whose inscrutable ways discover real good in seeming evil. But this is not Malebranche's view. 'A monster', he declares, 'is an imperfect work, whatever may have been God's purpose in creating it.'

Some philosophers, perverted by an extravagant metaphysics, come and tell me that God wills evil as positively and directly as the good; that he truly only wills the beauty of the universe . . . [and] . . . that the world is a harmony in which monsters are a necessary dissonance; that God wants sinners as well as the just; and that, just as shadows in a painting make its subjects stand out, and give them relief, so too the impious are absolutely necessary in the work of God, to make virtue shine in men of good will.[105]

Those who reason along these lines, in Malebranche's view, are trying to resolve moral dilemmas by appealing to aesthetic similes; but the method will not serve. 'Shadows are necessary in a painting

---

[104] Rodolphe du Tertre, *Réfutation d'un nouveau système de métaphysique proposé par le Père Malebranche* (Paris: Chez Raymond Mazières, 1715), 275–7. Du Tertre had been an ardent Malebranchist, but was ordered by his Jesuit superiors to relinquish his views; unlike his fellow-Jesuit and one-time friend Y. M. André, du Tertre followed orders.

[105] Cited in André Robinet, *Système et éxistence dans l'œuvre de Malebranche* (Paris: Vrin, 1965), 104.

and dissonances in music. Thus it is necessary that women abort and produce an infinity of monsters. What a conclusion!' And he ends by insisting that 'I do not agree that there is evil only in appearance'.[106] Hence *volonté générale* alone, which wills (positively) the good and only *permits* evil (as the unavoidable consequence of general and simple laws), is the sole avenue of escape from theodicy problems if one calls evil *real*. For Malebranche in the *Traité de la nature et de la grâce*, only *généralité* is positively good, truly justifiable.

Another of the aspects of *volonté générale* which Malebranche's critics found distressing was the possibility that it had been 'derived' or extracted from a Cartesian notion of general laws of uniform motion (in physics), and simply grafted on to, or inflicted on, the realm of grace.[107] And this suspicion was borne out by a careful reading of some passages from *Nature et grâce*. In the 'Premier Discours', Malebranche finds a 'parallel' between 'generality' in nature and in grace: but he *begins* with nature, and finds in grace no more than a kind of analogue to nature. 'Just as one has no right to be annoyed by the fact that rain falls in the sea, where it is useless,' Malebranche argues, so 'also' one has no right 'to complain of the apparent irregularity according to which grace is given to men.' Useless rain and useless grace both derive from 'the regularity with which God acts', from 'the simplicity of the laws which he follows'. And Malebranche reinforces the nature–grace parallel, in which nature seems to be the 'model' for grace, by calling grace a 'heavenly rain which sometimes falls on hardened hearts, as well as on prepared souls'.[108] This horticultural language, of course—which Malebranche himself said he used to persuade (mainly) Cartesians, not Scholastic theologians[109]—did nothing to dispel the suspicion of traditionalists like Bossuet that Cartesian 'generality' and 'uniformity' might be used in radical ways, to the detriment of traditional teachings about grace based on Scripture and patristic writings. This kind of suspicion—best expressed by Bossuet himself when he says, in a letter dealing with Malebranchism, that he sees 'a great struggle against the Church being prepared in the name of Cartesian philosophy'[110]—was certainly not relieved by Malebranche's insistence

[106] Ibid. 105.
[107] This was the fear of both Arnauld and Bossuet; see part II of this Introduction.
[108] *Nature et grâce*, I, sect. XLIV, 50. [109] Ibid., 'Avertissement', 7.
[110] Bossuet, letter to the Marquis d'Allemans, in *Œuvres complètes de Malebranche*, xviii. 445.

that 'what Moses tells us in Genesis is so obscure' that the beginning of the world can be explained *à la Descartes* better than any other way.[111] 'Obscurity', of course, is no more welcome than 'anthropology' or 'as if'.

The fear of orthodox Christian moralists that Malebranche had permitted a Cartesian 'physics' to invade and infect the sphere of metaphysics (including ethics) was of course not wholly groundless: after all, in the *Recherche de la vérité* Malebranche 'Cartesianizes' everything, not least human volition and action:

> Just as the author of nature is the universal cause of all the movements which are in matter, it is also he who is the general cause [*cause générale*] of all the natural inclinations which are in minds. And just as all movements proceed in a straight line [*en ligne droite*], if there are no foreign and particular causes which determine them, and which change them into curved lines through their opposing forces; so too the inclinations which we receive from God are right [*droites*], and they could not have any other end than the possession of the good and of truth if there were not any foreign cause, which determined the impression of nature towards bad ends.[112]

Here, of course, like Kant a century later, Malebranche is playing with the different senses of *droit* (meaning both 'straight' and 'right') and of curved (which can mean 'crooked' in a moral sense.[113] And this same kind of playing can be found in Rousseau's most famous single assertion about 'general will': 'La volonté générale est toujours droite, mais le jugement qui la guide n'est pas toujours éclairé.'[114] But the key point in connection with Malebranche is that the language of Cartesian physics has been imposed on morality and psychology: that (however briefly) Malebranche resembles Hobbes in accounting for everything in terms of 'general' *motion*. And that *généralité*, in Malebranche, always has a supremely important weight: if the God of Pascal and Arnauld permanently abandons a primitive *volonté générale* to save 'all' in favour of (very particular) 'pity' for the elect, Malebranche's God moves as quickly as possible

---

[111] Malebranche, *Réponse au Livre I des réflexions philosophiques*, viii–ix. 780.

[112] Malebranche, *De la recherche de la vérité*, I. i. 2, in *Œuvres complètes de Malebranche*, i. 45.

[113] Kant, *Die Metaphysik der Sitten*, 'Einleitung in der Rechtslehre', sect. E, in *Immanuel Kants Werke*, ed. Ernst Cassirer (Berlin: Bruno Cassirer Verlag, 1922), vii. 34.

[114] Rousseau, *Du contrat social*, in *Political Writings*, ed. C. Vaughan (Oxford: Basil Blackwell, 1962), ii. 50.

away from an embarrassingly particularistic Creation, and towards generality and simplicity.

Malebranche Accused of 'Humanizing' Theology

It is interesting that some of the contemporary opponents of Malebranche—particularly the orthodox Cartesian Pierre-Sylvain Régis—thought that the notion of a just and justifiable divine *volonté générale* was 'legal' in a wholly bad sense: that Malebranche had confused divine 'governance' with ordinary human governance, and hence subverted theology. 'I shall not say', Régis observes, 'that God acts by *volontés générales*, or by *volontés particulières*, because these two kinds of will cannot be suitable to a perfect being.'[115] If God acted only through *volontés générales*, Régis claims, this would mean 'that he willed things only in a general way, without descending to anything particular, as a king governs a kingdom through general laws, not having the power to guide each subject'. A mere king, Régis goes on, falls back on general laws and *volontés générales* only because of political impotence; but 'God cannot have *volontés générales* . . . because these *volontés* suppose an impotence in God which I cannot attribute to him'.[116] Since the notion that God operates through *volontés particulières* is no better, in Régis's view— 'it would follow that the nature of God would be composed of as many different wills as there are particular things which God wills, which is repugnant to his simplicity'[117]—it must be the case that 'God acts by a simple, eternal and immutable will which embraces indivisibly and in a single act everything that is and will be'.[118]

Malebranche, as it happens, had an answer to this kind of charge. In the seventh of his *Méditations chrétiennes et métaphysiques* (1683), he warns that when one says that God 'permits certain natural disorders, such as the generation of monsters, the violent death of a good man, or something similar', one must not imagine that there is an autonomous 'nature' to which God has 'given' some of his power and which acts independently of God, 'in the same way that a prince lets ministers act, and permits disorders which he cannot stop'.[119] God *could* stop all 'disorders' (though a prince cannot) by acting

---

[115] Pierre-Sylvain Régis, *Cours entier de philosophie ou système général selon les principes de M. Descartes* (Amsterdam: Huguetan, 1691), i. 92. For a commentary on Régis's thought, see Geneviève Lewis, *Le Problème de l'inconscient et le Cartésianisme* (Paris: Presses Universitaires de France, 1950).

[116] Ibid. (Régis).   [117] Ibid.   [118] Ibid. 93.

[119] *Méditations chrétiennes et métaphysiques*, 76.

through a multiplicity of *volontés particulières* which would remedy all particular evils. But acting in this fashion would derogate from the simplicity of his ways: God, Malebranche argues, 'does good because he wants his work to be perfect', and he 'permits' (rather than does) evil not because he 'positively and directly' wills it but because 'he wants his manner of acting to be simple, regular, uniform, and constant, because he wants his conduct to be worthy of him and to wear visibly the character of his attributes'.[120] Thus for Malebranche, to act by *volontés générales* and general laws does not manifest a quasi-human 'impotence' at all: God can will anything, but acting through *volontés particulières* would not be worthy of him. What he can do is simply a question of power; what he actually wills is a question of wisdom and justice.

If there were some critics of Malebranche who claimed that he had (illegitimately) thought of God after the manner of a mere earthly king, there were others who thought that 'rulership' analogies were (in themselves) perfectly acceptable, and that Malebranche had simply pitched upon false ones. In his *Réflexions sur le système de la nature et de la grâce* (1685), Arnauld argues that 'there is no contradiction whatever [in the fact] that God wills by a *volonté absolue et particulière* the contrary of what he wills *en général* by an antecedent will; just as a good king wills by an antecedent will that all his subjects live contentedly, though by a consequent will he executes those who disturb public tranquillity by murders and violence'.[121] Malebranche's theory of 'general' justice, in Arnauld's view, suffers from the defect of virtually equating *volonté générale*, general law, wisdom, justice, and 'the simplest means'; these, however, according to Arnauld, are not equivalent, and what 'wisdom' requires (e.g. the remedying of particular evils) may not be attainable by 'the simplest means'—either for God or for a human ruler.[122]

Malebranche's fatal confusion, for Arnauld, is the conflation of general will and general law: but the operation of a general law may contain (as it were) a divine *volonté particulière*. And in 'proving' this Arnauld has recourse to Scripture, which Malebranche had minimized. 'If one considers a particular effect', Arnauld begins in the *Réflexions*

---

[120] *Méditations chrétiennes et métaphysiques*, 77.

[121] In *Œuvres de Messire Antoine Arnauld*, xxxix. 198.

[122] Ibid. 174 ff. One must conclude, Arnauld insists, *contra* Malebranche, that God 'acts by *volontés particulières* in consequence of general laws' (175).

philosophiques et théologiques, 'and if one finds nothing but conformity to general laws of nature, one has reason to say, with respect to this effect, that God has acted according to general laws.' But, Arnauld goes on, since this particular effect has many 'remote causes', one would have to be 'assured' that there has never been a particular divine 'intervention' in this causal sequence, before one could say 'absolutely' that any particular effect was '*only* a consequence of the general laws of nature'. One would have, in short, to be omniscient. Now who, Arnauld asks triumphantly, can 'assure us of this, without a prodigious temerity, and without ruining the faith we have in Providence?'[123]

But Arnauld does not content himself with the impossibility of proving that Providence has *not* intervened somewhere in the causal chain; he relies mainly on Scripture. And it is precisely the Old Testament which 'recounts to us that a stone, falling high from a tower, smashed the head of Abimelech, son of Gideon, who had had all his brothers, save one, killed'. One cannot reasonably 'doubt', Arnauld argues, that this stone 'observed the general laws of the movement of heavy things', and that it crushed Ambimelech's head 'according to the laws of the communication of movement'; but this generality of law does not *exclude* a divine 'particular will' at all:

One can thus say that God acted, in injuring this wicked man, according to the general laws of nature, which he himself established. But does it follow from this that he acted only according to these laws, and that he had not the slightest *volonté particulière* in this matter? To judge of this, let us look farther back. This rock fell from this tower. Was it by itself? No; it was a woman who threw it. Now who can doubt that God led the will and the hand of this woman, if one considers that Scripture teaches us that this happened through a just vengeance of God, which had been predicted by the youngest of the children of Gideon, who had escaped the cruelty of his brother?[124]

If one looks back—or could look back—one would often find a particular divine 'contribution' to effects that *seem* to be 'only consequences of the general laws of nature'; and it is Scripture which teaches us where to find these 'hidden' particular interventions. To deny these interventions is to deny that God can realize justice in this world—by punishing Abimelech, for example. Malebranchian generality thus undercuts justice and wisdom; it forbids God to do in particular what justice requires, makes him the slave of his own

[123] Ibid. 177.   [124] Ibid.

'simplicity'. And if one wants to see how these *volontés cachées* of God operate in human history, Arnauld adds in a later chapter, one should repair to Bossuet's *Histoire universelle*—so full of 'light' and 'insight'—which reveals particular providence always operating behind 'the human causes of the establishment and decline of great empires'.[125] For Arnauld, in short, it is a Malebranchian confusion to identify general law and general will; for *loi générale* can carry out a divine *volonté particulière*. And that means that Descartes and Augustine cannot be fused: Cartesian *généralité* indeed governs *la physique*, but in the realm of *la morale* God acts wholly *particulière-ment*—even if he relies on his own general physical laws in so doing. Between Arnauld and Malebranche, then, these is no middle ground that can be jointly occupied: for Arnauld, Scripture limits what philosophy can reveal about God; for Malebranche, it is philosophy which limits Scripture and its 'anthropologies'.

Malebranche's Final Response to His Critics: the Reflections on Physical Promotion *(1715)*

In his last work, the *Réflexions sur la prémotion physique*, which was published in the year of his death (1715), Malebranche found an opportunity to show that his notions of *volonté générale* and general law have a general *moral* significance. The *Réflexions* were a commentary on Laurent Boursier's quasi-Jansenist *De l'action de Dieu sur les créatures* (1713)—a large section of which attempted to refute Malebranche's theory of the divine *modus operandi*. In *De l'action de Dieu* Boursier treats God as a 'sovereign' whose will is unrestricted by any necessity to act only through general laws ('God has willed [the world] thus, because he willed it'),[126] and argues that Malebranche's notion of divine 'wisdom' renders God 'impotent'. 'The sovereign who governs', Boursier claims, whether God or a 'prince', 'causes inferiors to act as he wills', and he does this through 'command': 'he interposes his power in order to determine them'. And 'inferiors', for their part, act only 'because they are excited and determined by the prince . . . they act in consequence of his determination'.[127]

[125] In *Œuvres de Messire Antoine Arnauld*, xxxix. 313.

[126] Laurent Boursier, *De l'action de Dieu sur les créatures* (Paris: Babuty, 1713), 70. (Substantial extracts from Boursier's work are printed as an appendix in *Œuvres complètes de Malebranche*, xvi. 199 ff.)

[127] Ibid. 36.

Since God is a powerful 'sovereign' who has willed the world to be what it is simply 'because he has willed it', one cannot say that he prefers a Malebranchian 'generality' or 'the simplest means', or indeed that he prefers anything at all; the 'greatness and majesty of the supreme being' must make us realize that 'everything that he can will with respect to what is outside himself' is 'equal' to him.[128] But Malebranche, Boursier complains, does not see that God can equally will whatever is in his power. 'What an idea of God! He wishes, and he does not accomplish; he does not like monsters, but he makes them; he does not attain the perfection which he desires in his works; he cannot fashion a work without defects . . . his wisdom limits his power. A strange idea of God! An impotent being, an unskilful workman, a wisdom based on constraint, a sovereign who does not do what he wills, an unhappy God.'[129]

In his response to Boursier's theory of 'sovereignty' based on will, command, and power, Malebranche actually abandons the terms *volonté générale* and *volonté particulière* (conceivably because of the constant criticisms of Régis, Arnauld, *et al.*); but he does not abandon at all the concepts for which the terms stood, and so *volonté générale* and general law become 'eternal law', while *volonté particulière* becomes *volonté absolue et bizarre*[130] (which is more striking still). 'My present design', Malebranche says, 'is to prove that God is essentially wise, just and good . . . that his *volontés* are not at all purely arbitrary—that is to say that they are not wise and just simply because he is all-powerful . . . but because they are regulated by the eternal law . . . a law which can consist only in the necessary immutable relations which are among the attributes and perfections which God encloses in his essence.'[131] The ideas which we have of wisdom, justice, and goodness, Malebranche goes on to say, 'are quite different from those that we have of omnipotence'.[132] To say that the *volontés* of God are 'purely arbitrary', that 'no reason can be given for his *volontés*, except his *volontés* themselves', and that everything that he wills and does is just, wise, and good because he is omnipotent and has a 'sovereign domain' over his creatures—to say all this, Malebranche argues, is 'to leave the objections of libertines in all their force'.[133]

---

[128] Ibid. 47.
[129] Ibid. 79.
[130] *Réflexions sur la prémotion physique*, 93.
[131] Ibid. 101.
[132] Ibid. 104.
[133] Ibid.

The notion that God wills in virtue of 'eternal law', not simply through the bare possession of 'sovereign domain', leads Malebranche to a criticism of Hobbes (and Locke) which is an interesting expansion of his notion of *volonté générale*. 'If', Malebranche says, 'God were only omnipotent, and if he were like princes who glory more in their power than in their nature', then 'his sovereign domain, or his independence, would give him a right to everything, or he would not act as [an] all-powerful [being]'. If this were true of God, Malebranche continues, then 'Hobbes, Locke, and several others would have discovered the true foundations of morality: authority and power giving, without reason, the right to do whatever one wills, when one has nothing to fear'.[134] This legal-positivist view of either human or divine justice Malebranche characterizes as 'mad'; and those who attribute this mode of operation to God 'apparently prefer force, the law of brutes (that which has granted to the lion an empire over the animals), to reason'.[135]

Now, however unfair this may be to Hobbes, and still more to Locke—though at least Hobbes does actually say, in chapter 31 of *Leviathan*, that 'irresistible power' carries with it a 'right' to 'dominion'[136]—Malebranche's last work shows that he thought that rule through *volontés* which are *particulières* or *absolues* or (even) *bizarres* was wrong in either human or divine governance, that rule through 'eternal laws' which are of general validity is right. Of course Malebranche was not alone in this: since Descartes's time a controversy had raged over the question whether there *are* any 'eternal laws' which God 'finds' in his understanding and 'follows' in his volitions.[137] Leibniz (following Plato's *Euthyphro*) put forward a theory of general, non-arbitrary divine justice in his *Theodicée* (1710) which was very close to Malebranche's, and criticized Hobbes along (roughly) Malebranchian lines in his *Opinion on the Principles of Pufendorf*.[138] So arguments against 'Hobbism' based on the notion

[134] *Réflexions sur la prémotion physique*, 98.   [135] Ibid. 93.
[136] Hobbes, *Leviathan*, ed. Michael Oakeshott (Oxford: Basil Blackwell, 1957), ch. 31, p. 234: 'To those therefore whose power is irresistible, the dominion of all men adhereth naturally by their excellence or power.' See also John Locke, *The Reasonableness of Christianity*, in *The Works of John Locke* (London: C. Rivington *et al.*, 1824), vi *passim*.
[137] For a fuller treatment of this point, see the author's 'Introduction' to *The Political Writings of Leibniz*, 6 ff.
[138] Plato, *Euthyphro*, 9E–10E; Leibniz, *Opinion on the Principles of Pufendorf*, in *The Political Writings of Leibniz*, trans. and ed. Riley, 64 ff.: 'Neither the norm of conduct itself, nor the essence of the just, depends on his [God's] free decision, but

that there are 'eternal laws' of justice were certainly not scarce at the turn of the eighteenth century, and Malebranche was in perfect accord with Leibniz in disputing Hobbes (and Descartes) on this point.[139]

In connection with his doctrine that God never operates through a *volonté* which is *absolue* or *bizarre*, but only through love of the 'eternal law' which is 'coeternal' with him, Malebranche designs one of the strikingly imaginative stage-settings that even Voltaire found impressive:

If God were only all-powerful, or if he gloried only in his omnipotence, without the slightest regard for his other attributes—in a word, without consulting his consubstantial law, his lovable and inviolable law—how strange his plans would be! How could we be certain that, through his omnipotence, he would not, on the first day, place all of the demons in heaven, and all the saints in hell, and a moment after annihilate all that he had done! Cannot God, *qua* omnipotent, create each day a million planets, make new worlds, each more perfect than the last, and reduce them each year to a grain of sand?[140]

Fortunately, according to Malebranche, though God is in fact all-powerful and 'does whatever he wills to do', none the less he 'does not will to do anything' except 'according to the immutable order of justice'. And this is why Malebranche insists, in four or five separate passages of the *Réflexions sur la prémotion physique*, that St Paul always said 'O altitudo divitiarum Sapientiae et Scientiae Dei', and not at all 'O altitudo voluntatis Dei': will can be wilful, if its only attribute is power, and that attribute is the one that Boursier (and Hobbes) wrongly endow with excessive weight.[141]

Strictly speaking, Malebranche and Leibniz share enemies (especially Hobbes), rather than agree perfectly; they are only in general accord on 'general will'. Even in the *Theodicée*, which maximizes the area of agreement, Leibniz takes care to distance himself just a little from *Nature et grâce*: it is quite true, Leibniz urges, that 'the events

rather on eternal truths, objects of the divine intellect . . . Justice, indeed, would not be an essential attribute of God, if he himself established justice and law by his free will.' For an appreciation of the limits of Leibniz's Platonism, see the author's 'An Unpublished MS of Leibniz on the Existence of God', in *Studia Leibnitiana*, 15: 2 (Hanover, 1983), 215–20.

[139] Cf. Alquié, *Le Cartésianisme de Malebranche*, 'Le Cartesianisme ruiné', 226 ff.

[140] *Réflexions sur la prémotion physique*, 100.

[141] Ibid. 172, 93, 122, etc.

which are born of the execution of general laws are not at all the object of a *volonté particulière* of God' and that 'one can even imagine that this way of acting through *volontés générales* seemed preferable to him (though some superfluous events . . . had to result from it) to another way which was more complex'. However, Leibniz goes on, he will not say, with Malebranche, that God 'derogates' from *lois générales* when and if he performs a miracle; even miracles, Leibniz insists, are only the 'applications' of a divine law, though that law may remain unknown to finite intelligences ('the character of miracles . . . is that one cannot explain them through the natures of created things').[142]

The notion that human finitude may keep men from seeing the real generality of the divine laws which give rise to 'miracles' is plainer and clearer in some of Leibniz's private notes on Malebranche. In his 1685 observations on Malebranche's *Réponse au livre des vrais et des fausses idées*, Leibniz first summarizes Malebranche's doctrine, then notes in the margin that

everything done by wisdom is done by *des loix générales*, or rules or principles; and God always acts wisely. Thus even miracles are in the general order, that is to say in general laws. But that which makes them miracles, is that they do not follow the notions of [human] subjects and cannot be predicted by the greatest finite mind that one can simulate.[143]

And the following year, in notes on some of Antoine Arnauld's letters to Malebranche, Leibniz relates to mathematics his belief that the merely apparent 'particularity' of miracles arises from the inability of finite minds to conceive truly general—divinely general—laws:

In my opinion, none of the actions of God are exceptions, but conform to general rules. And just as there is no line, freely made by hand, however irregular it appears to be, which cannot be reduced to a rule or a definition, in the same way the consequences of God's actions comprise a certain quite regular disposition, without any exception.[144]

Here Leibniz's view was no doubt that if Malebranche had been a better mathematician, he would have operated with a more adequate idea of generality.

---

[142] Cited in Robinet, *Malebranche et Leibniz*, 408.
[143] Ibid. 202.   [144] Ibid. 222.

Leibniz explicitly moralizes his notion of God's generality (even in miracles) in a MS from *c*.1700 entitled *Conversation sur la liberté et le destin*. After talking about the 'order of justice' in the best of all possible worlds which God has chosen to produce, and after enlarging on the 'usefulness' of divinely appointed 'pains and compensations' ('right is always based on the general utility'), Leibniz goes on to discuss the *volontés générales* of God, which 'serve as a rule', and his *volontés particulières*—which, however, are 'not at all an exception to the rule' (if one understands true generality). God's two kinds of will, Leibniz insists, are 'different without being contrary', and one can even say that the particular is 'subordinated' to the general. As for human conduct, Leibniz goes on, 'we can only govern ourselves through the known will of God, which is general, that is to say through the orders which he has given us' (such as the Commandments).[145]

Despite some differences with Malebranche, none the less, Leibniz could send a copy of the *Theodicée* to the Oratorian in the confident belief that most of it would prove congenial; and Malebranche's acknowledgement of Leibniz's present ('you prove quite well . . . that God . . . must choose the best') showed Leibniz right.[146] A shared Augustinian Platonism and love of eternal mathematical order formed the rapport between Malebranche and Leibniz; and if Malebranche was a more nearly orthodox Cartesian than his Hanoverian correspondent, even the Oratorian shared Leibniz's distaste for the Cartesian notion that God creates mathematical, logical, and moral truth *ex nihilo*.[147] (That shared Augustinian Platonism also accounts, in part, for a common devotion to *généralité* on the part of both Malebranche and Leibniz: in the Platonic tradition it was axiomatic that the proper object of immaterial reason is general or universal truth, whereas the proper object of physical sensation is imagery of particular things. Here, then, Platonism shores up the 'Cartesian' notion of a generally-willing God.)

In defence of uncreated 'eternal verities', indeed, Malebranche— for all his Cartesianism—joined forces with Leibniz and parted company with the Cartesians, who founded even the character of

---

[145] Cited in Gaston Grua, *Leibniz: Textes inédits* (Paris: Presses Universitaires de France, 1948), ii. 483.

[146] Cited in Robinet, *Malebranche et Leibniz*, 417.

[147] On this point see Alquié, *Le Cartésianisme de Malebranche*, 226 ff.

truth itself on the omnipotent will of God. As Descartes had written in his *Reply to the Six Objections*,

It is self-contradictory that the will of God should not have been from eternity indifferent to all that has come to pass or that will ever occur, because we can form no conception of anything good or true . . . the idea of which existed in the divine understanding before God's will determined him to act. . . . Thus, to illustrate, God did not will . . . the three angles of a triangle to be equal to two right angles because he knew that they could not be otherwise. On the contrary, it is because he willed the three angles of a triangle to be necessarily equal to two right angles that this is true and cannot be otherwise.[148]

Leibniz devoted the opening portion of his *Meditation on the Common Concept of Justice* to a refutation of this view—a refutation in which Malebranche would have joined.

It is agreed that whatever God wills is good and just. But there remains the question whether it is good and just because God wills it or whether God wills it because it is good and just; in other words, whether justice and goodness are arbitrary, or whether they belong to the necessary and eternal truths about the nature of things.[149]

One must, Leibniz said, hold to the second view, since, if the good were not the motive of God's will, his decisions would be only 'a certain absolute decree, without reason'.[150] Leibniz's position on this question is far from original: it stretches from Plato's *Euthyphro* to Duns Scotus, and had been recently restated by Grotius.[151] But Malebranche was in perfect agreement with Leibniz on this point: in both, Platonism limits Cartesianism.

II

In treating Malebranche—particularly when *Nature et grâce* is the focus of attention—it is common enough to speak as if his whole philosophy confined itself to elevating *volonté générale* and execrating *volonté particulière*. (In their critiques of Malebranche, as will be seen in Part III (below), Bossuet and Bayle were to single out *généralité* as

---

[148] Trans. Eaton, 265–6.

[149] In *The Political Writings of Leibniz*, trans. and ed. Riley, 45–6.

[150] Leibniz, 'On the Philosophy of Descartes', in *The Philosophical Works of Leibniz*, 2nd edn., trans. G. M. Duncan (New Haven, Conn.: Yale University Press, 1908), 3.

[151] Grotius, *De Jure Belli ac Pacis* I. i. x.

the main problem, or defect, in the Oratorian's thought.) Pierre Jurieu, writing at the end of the seventeenth century in his *Traitté de la nature et de la grâce*, insisted that 'one can scarcely say how much this thought [of general will] pleases this philosopher, for he loves it to the point of idolatry, and causes it to appear everywhere . . . It is the sole foundation of his system.'[152] Pierre-Valentine Faydit, publishing his characteristically venomous *Presbytéromachie* at the turn of the eighteenth century, argued that Malebranche will not 'admit any *volontés particulières* in God, outside the case of miracles, which are, according to him, almost as rare as in Spinoza'; that Malebranche's God is a 'universal agent' who acts only through 'des loix générales'.[153] And Sainte-Beuve, writing *Port-Royal* in the middle of the nineteenth century, urged equally that 'Malebranche loves general laws, the *volontés générales* of God, once established; he does not want God to alter them, whether two times or a thousand. . . . He wants the supreme watchmaker to make the world run by itself, or almost all alone, from the first push.'[154]

But the notion of 'general will' is not, for Malebranche, a complete or exhaustive doctrine; and even in *Nature et grâce* itself one finds, in addition to *généralité* and 'Cartesian' simplicity, the notions of 'order' (or 'relations of perfection') and of 'liberty', as well as the idea that men are merely the 'occasional' causes of their own actions (while God the Father is *cause générale* of nature and grace), and that Jesus Christ *qua* man is the 'occasional cause' of the distribution of grace to particular persons.[155] Obviously, then, light needs to be thrown on those ideas in *Nature et grâce* which go beyond generality and simplicity; but one must also show the rapport between these 'new' ideas and the *généralité* for which Malebranche was famous (or notorious). And for this one must consult not just *Nature et grâce*,

---

[152] Pierre Jurieu, *Traitté* [sic] *de la nature et de la grâce* (Utrecht: Chez François Halma, 1687), 160.

[153] Pierre-Valentine Faydit, *La Presbytéromachie*, in *Annales de philosophie chrétienne*, 7 (Paris, 1863), 50 ff.

[154] Sainte-Beuve, *Port-Royal* (Paris, 1908), bk. VI, p. 387.

[155] For these 'new' aspects of Malebranche and *Malebranchisme*, see Robinet, *Système et éxistence dans l'œuvre de Malebranche*, *passim*; Martial Guéroult, *Malebranche: Les cinq abimes de la Providence* (Paris: Aubier, 1959), iii. 147 ff.; Pierre Blanchard, *L'Attention á Dieu selon Malebranche* (Lyon: Desclée de Brouwer, 1956), *passim*; Ginette Dreyfus, 'Le Problème de la liberté de l'homme dans la philosophie de Malebranche', in *Malebranche: L'Homme et l'œuvre, 1638–1715* (Paris: Vrin, 1967), 153 ff.; Geneviève Rodis-Lewis, 'Malebranche "moraliste"', in *Dix-septième siècle*, 159 (1988), 175–90.

but also—especially to gain a fuller idea of Malebranchian 'order', and of liberty as the 'suspension' of consent—the *Traité de morale* (1684), the *Entretiens sur la métaphysique* (1688), and the *Prémotion physique* (1715). For it is in those later works that notions merely hinted at in *Nature et grâce* are more clearly and fully formulated. (The notion of 'order', for example, is insisted on in *Nature et grâce*; but what the term means is left obscure in that work. That meaning was made steadily clearer in the thirty-five years that separate *Nature et grâce* (1680) and the *Prémotion physique* (1715).)

The Place of the Traité de morale *in Malebranche's Thought*

The less than total importance of *volonté générale* in Malebranche becomes clear if one turns from the *Traité de la nature et de la grâce*, which is indeed mainly dominated by the notion of 'general will', to a work such as the *Traité de morale*, where one finds different but equally characteristic Malebranchian practical ideas. And since the *Traité de morale* was produced[156] at the very time (1683–4) that Malebranche was writing the third and fourth 'Éclaircissements' of *Nature et grâce*, there is a very smooth transition from the one work to the other. In the opening chapter of the '*Première Partie*' of the *Traité de morale*, indeed, Malebranche begins with the now familiar general–particular dichotomy, and only by a series of small steps arrives at the notion that there may be something of philosophical value *beyond* the 'constancy' and 'uniformity' of *volonté générale* and *loi générale*: and this something beyond he calls 'order' or 'relations of perfection'.

'If', Malebranche begins the *Traité* by observing, 'God moved bodies by *volontés particulières*, it would be a crime to avoid by flight the ruins of a collapsing building; for one cannot, without injustice, refuse to return to God the life he has given us, if he demands it.' If God positively willed everything in particular, 'it would be an insult to God's wisdom, to correct the course of rivers, and turn them to places lacking water: one would have to follow nature and remain at rest'. Since, however, God acts, not through *volontés particulières* but through *des lois générales*, 'one corrects his work, without injuring his wisdom; one resists his action, without resisting his will; because he

[156] For an account of its composition and publication, see *Œuvres complètes de Malebranche*, xi, 'Introduction'. The only extensive commentary on the *Traité* in English is Craig Walton's helpful *De la recherche du bien: A Study of Malebranche's Science of Ethics* (The Hague: Martinus Nijhoff, 1972), *passim*.

does not will positively and directly everything that he does'.[157] He permits disorder, but he loves order.

The case is quite different, however, in Malebranche's view, if one 'resists' or 'corrects' the action of men. 'What is true of God is not so of men, of the general cause as of particular causes.' When one resists the action of men, one 'offends' them: 'for, since they act only by *volontés particulières*, one cannot resist their acts without resisting their plans'. But in 'resisting' God's general laws, manifested in something like the collapse of a building, one not only offends 'not at all', one even favours God's plans. And this is simply because the general laws which God follows do not always produce results which 'conform' to order, or to 'the best work'.[158] (After all, as Malebranche remarks in *Nature et grâce*, 'if one drops a rock on the head of passers-by, the rock will always fall at an equal speed, without discerning the piety, or the station, or the good or evil dispositions of those who pass by'. And he gives this same thought a complacent cast in the *Méditations chrétiennes*, where he urges that God, by permitting general laws to operate, lets 'the ruins of a house fall on a just person who is going to the aid of an unfortunate, as well as on a villain who is going to cut the throat of an *homme de bien*'.[159]) Hence there is no moral obligation, in Malebranche's opinion, to allow *les lois générales* to 'cause death', or even to let their operation 'inconvenience' or 'displease' us. Our duty, Malebranche concludes, 'consists then in submitting ourselves to God's law, and to following order'; and we can know this order only through 'union' with 'the eternal Word, with universal reason'—the one thing all men share, whatever their particular dispositions.[160]

But what does Malebranche mean in calling this 'order'—something that transcends the *généralité* of *Nature et grâce*—a 'relation of perfection'? Now one first encounters Malebranche's theory of moral rapports in the opening book of *Recherche de la vérité*, where he argues (briefly) that while truth 'consists only in the relations which two or several things have between themselves', moral goodness by contrast 'consists in the relation of suitability [*rapport de convenance*] which things have to us [men]'.[161] Here the key notion is *rapport de convenance*, and *rapports de perfection* do not yet appear; it is indeed,

[157] *Traité de morale*, 25.   [158] Ibid. 26.

[159] *Nature et grâce*, I, sect. LVII, 63; *Méditations chrétiennes et métaphysiques*, VII. 19, cited in F. Alquié, *Malebranche*, (Paris: Seghers, 1977), 124.

[160] Cited in Alquié, ibid.   [161] *De la recherche de la vérité*, i. 52–3.

only in the *Traité de morale* that the first important exposition of Malebranchian 'relations' is to be found.[162]

'In supposing that man is reasonable', the *Traité* argues, and even that he belongs to a *société spirituelle* with God, which 'nourishes' all 'minds', one cannot deny that man 'knows something of what God thinks, and of the way in which God acts'. For 'in contemplating the intelligible substance of the Word, which alone makes me reasonable', Malebranche continues, 'I can clearly see the relations of size [*rapports de grandeur*] which exist between the intelligible ideas which it [the Word] encloses'; and these relations are 'the same eternal truths that God sees'. For God sees, as does a man, that 'two times two makes four'. A man can also discover, Malebranche insists, 'at least confusedly', the existence of 'relations of perfection [*rapports de perfection*]' which constitute the 'immutable order that God consults when he acts—an order which ought also to regulate the esteem and love of all intelligent beings'.[163]

This is, perhaps, more eloquent than clear; but in a succeeding passage Malebranche fleshes out the notion of 'relations of perfection'. The reason that it is true that 'a beast is more estimable than a stone, and less estimable than a man' is that 'there is a greater relation of perfection from the beast to the stone, than from the stone to the beast', and that there is 'a greater *rapport de perfection* between the beast compared to the man, than between the man compared to the beast'. Or, in simpler language, men enjoy a greater measure, a greater degree, of 'perfection', than beasts, and beasts more perfection than stones. Plainly Malebranche envisions a hierarchy of more or less 'perfect' beings—their 'perfection' defined in terms of their capacity for 'union' with 'the Word' or 'universal reason'—and holds that one should 'regulate his esteem' in view of degrees of perfection. Thus, for Malebranche, whoever 'esteems his horse more than his coachman' does not really 'see' the *rapport de perfection* 'which he perhaps thinks he sees'. And, linking this up with his familiar general–particular distinction, Malebranche adds that the unreasonable horse-lover fails to see *la raison universelle*, that he takes his own *raison particulière* for his rule. But, Malebranche goes on, to abandon *la raison universelle* and 'order' for *la raison particulière* is to manifest *amour-propre*, 'error', and 'lawlessness':

---

[162] *Traité de morale*, 19.   [163] Ibid. 21.

thus the language of *Nature et grâce* reappears, and begins to colour 'order' and 'relations of perfection' themselves.[164]

From all of this, in any case, Malebranche concludes—following St Augustine's following of Plato—that 'it is evident that there is a true and a false, a just and an unjust', and that this holds 'with respect to all intelligences'. Just as what is true for God is true for angels and men, so too 'that which is injustice or disorder with respect to man is also such with respect to God himself'. Just as 'all minds' discover the same *rapports de grandeur*, so those same minds discover 'the same truths of practice, the same laws, the same order', when they see the *rapports de perfection* enclosed in the Word.[165]

The 'love of order', then, according to Malebranche, is 'our principal duty': it is 'mother virtue, universal virtue, fundamental virtue'. (This order, these 'related' perfections, actually *exist* only in God; hence the love of God, of perfection, and of order are equivalent, and together constitute Malebranche's version of 'charity'—a charity which is extended to men as citizens of God's *société spirituelle*.) 'Speculative truths' or *rapports de grandeur* do not 'regulate' our duties; 'it is principally the knowledge and the love of relations of perfection, or of practical truths, which constitute our perfection'. Hence Malebranche's closing peroration: 'Let us then apply ourselves to know, to love and to follow order; let us work for our perfection.'[166]

Malebranche and Leibniz on the Concept of 'Order'

Is there a 'relation' between *rapports de grandeur* and *rapports de perfection*? In Malebranche's great contemporary and correspondent Leibniz, the answer is plainly 'yes', for Leibniz argues (in a 1696 letter) that 'order and harmony are . . . something mathematical and which consist in certain proportions';[167] and he adds in *Opinion on the Principles of Pufendorf* (1706)—a piece which attracted a European reputation thanks to Barbeyrac's French translation—that 'justice follows certain rules of equality and of proportion which are no less founded in the immutable nature of things, and in the ideas of the divine understanding, than the principles of arithmetic and

---

[164] Ibid.   [165] Ibid. 19.

[166] Ibid.24. On this point see the useful remarks in C. J. McCracken, *Malebranche and British Philosophy* (Oxford: Clarendon Press, 1983), 285.

[167] Leibniz, letter to the Electress Sophie, in *Textes inédits*, ed. Grua, i. 379.

geometry'.[168] In Malebranche himself, the initial answer appears to be 'no', for he calls *rapports de grandeur* 'quite pure, abstract, metaphysical', while *rapports de perfection* are 'practical' and serve as 'laws'.[169] But one might object that the notions of *rapports de perfection* and of 'order' are also 'quite abstract': as Jeremy Bentham later observed, 'the worst order is as truly order as the best'.[170]

In fact Malebranche finally abandons the abstractness of 'order', and his less than concrete characterization of 'relations of perfection'; and, in the work commonly accounted his masterpiece—the *Entretiens sur la métaphysique* (1688)—he moves in the direction of Leibniz's (virtual) identification of 'proportion' or 'equality' in mathematics and in notions of rightness. Malebranche begins the thirteenth section of *Entretien VIII* by calling *rapports de grandeur* 'speculative' and *rapports de perfection* 'practical' (as in *Traité de morale*), but then goes on to the view that 'relations of perfection cannot be known clearly unless they are *expressed* in relations of size'. That two times two equals four, Malebranche continues, 'is a relation of equality in size, is a speculative truth which excites no movement in the soul—neither love nor hate, neither esteem nor contempt'. But the notion that man is 'of greater value than the beast', he goes on, is 'a relation of inequality in perfection, which demands not merely that the soul should accept it, but that love and esteem be regulated by the knowledge of this relation or of this truth'.[171] Since, for Malebranche, we ought to love perfection, we ought to love beings closer to divinity in the scale of being, in preference to 'lower' beings and things. In this way the unfamiliar notion of *rapports de perfection* is assimilated to the much more familiar idea of a 'great chain of being'; if this makes Malebranchism more ordinary, it also makes it more concrete and intelligible.[172]

To be sure, this concreteness had already been intimated in the tenth 'Éclaircissement' of *Recherche de la vérité*, where Malebranche

---

[168] Trans. and ed. Riley, 71.

[169] *Méditations chrétiennes et métaphysiques*, Méditation IV, sect. 8, p. 39: 'Or il y a cette différence entre les rapports de grandeur et les rapports de perfection, que les rapports de grandeur sont des veritez toutes pures, abstraites, métaphysiques, et que les rapports de perfection sont des véritez et en même tems des Loix immuables et nécessaires.'

[170] Bentham, *Book of Fallacies*, in *Works* (Edinburgh: Tait, 1843), ii. 441.

[171] *Entretiens sur la métaphysique*, in *Œuvres complètes de Malebranche*, xii–xiii. 190–1.

[172] See A. O. Lovejoy, *The Great Chain of Being* (New York: Harper, 1960), *passim*.

argues that 'the perfections which are in God, which represent
created or possible beings, are not all equal, as representative of
those beings'. For the 'perfections' which 'represent' bodies, he goes
on, 'are not so noble as those which represent minds'. After
admitting that it is somewhat difficult to conceive exactly how the
mind of a 'perfect being' contains 'perfections' which 'represent'
beings that are necessarily imperfect—a point that John Locke later
complained of—Malebranche concludes that 'if it is true, then, that
God . . . encloses in himself all beings in an intelligible manner, and
that all of these intelligible beings . . . are not in every sense equally
perfect, it is evident that there will be an immutable and necessary
order between them'. And he adds that 'just as there are necessary
and eternal truths, because there are *rapports de grandeur* between
intelligible beings', so too 'there must be an immutable and
necessary order, because of the *rapports de perfection* which exist
between these same beings'. It is thus in virtue of 'an immutable
order that minds are nobler than bodies, as it is a necessary truth that
two times two makes four'.[173] 'Order', then, requires respect for
degree of perfection attained (or at least enjoyed) by every created
being in the great chain of being. This is at its clearest in the *Traité de
morale*, where 'order' gives a new meaning to Christian 'charity':

The charity which justifies [men], or the virtue which renders just and
virtuous those who possess it, is properly a ruling love of the immutable
order. . . . The immutable order consists of nothing else than the relations of
perfection which exist between the intelligible ideas that are enclosed in the
substance of the eternal Word. Now one ought to esteem and love nothing
but perfection. And therefore our esteem and love should be conformable to
order. . . . From this it is evident that charity or the love of God is a
consequence of the love of order, and that we ought to esteem and love God,
not only more than all things, but infinitely more than all things. . . .
  Now there are two principal kinds of love, a love of benevolence, and a
love which may be called a love of union. . . . One loves persons of merit
through a love of benevolence, for one loves them even though they are not
in a condition to do us any good. . . . Now God alone is [truly] good, he
alone has the power to act in us . . . thus all love of union ought to incline
towards God.[174]

---

[173] *De la recherche de la vérité*, 'Dixième Éclaircissement', iii. 137–8. For a fine
commentary on this passage, see Henri Gouhier, *La Philosophie de Malebranche et son
expérience réligieuse* (Paris: Vrin, 1948), 236–43.
[174] *Traité de morale*, 41–2.

Even in these passages which stress the notions of charity, order, and perfection, and which seems to have left the general–particular dichotomy far behind, Malebranche finds an occasion for animadversions against *particularisme*. Just as everyone can see that twice two are four, Malebranche urges, so too everyone can see that 'one ought to prefer one's friend to one's dog'; the mathematical *rapport de grandeur* and the moral *rapport de perfection* both rest in 'a universal reason that enlightens me and all intelligences whatever'. This 'universal' reason, which is 'coeternal' and 'consubstantial' with God, and which all intelligences 'see', is to be strictly distinguished from 'particular reasons'—the not very reasonable reasons that 'a passionate man follows'. And the passionate man turns out to be the familiar horse-lover:

When a man prefers the life of his horse to that of his coachman, he has his reasons, but they are particular reasons that every reasonable man abhors. They are reasons that fundamentally are not reasonable, because they are not in conformity with the sovereign reason, or the universal reason, that all men consult.[175]

Malebranche, then, will not countenance any *raisons que la raison ne connaît point*. If in this passage he appeals to what is 'universal' and not merely 'general', he still finds time to lump *des raisons particulières* with 'passion' and the 'abhorrent'. And toward the end of the tenth 'Éclaircissement', even the notion of the 'universal' yields, and *le général* makes its way back in: one can finally see, Malebranche urges, 'what the immutable order of justice is, and how this order has the force of law through the necessary love that God has for himself'. Since men ought to love the order that God loves, 'one sees how this law is general for all minds, and for God himself'; one sees that to abandon the idea of 'eternal' and 'immutable' order, common to all intelligences, is to 'establish *pyrrhonisme* and to leave room for the belief that the just and the unjust are not at all necessarily such'.[176] Thus even the treatment of 'relations of perfection' manages to hold on to Malebranche's anti-particularism, and to reflect his equation of generality with justice in *Nature et grâce*.

---

[175] *De la recherche de la vérité*, 'Dixième Éclaircissement', 131. This passage is well treated by Desmond Connell, *The Vision in God* (Louvain: Éditions Nauwelaerts and Beatrice-Nauwelaerts, 1967), 297.
[176] Ibid. (*Recherche*), 140.

The Relations of 'Order' and 'Generality' in Malebranche's Theology

But what, finally, is the 'relation' between these relations of size and perfection—the latter constituting 'order'—and the rule of divine 'general will' in the realms of nature and grace? One cannot simply say that 'nature' is to *rapports de grandeur* as grace is to *rapports de perfection*, because the created world is not 'orderly': it contains monsters and hardened hearts. 'The present world is a neglected work,' Malebranche insists. 'Man . . . inhabits ruins, and the world which he cultivates is only the *débris* of a more perfect world.'[177] The main passage in which Malebranche tries to 'relate' relations to the 'general will' is to be found in the *Méditations chrétiennes et métaphysiques*—this time *Méditation* VII:

> God has two kinds of laws which rule him in his conduct. The one is eternal and necessary, and this is order; the others are arbitrary, and these are the general laws of nature and of grace. But God established the latter only because order required that he act in that way.[178]

This 'works', of course, only if order entails the simplicity (of divine action) that makes general laws better than a multiplicity of particular ones. In any case the formulation of *Méditation* VII contains a great tension: 'order' or 'perfection' is 'eternal' and 'necessary', while the *volontés générales* which govern nature and grace are 'arbitrary'. But the burden of *Nature et grâce* is to show that *volonté générales* are, unlike *volontés particulières*, precisely *not* 'arbitrary'—instead, that they are wise, constant, and just. 'Arbitrary', perhaps unfortunately, calls to mind Malebranche's characterization of the *volonté particulière* of some earthly sovereigns: 'une volonté aveugle, bizarre et impérieuse'.[179] But 'arbitrary' may simply mean 'not necessary' and 'not eternal'; after all, the world itself is neither necessary nor eternal[180] (this would be a 'Spinozistic' denial of creation, in Malebranche's view), and therefore the 'general wills' which govern the world's realms, nature and grace, cannot be necessary or eternal either.

---

[177] *Méditations chrétiennes et métaphysiques*, Méditation VII, sect. 12, p. 73.
[178] Ibid. 76.
[179] *Nature et grâce*, 'Troisième Éclaircissement', 189.
[180] Ibid. I, sect. IV, 18: 'If you remain in agreement that the world cannot be a necessary emanation from the divinity, you will see quite well that it was not necessary that it be eternal, though it ought never to end' (*'First Discourse'*, sect. IV).

48 *Introduction*

Even if, however, the 'arbitrariness' of *volonté générale* simply means non-eternity and non-necessity, one can still ask: why, if *volonté générale* and *lois générales* are inferior to 'order' and to *rapports de perfection*—as must be the case—should God have 'realized' a world which can have nothing more than a shadow of a 'relation' to order and perfection (or perhaps *no* intelligible relation, unless order generates simplicity and simplicity generality)? Malebranche himself, of course, asks this radical question at the very beginning of *Nature et grâce*; and he concludes that there *is* no 'relation' between God and the world, between infinity and finitude.[181] He realizes throughout *Nature et grâce* that he must show that it is in some sense 'better' that a sin-disordered world, now governed by *volonté générales* which permit monsters and grace falling uselessly on hardened hearts, should exist rather than never have been. His 'solution' is of course Christian, even peculiarly Christian: the ruined world as *redeemed* by Christ is of greater worth than the non-existence (or never-existence) of that world. Since the Incarnation constitutes philosophical 'salvation' for Malebranche, quite literally 'saves' his system, and gives a perfect being a motive for creating a 'ruined' world, a great deal—indeed, everything—turns on the advent of Christ; for Malebranche *culpa* is not simply *felix*, but essential.[182] 'The world as saved by Jesus Christ', Malebranche insists in the *Entretiens sur la métaphysique*, 'is of greater worth than the same universe as at first constructed, otherwise God would never have allowed his work to become corrupted.'

Man . . . is a sinner, he is not such as God made him. God, then, has allowed his work to become corrupt. Harmonize this with his wisdom, and his power, save yourself from the difficulty without the aid of the man-God, without admitting a mediator, without granting that God has had mainly in view the incarnation of his son. I defy you to do it even with the principles of the best philosophy.[183]

It is in view of this that Malebranche can insist that while it is true that 'everything is in disorder', this is the consequence of 'sin':

---

[181] *Nature et grâce*, 'Troisième Éclaircissement', 11 ('addition'): 'The world is not worthy of God: there is not even any proportion with God, for there is no relation between the infinite and the finite.'

[182] On this point see the fine pages in Gouhier, *La Philosophie de Malebranche et son expérience réligieuse*, 97–103.

[183] *Entretiens sur la métaphysique*, 207.

'order itself requires disorder to punish the sinner'.[184] This, then, would be the 'relation' between *rapports de perfection* and a very imperfect (though still generally governed) world: order necessitates disorder, and so mere 'general will' is justifiable. Even so, one can ask: is 'disorder' the unintended, unwanted, unwilling *upshot* of God's 'simplicity' and 'generality' of operation (as *Nature et grâce* insists), or is it the intended, wanted, and willed divine punishment of human sin? Or is it precisely human sin—divinely previewed— which justifies God in creating a disordered world which can be no *more* than 'simple' and 'general'? This final version—in which 'Cartesian' generality is fused with something much more specifically Christian—might seem to be the most comprehensive and adequate: for, particularly in the *Méditations chrétiennes*, Malebranche suggests that the (generally governed but) 'ruined' world expresses or symbolizes human depravity. He makes this suggestion in a wonderfully imaginative descriptive passage:

The present world is a neglected work. It is the abode of sinners, and it was necessary that disorder appear in it. Man is not such as God made him: thus he has to inhabit ruins, and the earth he cultivates can be nothing more than the debris of a more perfect world. . . . It was necessary that the irregularity of the seasons shorten the life of those who no longer think of anything but evil, and that the earth be ruined and submerged by the waters, that it bear until the end of all centuries visible marks of divine vengeance.[185]

Though divine wisdom does not appear in the ruined world 'in itself', Malebranche adds, none the less in 'relation' to both 'simplicity' *and* the punishment of 'sinners', the world is such that only an 'infinite wisdom' could comprehend all its 'beauties'.[186] At least this argument, whatever its implausibilities, is more successful than Leibniz's demi-Christian one: demi-Christian in the sense that Leibniz insists that 'universal justice'—for God and men alike—consists in the 'charity of the wise' (*caritas sapientis*), but then is hard-pressed to explain why a 'charitable' God would create a necessarily imperfect world which can be (at best) 'best' (the 'best of all possible worlds'), though not good (absolutely). In explaining God's decision to create, Leibniz stresses God's glory and the notion that the world 'mirrors' that glory; here, however, charity has

---

[184] *Méditations chrétiennes et métaphysiques*, 39.
[185] Ibid. 73.   [186] Ibid.

vanished altogether.[187] At least Malebranche's deployment of Christ as redeemer—of both men and Malebranchism—does not attempt, *per impossibile*, to combine 'charity' and 'glory'.

One can still ask, of course, why an *être parfait* would see, as a manifestation of 'order', an historical drama in which fallen and corrupt beings are redeemed through the sacrifice of Christ *qua* 'perfect victim';[188] but this would be to question Christianity more closely than Malebranche was ever prepared to do. As early as 1687, Fénelon complained that, whether one considers Malebranche's version of the Incarnation theologically or scripturally, it is radically problematical. From a theologian's perspective, Fénelon argues that 'if one examines exactly what glory is truly added by the Incarnation' to the 'infinite and essential glory' of God, one finds that it 'only adds an accidental and limited glory'; what Christ suffered, though 'infinite in price', is 'not at all something infinitely perfect, which can be really distinguished from the perfection of the divine person'. And scripturally, for Fénelon, Malebranche is no better off: Malebranche argues that 'it would be unworthy of God to love the world, if this work were not inseparable from his son', Fénelon suggests, but 'Jesus Christ teaches us, on the contrary, that "God so loved the world, that he gave it his only son"'.[189]

Malebranchism, indeed, seems to suffer from a great difficulty: Malebranche wants to operate only with an *être parfait*, and imagine what such a perfect being *would* do—leaving out all scriptural 'anthropology'. And yet the idea of an *être parfait* acting uniformly through general laws leads to deism, not to Christianity: the concept of a perfect being does not yield a 'son' of God who, *qua* 'perfect victim', redeems a ruined and sin-disordered world. 'Anthropological' Scripture does indeed yield Christ and his earthly works; but anthropology is a concession to 'weakness' and 'anthropomorphism'. Only Christ 'saves' Malebranche's system, and gives the Father a motive for creating a world unworthy of him; but Christ is not (and cannot be) spun out of the bare idea of 'perfection'. Malebranche thus needs historical Christianity, even as he claims to rely solely on the concept of *l'être parfait*. It is this need which drives him to the

---

[187] On this point see Introduction to *The Political Writings of Leibniz*, trans. and ed. Riley, 16–17.

[188] Malebranche, *Entretiens sur la métaphysique*, 97.

[189] Fénelon, *Réfutation du système du Père Malebranche*, in *Œuvres de Fénelon*, ii. 284. Fénelon is thinking, of course, of John 3: 16.

astonishing claim—in the *Traité de morale*—that God the Father 'never had a more agreeable sight than that of his only son fastened to the cross to re-establish order in the universe'.[190]

If, finally, 'order' and 'relations of perfection' seem to have toppled mere 'general will' from the high place it occupies in *Nature et grâce*, one can still recall that God, who 'encloses' all perfection and order, is called by Malebranche *le bien général*, while mere earthly goods are styled *les biens particuliers*. So even here 'generality' recovers some of its lost lustre; it is preserved even as it is cancelled. For, as Malebranche has 'the Word' itself say to a *dévot* in the *Méditations chrétiennes*, 'God inclines you invincibly to love *le bien en général*, but he does not incline you invincibly to love *les biens particuliers*'.[191] If *généralité* does not shape the whole of what is right in Malebranche, at least *particularisme* is constantly and uniformly condemned—as it had been in *Nature et grâce*.

The Relation of Generality to 'Occasionalism' in Malebranche

Even if what Malebranche says about 'order' and *rapports de perfection* deprives 'general will' of some of the importance it seemed to have in *Nature et grâce*, that *volonté générale* is still the regulator of the realms of nature and grace, and thus remains quite significant. But what is the 'relation' (perhaps the key Malebranchian notion) between the 'general will' and the 'occasionalism' for which Malebranche is celebrated? That there must be some such rapport is evident in *Nature et grâce* itself: Malebranche opens the 'Second Discourse' by observing that 'since God alone acts immediately and by himself in minds, and produces in them all the different modifications of which they are capable, it is only he who diffuses light in us, and inspires in us certain feelings which determine our different volitions'. Adding that God alone is the 'true cause', Malebranche concludes that 'since the general cause [God] acts by laws or by *volontés générales*, and since his action is lawful, constant, and uniform, it is absolutely necessary that there be some occasional cause which determines the efficacy of these laws, and which serves to establish them'.[192] If 'occasional' or 'second' causes—for example human beings—did not act *particularly*, then there would be no 'relation' between general laws and particular actions. Malebranche,

---

[190] *Traité de morale*, 41.   [191] *Méditations chrétiennes et métaphysiques*, 65.
[192] *Nature et grâce*, II, sect. I, 66–7. On Malebranche's 'occasionalism', see Dreyfus, *La Volonté selon Malebranche*, ch. 6 ('Dieu seule cause éfficace').

indeed, in one of his defences of *Nature et grâce*, even insists that God 'cannot' act by 'the simplest means' or by 'general laws' until there are 'occasional causes' which determine the efficacy of divine *volontés générales*.[193] These occasional causes, obviously, must be established by creative divine *volontés particulières*; but since such willings are 'base' and 'servile', God abandons them as soon as generality and simplicity become available.[194]

What, then, is the role of 'occasionalism' in relation to 'general will'? Originally, of course—that is, in orthodox Cartesianism—occasionalism was only a theory of perception and of will: if, as in Descartes, the 'essence' or 'nature' of body is *extension*, and the essence of mind is *thought*, then 'mind' and 'body' cannot 'modify' each other, since 'thought' is not a modification of extension, and extension is not a modification of thought.[195] Given a strict mind–body dualism, the obvious question is: how can minds 'perceive', if perception is viewed as a physical 'modification' of the eye or the ear, as motion 'in' a sense-organ (as in Hobbes's bawdy insistence that 'there is no conception in a man's mind, which hath not . . . been begotten upon the organs of sense');[196] and again, how can minds 'move' bodies—through 'volition'—if thought cannot 'modify' extended substances? The obvious answer for an occasionalist must be that 'perception' (so-called) is not *really* a modification of mind by 'sensed' matter, and that 'volition' is not *really* efficacious: that, instead, God presents to the mind the 'idea' of the thing 'seen' on the *occasion* of its being 'seen', just as he moves bodies (for us, as it were) on the occasion of our willing. This 'occasionalism' does not, of course, require a constantly intervening *Deus ex machina* who scurries about the universe giving 'efficacy' to 'occasional' causes: indeed Malebranche's theory of *general* law means that God has established a permanent, general 'relation' between mind and body, so that these naturally unrelated substances constantly operate in conjunction. Thus, for Malebranche, *whenever* one 'wills' to move his arm, it moves—thanks to a constant, general (though non-

---

[193] *Réponse au livre I des réflexions philosophiques*, 780.

[194] See Dreyfus, *La Volonté selon Malebranche*, 105.

[195] See the excellent notes on Cartesianism by Pierre Costabel which accompany vol. xvii pt. 1 of the *Œuvres complètes de Malebranche*, 30–7, 199–236 ('notes de l'éditeur'). See also Alquié, *Le Cartésianisme de Malebranche*, 243 ff., who shows that Descartes himself cannot be considered a true occasionalist.

[196] Hobbes, *Leviathan*, ed. Oakeshott, 7.

natural) conjunction between mind and body, which God has established by a 'general will'. 'It is only God', Malebranche says in the *Conversations chrétiennes*, 'who can act in the [human] soul . . . through his general will which makes the natural order.'[197]

To be sure, it was not simply in order to be a 'Cartesian' that Malebranche was an occasionalist; indeed his motivation was as much theological as (purely) philosophical. For Malebranche's view was that the attribution of independent causal efficacy to non-divine beings is *impious*; and to make that clear he employed the legal idea of 'sovereignty'. 'The idea of a sovereign power is the idea of a sovereign divinity', Malebranche urges in *De la Recherche de la vérité*, 'and the idea of a subordinate power is the idea of an inferior divinity . . . Thus one admits something divine in all the bodies that surround us, when one admits . . . real beings capable of producing certain effects by the [causal] force of their nature; and one thus enters insensibly into the sentiment of the pagans.'[198] It is true, Malebranche adds, that 'faith corrects us'—by reminding us of the Pauline notion that *in God* we 'move' and 'have our being'; none the less if one reads too much Aristotle 'the mind is pagan' even if 'the heart is Christian'. And this is why one must prefer St Augustine— 'this great saint [who] recognized that the body cannot act upon the soul, and that nothing can be above the soul, except God'.[199] Small wonder that Malebranche read Descartes as an 'Augustinian', and the Aristotle-loving Scholastics as thinly veiled pagans.

One of the best brief and non-technical accounts of 'occasionalism' is offered by Malebranche in the *Traité de morale*:

The [human] mind can be immediately related to God alone . . . for mind cannot be related to body, except by being united to God himself. It is certain for a thousand reasons that when I suffer, for example, the pain of being pricked, it is God who acts in me, in consequence none the less of laws of the union of soul and body. . . . But the body itself cannot be united to the mind, nor the mind to the body. They have no relation between them, nor any creature [a relation] to any other: I mean a relation of [true] causality . . . It is God who does everything. His will is the link of all unions.[200]

---

[197] In *Œuvres complètes de Malebranche*, iv. 83.
[198] Cited in Alquié, *Malebranche*, 116.
[199] Ibid. 117.   [200] *Traité de morale*, 117.

And all of this, of course, is only an elaboration of Malebranche's
first statement of 'occasionalist' doctrine in Book VI of *Recherche de
la vérité*:

There is only one true God, and one cause who is truly a cause: and one must
not imagine that what precedes an effect is the true cause of it. God cannot
communicate his power to creatures, if we follow the light of reason: there
cannot be [many] true causes, there cannot be gods. But even if he could do
this, we cannot conceive that he would will it. Bodies, minds, pure
intelligences—none of these can do anything. It is he who has made minds
that enlightens and moves them . . . It is, finally, the author of our being
who executes our wills.[201]

Malebranche begins, then, like the Cartesians, by viewing
occasionalism as a theory of perception and of volition; but
occasionalism finally serves a huge range of functions in Malebranchism, some of them non-Cartesian. As a theory of knowledge
and perception, Malebranchian occasionalism leads to the famous
idea that 'we see all things in God';[202] as a theory of volition it holds
that God 'moves our arm' ('it seems to me quite certain that the will
of minds is not capable of moving the smallest body that there is in
the world');[203] as (part of) the theory of grace it maintains that the
'human soul' of Jesus Christ is the 'occasional cause' of the
distribution of grace to 'particular' persons.[204] (It is this last
element—argued at length in the 'Second Discourse' of *Nature et
grâce*—which is non-Cartesian, or at least extra-Cartesian, since
Descartes was politic enough to say next to nothing about 'grace'.[205])

---

[201] *De la recherche de la vérité*, VI. ii. 3, ii. 318.

[202] See Gouhier, *La Philosophie de Malebranche et son expérience réligieuse*, 211–43.
Gouhier correctly gives great weight to the following lines from the 'Dixième
Éclaircissement' of the *Recherche*: '. . . this principle that it is only God who
enlightens us, and that he only enlightens us through the manifestation of an
immutable and necessary reason or wisdom, seems to me . . . so absolutely necessary
to give to any truth whatsoever a certain and unshakable foundation, that I believe
myself to be indispensably obliged to explain it and to sustain it.'

[203] Malebranche, *De la recherche de la vérité*, ii. 318, 315.

[204] *Nature et grâce*, II (entire), 65–99.

[205] Descartes is carefully orthodox (and a little vague) in his letter to Père Mersenne
(Mar. 1642): 'Pelagius said that one could do good works and merit eternal life
without grace, which was condemned by the Church; as for me, I say that one can
know by natural reason that God exists, but I do not therefore say that this natural
knowledge merits in itself, and without grace, the supernatural glory that we expect in
heaven. For, on the contrary, it is evident that, this glory being supernatural, it
requires more than natural powers to merit it' (in Descartes, *Œuvres et lettres*, ed.
André Bridoux (Paris: Pléiade, 1953), 1144).

Malebranche on Knowledge and Perception

One can begin, as does Malebranche himself, with knowledge and perception. And the most important passage in which he treats the significance of the notion that we see 'all things in God' is a remarkable commentary on St Augustine in (yet another) of his defences of *Nature et grâce* against Antoine Arnauld—this time the *Trois lettres* of 1685. Malebranche begins, indeed, by allowing that St Augustine himself did not claim to 'see' or 'find' all things in God: 'I realized', Malebranche grants, 'that this Father spoke only of truths and of eternal laws, of the objects of the sciences, such as arithmetic, geometry, morality; and that he did not urge that one saw in God things which are corruptible and subject to change, as are all the things that surround us.'[206] He himself, Malebranche goes on to concede, does not claim that one 'sees' corruptible and changing things in God: 'to speak exactly, one sees in God only the essences' of things; and those essences or *ideas* of things alone are 'immutable, necessary, and eternal'. One sees in God only 'that which represents these things to the mind . . . that which renders them intelligible'.[207] (Or, as Malebranche put the matter in his 1714 correspondence with Dortous de Mairan, 'I see immediately [in God], only the idea, and not the *ideatum*, and I am persuaded that the idea has been for an eternity, without [any] *ideatum*.'[208]) Corruptible things are problematical because they change, though the 'essence' of them does not; but incorruptible, unchanging things one sees *simply* in God. 'One can see only in an immutable nature, and in eternal wisdom, all the truths which, by their nature, are immutable and eternal.' It would not be difficult to prove, 'as St Augustine did', that 'there would no longer be any certain science, any demonstrated truths, any assured difference between the just and the unjust—in a word, truths and laws which are necessary and common to all minds—if that which all intelligences contemplate were not . . . by its nature absolutely immutable, eternal, and necessary'.[209] And all of this, of course, simply reinforces the view—already examined—that God

[206] Malebranche, *Trois lettres touchant la défense de M. Arnauld*, in *Œuvres complètes de Malebranche*, vi–vii. 199–200. Malebranche says in a footnote that he is relying particularly on Augustine's *De Libero Arbitrio* and *De Trinitate*; Arnauld, by contrast, builds his Augustinianism on the late, proto-Jansenist *De Correptione et Gratia*.

[207] Ibid. (*Trois lettres*).

[208] In *Œuvres complètes de Malebranche*, xix. 910.

[209] Malebranche, 199.

and men 'see' the 'same' *rapports de grandeur* and the same *rapports de perfection*, view the same 'speculative' and 'practical' truths.

Malebranche maintained this view of the *moral* importance of a 'vision' in which nothing is 'seen', which is not a modification of 'mind' by 'body', to the end of his philosophical career. In the fragmentary remains of a 1713 letter to Fénelon, he argues that 'if the mind forms its ideas by a vital act', and if 'our ideas as distinguished from our perceptions are only chimeras', then 'Pyrrhonism' will be established. If *all* ideas are simply mind modified by matter, then 'Hobbes and Locke, authors greatly esteemed by many men, will be right'.[210] And if they *are* right 'there will be no more true, nor false, immutably such; neither just, nor unjust, neither science nor morality'. If 'empirical' notions of perception and knowledge carry the day, 'St Augustine will pass for a fanatical Platonist' who has taught his 'subtle atheism' to Malebranche himself. Hobbes and Locke, in Malebranche's view, simply extend the theory of Aristotle (and of his 'impious commentator' Averroës) that 'seeing objects is accomplished by means of impressed species . . . by the power of an active intellect which presents [ideas] to a passive intellect'. But this, Malebranche insists, is a 'fiction of men who wanted to discuss what they did not understand'.[211]

Locke, for his part, thought Malebranche's 'vision in God' just as impious as Malebranche thought Locke's 'sense perception'. In his *An Examination of Père Malebranche's Opinion of Seeing All Things in God*, Locke argues that 'God has given me an understanding of my own; and I should think it presumptuous in me to suppose I apprehended anything by God's understanding, saw with his eyes, or shared of his knowledge'. He goes on to ask—and this bears directly on Malebranche's notion that we 'see' moral *rapports de perfection* 'in' God—'in which of the perfections of God does a man see the essence of a horse or an ass, of a serpent or a dove, of hemlock or parsley?' For his part, Locke 'confesses', he cannot see 'the essence of any of these things in any of the perfections of God'. It is perfectly true, Locke goes on, that 'the perfections that are in God

---

[210] Malebranche, letter to Fénelon, in *Œuvres complètes de Malebranche*, xix. 842–3. The circumstances surrounding the composition of this letter are given in Yves Marie André, *La Vie du R. P. Malebranche*, ed. A. M. Ingold (Geneva: Slatkine, 1970), 355 ff.

[211] Ibid. (letter to Fénelon), 842–3.

are necessary and unchangeable'; but it is not true that 'the ideas that are . . . in the understanding of God . . . can be seen by us', and still less true that 'the perfections that are in God represent to us the essences of things that are out of God'.[212]

In another Malebranche criticism, Locke adds that the Malebranchian notion that God 'cannot' communicate to creatures the powers of real perception and real volition sets 'very narrow bounds to the power of God, and, by pretending to extend it, takes it away'. And he concludes his assault on occasionalism with a moral objection:

The creatures cannot produce any idea, any thought in man. How then comes he to perceive or think? God upon the occasion of some motion in the optic nerve, exhibits the colour of a marygold or a rose to his mind. How came that motion in his optic nerve? On occasion of the motion of some particles of light striking on the retina, God producing it, and so on. And so whatever a man thinks, God produces the thought: let it be infidelity, murmuring or blasphemy.[213]

For Locke, then, *tout en Dieu* is a moral enormity; for Malebranche it is a moral necessity. For Malebranche, as for Kant a century later, mere 'sense-perception' of a 'natural' world can never explain the possibility of the idea of moral necessity, since that idea does not 'arise' in perception. Kant argues in *Pure Reason* that ' "ought" expresses a kind of necessity . . . which is found nowhere in the whole of nature',[214] and Malebranche would have agreed wholly with that. Nor are other interesting Malebranche–Kant 'relations' lacking: both, though on different grounds, deny the possibility of 'seeing' things-in-themselves. To be sure, Kant was harshly critical of all neo-Platonic idealisms, whether Malebranchian or Berkeleyian; but this does not destroy all Malebranche–Kant rapports.[215]

It should finally be pointed out, before leaving *tout en Dieu* behind, that Malebranche sometimes draws important moral consequences *directly* from his occasionalism—as in the *Défense de*

[212] Locke, 'An Examination of P. Malebranche's Opinion of Seeing All Things in God', in *The Works of John Locke* (London: Otridge & Son *et al.*, 1812), ix. 211–55. For a fine commentary, see McCracken, *Malebranche and British Philosophy*, 119 ff.

[213] Locke, 'Remarks upon some of Mr. Norris's Books, Wherein He Asserts P. Malebranche's Opinion of Our Seeing All Things in God', in *The Works of John Locke*, x. 255.

[214] Kant, *Critique of Pure Reason*, trans. N. Kemp Smith (London: Macmillan, 1963), A547/B565, pp. 472–3.

[215] See Alquié, *Le Cartésianisme de Malebranche*, 491–520 ('Malebranche et Kant').

l'auteur de la recherche de la vérité (1684), where he asserts that 'to
love even one's father, one's protector, one's friend, as if they were
capable of doing us good', is to 'render them an honour due only to
God'. This mistake, according to Malebranche, follows from the
false supposition that 'the bodies which surround us can act as true
causes in us'. According to the occasionalist doctrine, this must be
false; and therefore, for Malebranche, one 'should love his brothers,
not as capable of doing us [any] good, but as capable of enjoying with
us the true good'.[216]

On occasion he makes occasionalism yield slightly different social
consequences: in the late (1708) *Entretien d'un philosophe chrétien et
d'un philosophe chinois*, he first argues for divine *volonté générale*, then
goes on to insist that 'it is absolutely necessary for the preservation of
the human race and the establishment of societies' that God 'act
ceaselessly' in terms of the 'general laws of the union of the soul and
the body', that if God did not, through the ceaseless operation of
general laws, *constantly* give men 'the same perceptions', this alone
'would destroy society'. 'A father would fail to recognize his child, a
friend his friend . . . take away the generality of natural laws [for
example of perception, which permits "recognition"] and everything
collapses in chaos.'[217] Here, as is evident, occasionalism and
généralité fuse to generate a *social* doctrine: even occasionalism, then,
leans heavily on the ideas of *Nature et grâce*.

Malebranche on Will and Freedom

Just as, for Malebranche, there is no empirical 'perception' in the
Hobbesian or Lockean sense, so too there is little notion of human
will. One says 'little' rather than 'no', however, because of an
obvious problem: if men are merely the 'occasional' causes of their
own actions, in what sense are they free agents who are accountable
for good action—for choosing (say) 'order' or *le bien général* in
preference to *amour-propre* and *les biens particuliers*? After all, as
Malebranche himself says in *Recherche de la vérité*, 'without liberty
there are neither good nor bad actions'.[218] (This is why almost the
entire 'Third Discourse' of *Nature et grâce* is given over to showing

---

[216] Malebranche, *Défense de l'auteur de la recherche de la vérité*, in *Traité de la
nature et de la grâce* (Rotterdam: Chez Rainier Leers, 1684), 23.

[217] Malebranche, *Entretien d'un philosophe chrétien et d'un philosophe chinois sur
l'éxistence et la nature de Dieu*, in *Œuvres complètes de Malebranche*, xv. 3–31.

[218] 'Quinzième Éclaircissement', iii. 225.

Disc 4. File 5.

that 'this expression, *our will is free*, signifies that the natural movement of the soul towards the good in general, is not invincible with respect to the good in particular'.[219]) Men are free, then, and hence possibly responsible, for Malebranche, in the sense that they must 'consent' to a 'motive': God 'inclines' men, he argues, through an Augustinian *délectation*, towards *le bien* or 'order' *en général*, and one must feel this delight before 'consent' is possible. (Or, as Malebranche puts it in an untranslatable passage, 'il faut sentir . . . avant que de consentir'.[220]) But, he insists, one can 'suspend' one's consent, be 'motivated' by a *délectation* without being irresistibly or 'invincibly' determined by it; hence Malebranche's most adequate definition of will—at least in his later work—is 'consenting to a motive'.[221] The 'essence' of liberty, he argues in *Réflexions sur la prémotion physique*, 'consists in a true power . . . which the soul has, to suspend or to give its consent to motives, which naturally follow interesting perceptions';[222] and this refines what he had said in *Nature et grâce*. In 'suspending' one's consent to an 'interesting' or even delectable 'motive', however, one does not actually *cause* anything to happen—as Malebranche is careful to make clear in the first 'Éclaircissement' of the *Recherche de la vérité*. If we allow a *délectation* which is *déreglé*—such as 'concupiscence'—to overwhelm us, and fail to suspend our consent to this motive in favour of 'order' or *rapports de perfection*, what, according to Malebranche, do we actually *do*?

Nothing. We love a false good, which God does not make us love by an invincible impression. We cease to look for the true good. . . . The only thing we do is stop ourselves, put ourselves at rest. It is through an act, no doubt, but through an immanent act which produces nothing physical in our substance . . . that is, in a word, through an act which does nothing and which makes the general cause [God] do nothing . . . for the repose of the soul, like that of the body, has no force or physical efficacy.[223]

This somewhat peculiar doctrine—in which human willing is 'an act, no doubt' but one which 'produces nothing physical'—is

---

[219] *Nature et grâce*, III, sect. III, 119.
[220] Malebranche, *Réflexions sur la prémotion physique*, 3 ff. Cf. p. 35: 'It is agreed that it is in the feelings and in the movements which God produces in us without us [*en nous sans nous*] that the material of sin consists, and that the formal [cause of sin] consists only in the consent that one gives: and all this because it does not depend on us to feel, but it does depend on us to consent.'
[221] Ibid. 50: 'To will is to consent to a motive.'   [222] Ibid. 47.
[223] *De la recherche de la vérité*, 'Premier éclaircissement', iii. 24–5.

necessitated by Malebranche's view that God alone is a true cause, but that, at the same time, men must in some way be accountable for their volitions.[224] In his last work, the *Réflexions sur la prémotion physique*, Malebranche tried specially hard to make this doctrine plausible by drawing a fine distinction between 'two powers' or 'two different activities' in the human 'soul'. He begins by asserting that 'the *willing* power of the soul, so to speak, its desire to be happy, its movement toward the good in general', is the first 'power' or 'activity', but it is a power which is 'certainly the effect of the Creator's will'. Thus this 'power' is 'only the action of God' *in* the soul: it is therefore 'like that of created bodies in motion . . . whose moving force . . . depends on the action of God'. It is a power *in* us, indeed, but not 'ours': it is, to recall a favourite Malebranchism, *en nous sans nous*.[225]

For human moral responsibility it is, for Malebranche, the 'second' power of the soul which is more interesting—because it is really ours.

The second power or activity of the soul . . . which constitutes the essence of liberty . . . consists in a true power, not to produce in itself, through its own efficacity, any new modifications; but it consists in a true power which the soul has, to suspend or give its consent to motives, which naturally follow interesting perceptions.[226]

Will, then, understood as 'consent to a motive', consists in passively permitting that motive to operate.

Even if, however, one can perhaps characterize this passive 'consent' as involving *'rien de physic'*, can one say the same of 'suspending' a motive (such as concupiscence) while one 'searches' after 'order' and *rapports de perfection*? Do 'suspending' and 'searching' involve *rien de physic*? Malebranche seems to be caught between God as the only 'true' cause, and the wish to avoid a 'Spinozistic' determinism in which men are unfree 'modes' of the divine substance and 'will' is therefore an illusion: hence his account of will as both passive and active (or perhaps suspended on a line between the passive and the active). But Malebranche thought, at least, that he was avoiding one of the chief errors of Jansenism:

[224] *Réflexions sur la prémotion physique*, 45.
[225] Ibid. 46–7. The best commentary on this part of Malebranche's thought is Dreyfus's *La Volonté selon Malebranche*, 274–83.
[226] Ibid. 47.

namely viewing the *délectation* of 'efficacious' grace as irresistible. An 'irresistible' motive, which one cannot 'suspend', or resist without 'contradiction', in Malebranche's view, truly destroys the possibility of freely loving order and *le bien général*, of meritoriously abandoning *les biens particuliers*.[227]

John Locke (again) thought Malebranche's attentuated notion of 'will' even more impious, if possible, than the notion of 'vision in God'.

A man cannot move his arm or his tongue; he has no power; only upon occasion, the man willing it, God moves it. . . . This is the hypothesis that clears doubts, and brings us at last to the religion of Hobbes and Spinoza, by resolving all, even the thoughts and will of men, into an irresistible fatal necessity.[228]

It is ironic, of course, that in the second edition (1694) of his *Essay Concerning Human Understanding*, Locke himself defines human liberty as the capacity to 'suspend' any 'particular' desire while one searches for happiness 'in general',[229] for the truly good. Here there is a strong Locke–Malebranche 'relation': strong enough to make one wonder whether, despite Locke's general hostility to Malebranchism, that doctrine did not (particularly) affect the Lockean notions of 'liberty' and 'will'. This rapport is at its clearest in the account of the alterations to the 1694 edition of the *Essay* which Locke provided in a letter to his friend Molyneux, the Dublin savant, in August 1693:

All that we desire is only to be happy. But though this general desire of happiness operates constantly and invariably in us, yet the satisfaction of any particular desire can be suspended from determining the will to any subservient action, till we have maturely examined whether the particular apparent good we then desire make a part of our real happiness.[230]

Is this not, overall, extraordinarily Malebranchian—coming from one who could mention Malebranchian 'freedom' in the same breath with Hobbes and Spinoza? There is, as in Malebranche, a 'general' desire for happiness; this general desire operates 'constantly and

[227] Ibid. 8–22.
[228] Locke, 'Remarks upon some of Mr. Norris's Books', 255–6.
[229] Locke, *An Essay Concerning Human Understanding*, ed. A. C. Fraser (New York: Dover, 1959), i, Bk. II, ch. 21, pp. 343 ff.
[230] Locke, *Correspondence of John Locke*, ed. E. S. de Beer (Oxford: Clarendon Press, 1979), iv. 722.

invariably' (like all Malebranchian general laws); all 'particular' desires can be 'suspended' (Malebranche's very terms); 'particular' goods may be merely 'apparent'—not part of 'real' or 'general' happiness. Despite a seemingly strong Malebranche–Locke rapport, however, Locke's final view may well have been that Malebranche has no grounds for insisting on the real existence of human 'will', and hence is not entitled to speak of 'suspension'—even as an 'immanent' act which 'does nothing', produces *rien de physic.*

Malebranche on the Distribution of Grace in Nature et grâce

Unusual as are Malebranche's notions of knowledge, perception, and will—from a Lockean perspective not just unusual but false and impious—perhaps the most peculiar part of his 'occasionalism' is his view that the 'human soul' of Jesus Christ is the 'occasional cause' of the distribution of (general) grace to particular persons—a doctrine worked out in the 'Second Discourse' of the *Traité de la nature et de la grâce.*[231]

In this part of *Nature et grâce* Malebranche begins his treatment of Christ as 'distributor' of grace by arguing that 'since it is Jesus Christ alone who can merit grace for us, it is also him alone who can furnish occasions for the general laws, according to which it is given to men'. The human soul of Jesus Christ

thus having different thoughts successively in relation to the different dispositions of which [men's] souls in general are capable, these different thoughts [in Christ] are accompanied by certain desires in relation to the sanctification of those souls. Now these desires being the occasional causes of grace, they must diffuse it in some persons *en particulier*, whose dispositions are like those which the soul of Jesus presently thinks.[232]

Since the 'different movements of the [human] soul of Jesus Christ' are the occasional causes of grace, one should not be astonished (according to Malebranche) if grace is sometimes 'given' by Christ to 'great sinners', or to 'persons who will not make the slightest use of it'. The reason for this is (again) a physicalist one, resembling Malebranche's treatment of grace as a variety of 'rain' in *Nature et grâce*: just as the 'mind' of an architect thinks 'in general of square stones' when 'those sorts of stones are actually necessary to his building', so too the 'soul' of Jesus Christ needs 'minds of a certain character' to serve as building-blocks of his Church—a

---

[231] *Nature et grâce*, II (entire), 65 ff.   [232] Ibid. II, sect. XIV, 73.

'temple of vast extent and of an infinite beauty'—and hence 'diffuses in them the grace that sanctifies them'.[233]

Here the reasoning sometimes seems a little odd. One can see why Christ would will *particularly* the gracious 'sanctification' of a former 'great sinner' whom he wants to use as a stone in his temple; but why would he will particularly the attempted sanctification of 'persons who will not make the slightest use' of grace? God the Father 'permits' grace to fall 'uselessly' because his operation is *general*, and the generality *excuses* the uselessness; but if God the Son confers useless grace particularly, through a 'desire' of his 'human soul', does this not lead to the possibility of charging Christ with 'acceptation of persons' and arbitrariness—even while the Father escapes this charge thanks to his 'simplicity' and uniformity? Certainly it is Malebranche's view that Christ wills many things particularly: 'we have', he urges, 'reason to believe, that the vocation of St Paul was the effect of the efficacity of a particular desire of Jesus Christ'.[234] Not everyone, of course, will be given such a vocation; for, as Malebranche argues, the 'different desires of the soul of Jesus' do not 'diffuse' grace 'equally upon all men'.[235] Finally, however—perhaps recalling what he had said about the 'levity' and inconstancy of *volonté particulière*—Malebranche attempts to distinguish between the 'particular' wills of Christ and what is 'permanent' in his volitions.

It is by present, passing, and particular desires of the soul of Jesus, that grace is diffused to persons who are not prepared for it, and in a way which has something singular and extraordinary about it. But it is by permanent desires that it is given regularly to those who receive the sacraments with the necessary dispositions. For the grace which we receive through the sacraments is not at all given to us precisely because of the merit of our action . . . it is because of the merits of Jesus Christ, which are liberally applied to us as a consequence of his permanent desires.[236]

In this passage one notices—apart from the effort to preserve the gratuity of grace—that Malebranche tries to bring the 'human soul' of Christ as *near* the Father as possible by speaking of *désirs permanens*: these are not quite *volontés générales*, of course, but they are an advance on *des désirs actuels, passagers et particuliers*. And this keeps Christ from being charged with any more *particularisme* than is

---

[233] Ibid. II, sect. XVII, 74.
[235] Ibid. II, sect. XIX, 88.

[234] Ibid. II, sect. XVIII, 75.
[236] Ibid. II, sect. XXIII, 91.

required in explaining something as particular as the vocation of St Paul. But those who say that in Malebranche 'generality' saves the Father, and brings down on Christ reasonable complaints of 'inequity' in distributing grace unequally, through mere 'desires' of his human soul, seem to have a point. (As Fénelon says in his *Réfutation du système du Père Malebranche*, 'if God had not given us a Saviour at all, all men would have been able to be saved through his general will to give them grace abundantly; and it is precisely because we have a Saviour that so many souls perish'.[237] Or, as Bossuet put it more tartly, 'We would all be saved, if we had no Saviour.'[238])

One can hardly say that Malebranche was unaware of this difficulty: in a manuscript from *c*.1680–3 entitled *De la prédestination*, he insists that while some people imagine that 'all the desires of Jesus Christ with respect to the distribution of grace are commanded of him in detail and through *volontés particulières* [of the Father]', such a view makes it impossible to 'justify divine providence'. And he ends the manuscript with the perfectly unequivocal assertion that 'it is thus in Jesus Christ as man that one must seek the reason for the distribution of grace, if one wants to justify the conduct of God in this matter; and this is what I have tried to do in the *Traité de la nature et de la grâce*'.[239] If the blame for all men's not being saved thus falls on Christ's human particularism, *ainsi* (apparently) *soit il*. (Small wonder that Malebranche's critics were shocked: if 'general' grace must be given to individuals by Christ's *volontés particulières*, and if *volontés particulières*, in turn, are 'complex, sterile, lawless, and inconstant', then the 'perfect victim' has been victimized one more time to 'save' the Father's *généralité*. Or so it must have seemed to Malebranche's adversaries.)

The problem, finally, is this: if men *ought* to 'incline' towards God (order, perfection), towards *le bien général*, and incline away from *les biens particuliers*, they need grace; to deny this would be a 'Pelagian'

---

[237] *Réfutation du système du Père Malebranche*, ch. 36.

[238] Cited in Dreyfus, 'Introduction' to Malebranche's *Traité de la nature et de la grâce* (1712 text), p. xxxiii. Cf. Sainte-Beuve, *Port-Royal: Le Cours de Lausanne, 1837–1838* (Paris: Librairie Droz, 1937), 501: 'Malebranche imaginait pourtant ce système pour rendre Dieu plus aimable et adorable; mais on peut remarquer qu'à son insu, il ne met si hors d'atteinte Dieu le Père que pour accumuler les difficultés sur le Fils.'

[239] Malebranche, *De la prédestination*, in *Œuvres complètes de Malebranche*, xvii, pt. 1, 560.

assertion of perfect human independence, of natural self-perfectibility. But since grace is given, on the Father's part, only by a *loi générale*, a *volonté générale*, and not particularly, is there any rapport between those who need grace (in order to love order) and those who get it? The Father, to be sure, cannot attend to this difficulty: that would turn him into a Calvinist who 'elects' a few (particularly) and damns all others. But Christ's particularism—through his 'human soul'— does not always pick out just those persons who need grace; as Malebranche says, Christ may choose 'great sinners' for his temple, and not those who want to love order.[240] At the same time, however, Malebranche wants to avoid the Jansenist 'heresy' that 'some commandments are not possible for the just'.[241] But one can wonder how completely he escapes this difficulty.

A General Overview of Malebranche's Thought

Looking back on *Nature et grâce* and on the works that followed it, it might seem that Malebranche 'naturalizes' grace—unlike St Augustine, for whom a corrupt nature is (partly) redeemed by grace. After all, Malebranche says that the 'rain' of grace sometimes falls on unprepared souls, just as (mere) rain sometimes falls on unprepared soils; that one has no right to complain of uselessness or of divine 'levity' in either case, since an *être parfait* ought to operate through general, constant, simple laws and wills. And *Nature et grâce* opens, of course, with a section called, 'On the necessity of general laws of nature';[242] physics comes first. Despite these first appearances, however, one soon learns that for Malebranche 'mere' nature has no *raison d'être* at all: it is unworthy, in its finitude, of God's infinity. A divine being has no motive to create a finite nature. And yet he has done so. For Malebranche—*finally* like Augustine on this point— the natural world only comes into being if it can be 'redeemed' by the sacrifice of a 'perfect victim', Jesus Christ; the natural world (including human beings) is only a kind of material from which Christ will build the Church. Without the Incarnation, for Malebranche, God cannot have a sufficient motive for world-creation: the Word must be made flesh to 'justify' flesh. And Jesus Christ (*qua* man) is above all the 'occasional cause' of the distribution of (originally general) grace to particular persons: without this grace-dispenser nature could not be at all (since it needs to be 'saved').

---

[240] *Nature et grâce*, II (entire), 65 ff.   [241] See Paquier, *Le Jansénisme*, 162.
[242] *Nature et grâce*, I (entire), 11 ff.

So what Malebranche really does is this: he 'naturalizes' grace by drawing horticultural parallels between souls and soils, but then nature itself could not be were it not to be redeemed by Christ's *gracious* sacrifice. By the end of Malebranche's enterprise, there is a perfect inversion of initial expectations: nature in itself becomes a pagan 'Chimera', and the Incarnation alone justifies a carnal sphere that the Father had no sufficient reason to 'realize'. And all of this is a further blow to Malebranche's effort to avoid all 'anthropology' and spin the whole of theology from an *être parfait* alone: without Christ crucified, the Father would be self-contemplative *ad infinitum*—in the manner of Aristotle's divinities in Book 10 of the *Ethics*. One cannot squeeze the real existence of a man-God out of the idea of an *être parfait*; finally Malebranche is driven back on the Scripture about which he had such radical doubts.

In the end Malebranchism seems to be riven by terrible tensions; and it may be that the Cartesian, Platonic, and Augustinian elements that he tried to fuse will not remain at rest in a stable compound. Nature begins by seeming to dominate grace, but this is ultimately inverted; real human liberty seems to struggle against the occasionalist doctrine that God alone is a 'true cause'; Scripture is initially minimized only to be tacitly rehabilitated (in a 'story' of Christ that Malebranche cannot do without); *généralité* is at first wonderful, but later 'arbitrary' when compared to 'order'; Christ is both the *raison d'être* of any finite world 'beyond' God, and the limiter of general salvation thanks to the *particularité* of his *volontés*.

It is not surprising, then, that Malebranche should have provoked both warm admiration and sharp hostility; and no account of *Nature et grâce* (and its successors) would be complete without a treatment of the 'reception' of *Malebranchisme* at the hands of Bossuet, Fénelon, Bayle, and (finally) Rousseau.

III

Among Malebranche's contemporaries, the most important critics of the *Traité de la nature et de la grâce* were Arnauld, Leibniz, Bossuet, Bayle, and Fénelon. Enough has already been said, perhaps, about Arnauld's (unlimited) hostility, and about Leibniz's (limited) approval; but the reservations of the remaining three still stand in need of illumination. Here the most important figures are Bossuet and Bayle. Both offer striking criticisms of Malebranchism, but from radically different perspectives: Bossuet was a pillar of the Catholic Church and an ally of the French monarchy, while Bayle was a Calvinist *émigré* to Holland who was tolerated by neither French Church nor state. Bossuet represented an eloquent perfect orthodoxy, while Bayle was an independent intellectual frequently accused of undercutting all orthodoxy (even Calvinist 'orthodoxy'). Despite these enormous differences, both developed influential critiques of Malebranchism during roughly the same period—from the early 1680s to their nearly coinciding deaths (Bossuet in 1704, Bayle in 1706). To be sure, Bayle began as a strong Malebranchist, then moved slowly but steadily away; while Bossuet began with antipathy, and ended with slight and partial sympathy. None the less they count as the most important critics of Malebranchian *généralité* after Arnauld and Leibniz; Fénelon's contribution, as will be seen, confined itself to a single work in 1686–7—the *Réfutation du système du Père Malebranche*.[243] (In later times the only Malebranche critic/appreciator of a stature comparable to that of the seventeenth-century critics was to be Rousseau—whose *Malebranchisme* will be treated in due course.)

Bossuet

If Antoine Arnauld was so influential that some of his partisans succeeded in having Malebranche's *Traité de la nature et de la grâce* placed on the Index at Rome in 1690,[244] the still more formidable opponent was Bossuet: Bishop of Meaux, preacher to the Court of Louis XIV, tutor to the Dauphin.[245] Bossuet showed an unabating hostility to Malebranchian *généralité*: first in his *Oraison funèbre de Marie-Thérèse d'Autriche* (1683), then in his correspondence with Malebranche's disciple the Marquis d'Allemans, finally in his commissioning of Fénelon's *Réfutation du système du Père Malebranche sur la nature et la grâce* (which Bossuet corrected and annotated in his own hard, but finally did not publish). And, of course, Bossuet's great *Discours sur l'histoire universelle* is built on the notion of a *Providence particulière* which Malebranche had tried so hard to overturn, just as his *Politique tirée des propres paroles de*

---

[243] See Gouhier, *Fénelon philosophe*, 33 ff.
[244] For details of the condemnation of Malebranche's work, see *Œuvres complètes de Malebranche*, 550–8.
[245] See the brief 'vie de Bossuet' in Jacques Le Brun's 'Introduction' to Bossuet's *Politique* (Geneva: Librairie Droz, 1967), pp. vii ff.

l'Écriture Sainte relied on the very scriptural 'anthropologies' that Malebranche had scorned.[246] It was only in 1697, when Malebranche published his *Traité de l'amour de Dieu*, which argued against Fénelonian 'quietism' and 'disinterested' love, that Bossuet—now locked in combat with Fénelon—finally began to countenance a part of Malebranchism, and even to make some use of the term *volonté générale*. That notion finally appeared not just in his magisterial *Défense de la tradition et des Pères*—which was left unfinished (with a massive fragment on grace in St Augustine) at his death in 1704—but also in his anti-Jansenist revisions of the Introduction to the Benedictine edition of the complete works of Augustine (*c.*1700).[247]

If Bossuet ended his career with a partial countenancing of Malebranchian *généralité*—though within very narrow limits—he also began that career with a view of the 'general' and the 'particular' which is not wholly unrelated to Malebranchism. In a sermon on 'Providence' preached at the Louvre in 1662, Bossuet argues that the 'remarkable difference' between *les causes particulières* and *la cause universelle* (God) is that 'particular causes'—such as heat and cold, human desires and counter-desires—oppose and cancel each other, while the 'universal' cause 'encloses both the whole and the parts within the same order'. And he pursues the distinction between the *particulière* and the *universelle* in a moral tone rather like that of Malebranche's *Nature et grâce*:

Whoever attaches himself to particular causes—or, let us say it more plainly, whoever wants to obtain a benefit from a prince; whoever wants to make his fortune in a circuitous way, finds other claimants who counter him, finds unforeseen collisions which cross him: a scheme fails to work in time, and the machine breaks down; intrigue fails to have its effect; hopes go up in smoke. But whoever attaches himself immutably to the whole and not to the parts; not to proximate causes—to the powerful, to favour, to intrigue—but to the *cause première et fondamentelle*, to God, to his will, to his providence, finds nothing which opposes him, nothing which troubles his plans.[248]

While this is not exactly Malebranchism, the merely 'particular' is cast in an unflattering light by being linked with 'circuitous-

---

[246] See the editor's Introduction to Bossuet, *Politics Drawn from the Very Words of Holy Scripture*, trans. P. Riley (Cambridge: Cambridge University Press, 1991).

[247] Notes (*c.*1700), (on the Benedictine edition of the works of Augustine) first published in *Revue Bossuet*, 1 (Paris, 1900), 159 ff.

[248] Bossuet, 'Sermon sur la Providence', in *Œuvres de Bossuet* (Pléiade edn.), 1070.

ness', 'collision', 'intrigue', and 'smoke', while the universal is 'providential'.

Only a year later, in 1663, Bossuet preached the *oraison funèbre* of his benefactor Nicolas Cornet, the Syndic of the Sorbonne who had first identified (Jansenists would say constructed) the 'five propositions'. Without specifically affirming, against the Jansenists, that God has a still-efficacious 'general will' to save all men, Bossuet none the less praises Cornet for the 'exquisite knowledge' of Scripture and of the writings of Saints Augustine and Thomas which permitted him, in conjunction with 'the best minds of the Sorbonne', to identify 'these five propositions', which go beyond 'the just limits by which truth is separated from error', and which manifest the 'singularity' and 'peculiarity' of 'new opinions'. To be sure, Bossuet concedes, the leading Jansenists were 'great men, eloquent, bold, strong, and luminous minds'; but they were also 'more capable of pushing things to the extreme' than of being moderate—though they were quite right to oppose the Jesuitical laxity that Bossuet equally castigates. In the face of the 'zealous and powerful' Jansenist 'party' within the Sorbonne, Bossuet goes on, Nicolas Cornet 'worked usefully among these tumults, convincing some through his doctrine, restraining others by his authority, animating and sustaining everyone through his constancy'.[249] The praise of the characters (if not the thoughts) of the Jansenists, coupled with an assault on Jesuitical latitudinarianism reminiscent of Pascal's *Lettres provinciales*, allows Bossuet to steer a middle course between 'terrible excesses' of rigour and worldliness;[250] nevertheless it could really please no orthodox Jansenist to hear the 'five propositions' stigmatized as 'singular', 'peculiar', and 'error'. For that must mean—if the 'fifth proposition' is as 'erroneous' as the rest—that it is *not* a 'semi-Pelagian' heresy to read 'God wills that all men be saved' *au pied de la lettre*. A Jansenist, indeed, would wish that St Paul had ceased his letter-writing with Romans 9, with the doctrine that God 'hath mercy on whom he will have mercy, and whom he will he hardeneth . . . hath not the potter power over the clay, of the same lump to make one vessel unto honour, and another

[249] Bossuet, *Oraison funèbre de Nicolas Cornet*, in *Œuvres de Bossuet* (Pléiade edn.), 51.
[250] Ibid. 44–50.

unto dishonour?'[251] For the clay of Romans can certainly be modelled into 'the elect'; it is Paul's letter to Timothy that is harder to shape to Jansenist ends. By condemning the fifth proposition, Bossuet tacitly reaffirms God's general will to save all men—rather in the manner of Malebranche.

By 1680, however, when Bossuet first read Malebranche's *Nature et grâce*, his thought had begun to change: he is said to have written *pulchra*, *nova*, *falsa* on his (published) copy; and by June 1683 he was expressing his doubts about divine general will (in general) and his 'horror' of Malebranchian *volonté générale* (in particular) in a letter to a fellow-bishop.[252] But the decisive (and very public) turn came in September 1683, with the rhetorically superb *Oraison funèbre de Marie-Thérèse d'Autriche*, pronounced by Bossuet during the funeral of the Queen of France at St Denis, in the presence of the Dauphin and of the Court. The central passage of this remarkable funeral oration (which was quickly published) is aimed clearly and obviously at Malebranchian *généralité*:

What contempt I have for those philosophers who, measuring the counsels of God by their own thoughts, make him the author of nothing more than a certain general order, out of which the rest develops as it may! As if he had, after our fashion, only general and confused views, and as if the sovereign intelligence could not include in his plans particular things, which alone truly exist.[253]

If in the *Oraison funèbre de Marie-Thérèse* Bossuet attacked Malebranche's *Nature et grâce* quickly and sharply, he expanded this attack into a more general theological programme in his *Traité du libre arbitre*.

It is useless, in explaining [divine] prescience, to place in God a general concourse whose action and effect are determined by our liberty. For neither a concourse so understood, nor the will to establish it, have determined anything, and in consequence do not serve at all in explaining how God knows particular things [*les choses particulières*]; such that, to establish the universal prescience of God, he must be given means which are certain, by which he can turn our will to all the particular effects which it may please

[251] Romans 9: 18, 21. One might reasonably say that the whole question of *volonté générale* is a theological by-product of later efforts to reconcile St Paul with himself—to make this passage from Romans coexist with 1 Timothy 2: 4.

[252] Bossuet, letter to Neercassel (June 1683), in *Œuvres complètes de Malebranche*, xviii. 248–9.

[253] In *Œuvres de Bossuet* (Pléiade edn.), 110.

him to ordain. . . . For he, whose knowledge and will always yield the ultimate precision in all things, does not content himself with willing that they be *en général*, but he descends . . . to that which is most particular.[254]

For Bossuet, providentialist particularism must not (mistakenly) take the form of Protestant fatalism: human freedom must be made congruent with divine Providence (in the more or less Thomistic way suggested by Bossuet's *Traité du libre arbitre*). One must somehow avoid both 'Pelagianism'—which only lets God 'concur' in radically free human actions—and Calvinism.

Let us recognize, then, in the Reformation—I say in the two parts, and as much in Calvinism as in Lutheranism—that false and dangerous science which, to show that it understands the highest mysteries of God, has found in his immutable decrees the ruin of human free will, and at the same time the extinction of the regrets of conscience.[255]

One must beware 'the shipwreck of the Calvinist, who, to maintain the prescience and the Providence of God, takes from man the liberty of choice, and makes God the necessary author of all human events. . . . [Calvinism] breaks against the rocks'.[256]

Bossuet's solution to the problem of *Providence particulière*— avoiding the polar errors of 'Calvinistic' necessity and 'Pelagian' human independence—is to be found in Thomistic premotion or 'physical predetermination'; the correct *via media* is this:

Since then a man is, from the time that God wills that he be, he is free, from the time that God wills that he be free: and he acts freely, from the time that God wills that he act freely; and he freely performs this or that action, from the time that God so wills it. For all the wills, both of men and angels, are included in the will of God, as in their first and universal cause; and they are free only because they are there included as free. . . . Such is the sentiment of those who are called Thomists . . . [and] . . . the principal foundation of this whole doctrine is so certain, that the whole School is in agreement on it.[257]

All of these considerations lead to what Bossuet takes to be the only coherent reconciliation of particular Providence and human freedom; and in the *Traité du libre arbitre* he insists that

[254] In *Œuvres de Bossuet* (Paris: Didot Frères, 1841), i. 108.
[255] Bossuet, *Deuxième avertissement aux Protestants*, in *Œuvres* (1841 edn.), iv. 326.
[256] Ibid.
[257] *Traité du libre arbitre*, 117 ff.

we conceive God as a being who knows all, who previews all, who provides for everything, who governs everything, who makes what he will of his creatures, [a being] to whom all the world's events must be related. If free creatures are not included in this order of divine Providence, one deprives him of the conduct of what is most excellent in the universe, that is, intelligent creatures. There is nothing more absurd than saying that he does not interfere with the governance of nations, the establishment or the ruin of states, how they are governed, and by which laws.[258]

By this point, as is evident, a 'merely' general Providence of a Malebranchian kind has been completely ruled out.

Bossuet actually sent a copy of the published version of his *Oraison funèbre de Marie-Thérèse d'Autriche* to Malebranche, who felt constrained to thank the Bishop for his thoughtful gift.[259] But Bossuet's criticism of the *généralité* of *Nature et grâce* was not always so public; and, indeed, the lengthiest of his refutations of 'general will' and *Providence générale* is to be found in a 1687 letter to the Malebranchian Marquis d'Allemans, who had tried to represent (or re-present) Malebranche's *Nature et grâce* in a way that Bossuet could accept. Bossuet begins this very long letter by complaining that d'Allemans has not in the slightest succeeded in making *Nature et grâce* more palatable; and he refers to Malebranche, with withering sarcasm, as 'your infallible doctor' and 'your master'. 'I notice in you', Bossuet tells the Marquis, 'nothing but an attachment, which grows every day more blind to your patriarch', though his 'ridiculous' theory of nature and grace is 'a perfect galimatias'.[260]

To be more exact, in Bossuet's view, Malebranche does not really offer nature *and* grace at all: he offers just nature, and grace vanishes. (The 'naturalization' of grace which was later to delight Voltaire only horrified Bossuet.[261]) It is bad enough, Bossuet complains, that Malebranche 'prides himself' on having 'explained

---

[258] Ibid. 106.

[259] Dreyfus, 'Introduction philosophique' to Malebranche, *Traité de la nature et de la grâce* (1680 text), 127 ff. ('l'opposition commune de Bossuet et de Fénelon').

[260] Bossuet, letter to the Marquis d'Allemans (May 1687), in *Œuvres complètes de Malebranche*, xviii. 444.

[261] Voltaire, *Dictionnaire philosophique*, article 'Grâce', cited in Alquié, *Le Cartésianisme de Malebranche*, 443–4; 'Toute la nature, tout ce qui éxiste, est une grâce de Dieu . . . La grâce de faire croître un arbre de soixante et dix pieds est accordée au sapin, et refusée au roseau. Il [Dieu] donne à l'homme la grâce de penser, de parler et de le connaître.' And Alquié himself adds (p. 444): 'Ici, l'assimilation de la nature et de la grâce est complète. Malebranche, assurement, n'opère pas cette identification. Mais, en naturalisant la grâce, il prepare de telles pensées.'

Noah's Flood through the operation of natural causes'; but if d'Allemans continues to follow Malebranche 'he will lead you to find, in those same causes', the Israelites' passage through the Red Sea, as well as all other scriptural 'marvels of this kind'. If, Bossuet goes on, one means by 'natural' causality the 'effects which happen through the force of the first laws of movement', then Malebranchian 'generality' will finally 'render everything natural, even to the resurrection of the dead and the healing of those born blind'.[262] (Bossuet turned out to be as prescient as he was conservative, for only eighty years later Rousseau was to argue in the Malebranche-coloured *Lettres écrites de la montagne* that the 'raising' of Lazarus was no 'supernatural operation' but a misreported 'live interment', and that one should doubt 'particular' changes in 'the order of nature'.[263])

Much of this 'heresy' (as Bossuet does not hesitate to call it) arises from misunderstanding the Cartesian 'method of doubt':

For on the pretext that one should admit only what one clearly understands—which, within certain limits, is quite true—each person gives himself freedom to say: I understand this, I do not understand that; and on this sole foundation, one approves or rejects whatever one likes. . . . Thus is introduced, under this pretext, a liberty of judging which involves advancing with temerity whatever one thinks, without regard for tradition.[264]

This, fairly clearly, refers to Malebranche's notion that one must conceive God through the 'idea' of an *être parfait*, and not through scriptural 'anthropologies'. But this preference for 'ideas', this contempt for tradition, leaves Bossuet 'terrified' and fearful of 'great scandal': heretics, he says, always 'begin with novelty', move on to 'stubbornness', and end with 'open revolt'.[265]

On occasion Bossuet tries to find in Descartes himself a supporter of the notion that 'good philosophy teaches us that God can demand of us belief in several things which are incredible and inconceivable'— such as the Incarnation and the Trinity, which matter even more than Noah's Flood or the parting of the Red Sea. In the *Principia*, Bossuet insists, there is a *beau passage de M. Descartes* which the Malebranchians would do well to remember: ' "Above all," says M.

---

[262] Bossuet, letter to d'Allemans, 444.

[263] Rousseau, *Lettres écrites de la montagne*, in *Rousseau: Œuvres complètes* (Paris: Éditions du Seuil, 1971), iii. 424 n.

[264] Letter to d'Allemans, 445.

[265] Ibid. 446.

Descartes, "we hold it as an infallible rule that that which God has revealed is incomparably more certain than the rest [of knowledge]; such that, if some spark of reason suggests something contrary to us, we are always ready to subject our judgement to that which comes from him".' In this passage, for Bossuet, a 'true philosopher' recognizes 'the limits within which human reason must keep itself'. Again for Bossuet, it is precisely those limits which the 'Cartesian' Malebranche has stepped over, with his *généralité* and his notion of what an *être parfait* 'must' do.[266]

Bossuet concludes his letter—spoken, he says, 'as one does to a friend'—with a final chilling remark about thinking that one can 'do' theology because one 'knows physics and algebra'; and he reminds Malebranche's disciple that one cannot 'favour' both Malebranchian *volonté générale* and Bossuet's own *Histoire universelle* (which d'Allemans had praised).

It is easy for me to show you that the principles on which I reason are directly opposed to those of your system. . . . There is a great difference in saying, as I do, that God leads each thing to the end which he proposes for it by the means which he [actually] follows, and in saying that he contents himself with giving some general laws, from which result many things which enter only indirectly into his plans. . . . I turn away from your ideas of general laws.[267]

Bossuet was perfectly right, of course, in characterizing his own *Histoire universelle* as a work built in *Providence particulière*, not on 'general laws'. 'Remember, Monseigneur,' Bossuet admonishes the Dauphin at the end of the *Histoire*, 'that this long chain of particular causes, which make and unmake empires, depends on the secret decrees of Divine Providence.' It is God who 'holds the reins of every kingdom and holds every heart in his hands'.[268] His action, moreover, in shaping universal history, is completely particular: 'should he wish to see a conqueror, he will spread terror before him . . . should he wish to see legislators, he will send them his spirit of wisdom and foresight'.[269] And Bossuet—after urging that, thanks

[266] Bossuet, 'Examen d'une nouvelle éxplication du mystère de l'Euchariste', finally published in *Revue Bossuet*, I (Paris, 1900), 152–3. (The MS seems to date from the 1670s.)

[267] Letter to d'Allemans, 447.

[268] Bossuet, *Discours sur l'histoire universelle*, in *Œuvres de Bossuet* (Versailles: J. A. Lebel, 1818), xxxv. 556.

[269] Ibid.

to secret Providence, rulers 'achieve either more or less than they plan', and that 'their intentions have always led to unforeseen consequences'—concludes with an apotheosis of *Providence particulière* which excludes all Malebranchian *généralité*.

Thus God reigns over every nation. Let us no longer speak of coincidence or fortune; or let us use those words only to cover our ignorance. What is coincidence to our uncertain foresight is concerted design to a higher foresight which encompasses all causes and all effects in a single plan. Thus all things concur to the same end; and it is only because we fail to understand the whole design that we see coincidence or strangeness in particular events.[270]

And that draws together the Providentialist 'particularism' of both the *Oraison funèbre de Marie-Thérèse d'Autriche* and the *Traité du libre arbitre*; it is the *summa* of Bossuet's thought.

By the 1690s Bossuet, now locked in a fratricidal theological struggle with Fénelon, allowed something of a *rapprochement* with Malebranche—whose works after the *Entretiens sur la métaphysique* had begun to have a slightly more 'orthodox' look.[271] Hence in his *Défense de la tradition et des Pères*, which he began in 1693 as a refutation of Richard Simon's *Histoire critique des principaux commentateurs du Nouveau Testament*, Bossuet allowed himself to use the concept of 'general will'—though mainly, it is true, in the thirteenth book, which he added to the manuscript in 1702. And even here Bossuet does not permit himself to use *volonté générale* in Malebranche's expanded sense—as something coextensive with wisdom, constancy, even justice; he is careful to restrict *généralité* to a narrowly circumscribed realm of grace. Indeed, he speaks simply about St Augustine's interpretation of the Pauline assertion that 'God wills that all men be saved'—the very claim that had inspired Malebranche to write *Nature et grâce*.[272]

St Augustine's 'difficulty', Bossuet argues, was that of knowing why 'the will to believe' was not given equally to all men, if God truly wills that 'all men be saved'. And St Augustine had two related 'problems' as well: first, how one can say that God 'wills' something

---

[270] Ibid. 557.
[271] The notion of *volonté générale*, for example, is used rather sparingly in the *Entretiens*.
[272] Malebranche, *Lettres du P. Malebranche* (Paris, 1709), 189.

that 'does not happen' (since some are damned, not saved); and second, how one can reconcile God's 'general will' with human 'free will'. But St Augustine, in Bossuet's view, overcomes all these difficulties quite admirably, by 'saying that God truly wills to save all men, but that, since he wants to do this without depriving them of their natural liberty, it is also through the latter that they perish'.[273] St Augustine 'supposes', Bossuet argues, that if all men are not saved, the obstacle comes not at all from 'the *volonté* of God, which is *générale*', but from 'the will of man' which 'opposes' God. (This 'opposition' finally gets punished, to be sure: precisely through some men's being damned.[274])

Bossuet grants that St Augustine does not invariably maintain that God has a 'general will' to save all men; indeed in *De Correptione et Gratia*, Bossuet concedes, Augustine seems to say that 'all' men in St Paul's assertion refers simply to 'the predestined'. But one must recall, Bossuet insists, that in late writings such as *Correction and Grace* St Augustine was combatting the Pelagians, who 'amused the world by calling nature "grace"), and who maintained that grace was given to all equally and indifferently. It was the aim of St Augustine, Bossuet continues, 'to preach the grace by which we are Christians'; and he finally concludes that while God as 'creator' willed generally that all men be saved, God as 'redeemer' reduced this 'all' to Christians particularly.[275] And this, of course, is fairly close to what Pascal says (in the *Écrits sur la grâce*) about the *volonté générale* to save 'all' being replaced, after the Fall, by a will to save a smaller number—though Bossuet, no Jansenist, is careful not to speak of the 'elect'.

It is worth remembering that in the year 1700—precisely when Bossuet was working on the *Défense de la tradition et des Pères*—he was asked to revise the preface to the new Benedictine edition of the works of St Augustine, and that in this revision he insisted strongly (against the Jansenists) on God's antecedent or 'conditional' general will to save all men.[276] Speaking of Augustine's late anti-Pelagian writings, Bossuet urges that 'One will grant without difficulty that St Augustine, in these works, insists principally on the consequent or

---

[273] Bossuet, *Défense de la tradition et des Pères*, in *Œuvres complètes de Bossuet* (Bar-le-Duc: Louis Guérin, 1870), v. 324.
[274] Ibid.   [275] Ibid. 357–9.
[276] Bossuet, notes on the Benedictine edition of St Augustine, *Revue Bossuet*, I (Paris, 1900), 159 ff.

absolute will of God [to save the few]. But . . . St Augustine, even against the Pelagians, recognized an antecedent *volonté générale* . . . to save all men.' And, complaining that the Benedictine editors have not given sufficient weight to a key passage from Augustine's *De Spiritu et Littera*, Bossuet insists that 'it is to be feared that they imitate Jansenius too much, by striving to render useless this place [in the text] of *The Spirit and the Letter*, which is expressly for the general will and for the notion of free will'.[277]

But if, in the last few years of his life, Bossuet began to make some use of *volonté générale*, that did little to weaken his (stronger) conviction that God rules the universe through *Providence particulière*; if in the end he was not as violently anti-Malebranchist as Antoine Arnauld, he never retracted his judgement that *Nature et grâce* was 'a perfect galimatias'.

Fénelon

In 1686–7 Bossuet, not wholly content with his own efforts to overturn Malebranchian *généralité*, commissioned a work from the Abbé Fénelon (as he then was); and this *Réfutation du système du Père Malebranche sur la nature et la grâce*—in some parts corrected or amplified by Bossuet—was to be Bossuet's greatest (if indirect) contribution to the shoring up of *Providence particulière*.[278] In the *Réfutation*, Fénelon begins with a reasonably fair résumé of *Nature et grâce*, but thinks that he has found a fatal flaw in Malebranche's admission that God acts only usually, but not invariably, through 'general wills' and general laws; that he sometimes—though 'rarely'—acts through *volontés particulières*.

But in what consists that which the author [Malebranche] calls 'rarely'? These words signify nothing, unless they mean that there is a certain number of *volontés particulières* which order permits to God outside the general laws, after which he can will nothing particularly. If order permits to God this small number of *volontés particulières*—order never permitting anything but the most perfect—it follows not only that these *volontés particulières* do not diminish in the slightest the simplicity of God's ways but even that it is more perfect of God to mix some *volontés particulières* in his general plan, than to limit himself absolutely to his *volontés générales*.[279]

---

[277] Ibid. 175.   [278] See Gouhier, *Fénelon philosophe*, 33 ff.
[279] Fénelon, *Réfutation du système du Père Malebranche*, in *Œuvres de Fénelon* (Paris: Chez LeFevre, 1835), ii. 258.

(In his corrections, Bossuet complains at this point that Fénelon should not confuse God's 'simplicity' with his 'perfection': 'multiplicity [of divine wills] may well not be contrary to perfection', Bossuet urges, 'but it is always [contrary] to simplicity'.[280] This is logically unimpeachable: the 'simple' is necessarily non-multiple; the 'perfect' may or may not involve multiplicity.)

Fénelon, still stressing 'simplicity' rather than 'perfection' goes on to imagine a hypothetical case in which 'order' has permitted God to have a hundred *volontés particulières*; and he then asks himself a rhetorical question: 'What, then, is this "simplicity" which is able to accommodate a hundred [particular] wills, which even requires them, but which invincibly rejects the hundred and first?'[281] And Fénelon adds, in a passage which is extremely effective, though not perhaps wholly fair, that

If God did not have these hundred *volontés particulières*, he would cease to be God; for he would violate the order which requires them, and would not act with the greatest perfection. If he had the hundred and first *volonté*, he would also cease to be God; for he would destroy the simplicity of his ways.[282]

It is certainly not the case, Fénelon goes on, that the hundred and first *volonté particulière* is 'of another nature' than the first hundred; all are equally 'exceptions to the general rule'. And he ends with the striking question: 'Is there a fatal number of exceptions which God is obliged to use up, after which he can will nothing except according to general laws? Would one dare to say this?'[283] Even if, as Bossuet's annotations and marginalia argue, a multiplicity of *volontés particulières* would contradict only 'simplicity', but not (necessarily) 'perfection', this is an effective passage.

The providentialist moral of all this is drawn by Fénelon several chapters later, in a section called, 'That which the author [Malebranche] says about *volontés particulières* destroys, through its consequences, all divine Providence'. Sometimes, Fénelon argues, Providence 'acts against general rules, through miracles', as in the parting of the Red Sea; and this particularism is obviously morally important, since the Jews deserved to escape from the Egyptians. But sometimes—and this seems to matter more—Providence creates

---

[280] Fénelon, *Réfutation du système du Père Malebranche*, in *Œuvres de Fénelon* (Paris: Chez LeFevre, 1835), ii. 258 n.
[281] Ibid. 258–9.   [282] Ibid. 259.   [283] Ibid.

a parallel between general laws and particular plans: she 'uses the wills of men, in which she inspires whatever please her, to cause even in matter itself movements which seem fortuitous, but which are related to events which God wills to draw from them'. It was exactly in this way, Fénelon insists, that Alexander the Great 'conceived the ambitious plan of conquering Asia: in that way he was able to fulfil the prophecy of Daniel'. If one examines 'all the revolutions of great empires'—which are, Fénelon adds, 'the greatest spectacle which can sustain our faith'—one sees that 'Providence has raised or levelled them to prepare the way for the Messiah, and to establish his endless reign'.[284] And in a footnote he indicates that, on this point, it is Bossuet's *Histoire universelle* that ought to be consulted.[285] (In this chapter, significantly, Bossuet found nothing at all to fault.)

It should not be assumed that Fénelon was merely pandering to Bossuet at the time of the *Réfutation*; for in the early 1700s, long after the permanent rupture with Bossuet, Fénelon continued to have the gravest doubts about Malebranchian *généralité*—as his 1708 letters to François Lami on grace and predestination show. What is interesting in these letters, however, is that Fénelon shows how attractive a generally-willing God might be—before finally repudiating this notion as anti-Augustinian and heretical.

God could limit himself to giving to all men, without [particularly] predestining any of them, the same grace, fully sufficient for all. He could say to himself: I shall give my heavenly reward to all those who by their free will answer to this [divine] help, and I shall deprive of this reward all those who, being in a position to merit it, do not will to make themselves worthy of it. On this supposition, could you accuse God of injustice? Not the slightest inequality would appear; not the slightest favouritism; not the slightest preference; everything would be general [*tout serait général*], effective, proportional to need, and abundant on God's part. There would be no inequality except on the part of men: all inequality would come from their free will.[286]

But while the Archbishop of Cambrai (as he had since become) begins by imagining this Malebranchian equation of justice and generality, he wants to be able to justify special divine grace given to

---

[284] Ibid. 270.   [285] Ibid. 270n.
[286] Fénelon, letters to Lami, in *Œuvres spirituelles* (n.p.: 1751; orig. edn. 1718), iv. 290.

the predestined or elect. And therefore a little later in one of the letters to Lami he says that

the special goodness of [divine] favouritism for the few, in no way diminishes the general goodness for all the others. The superabundance of aid for the elect, diminishes not at all the quite sufficient aid that all the others receive . . . Does the superabundance of [God's] goodness for another destroy the exact justice, the gratuitous and liberal goodness that he has for you, and the quite sufficient aid that he gives you?[287]

To deny this superadded, extra goodness that God gratuitously heaps on the elect, according to Fénelon, is to deny Augustinian predestination altogether; and that is a heresy.

Now it is obvious that the totality of men cannot be included in this special decree, and that this favouring cannot embrace the whole human race. Favour would no longer be favour, but a general love, if it extended generally to all men. The special will [of God] would be confused with the *volonté générale*. Election would be no more particular [*n'aurait rien de plus particulier*] than simple vocation.[288]

From a Malebranchian perspective, Fénelon begins well by imagining a God who links up justice, generality, and equal treatment; but then, to save the dogma of predestination, he severs the tie between *généralité* and justice, and tries to justify God's particularistic favouritism by appealing to Scripture ('many are called, but few are chosen'[289]). But Fénelon would doubtless reply that Malebranche saves God's 'generality' only by making the Son the distributor or occasional cause of grace through *volontés particulières*—only by shifting the burden of 'election' from one part of the Trinity to another. And to that Malebranche would retort that it is better to put the blame for some men's not being saved on Christ's human 'particularism' than to imagine a divided Father who both wills universal salvation and undermines it. What is clear is that Malebranche and Fénelon could never have reached agreement on this issue: Malebranche's *recherche de la généralité* forces him to shift 'election' on to Christ's humanity; since *généralité* has no conclusive weight for Fénelon, he can simply say that the Father's general 'favour' for all is particularly enlarged for the elect without the slightest injustice. Thus Fénelon and Bossuet, despite their

---

[287] Fénelon, letters to Lami, in *Œuvres spirituelles* (n.p.: 1751; orig. edn. 1718), iv. 294.

[288] Ibid. 321.   [289] Ibid. 320–1.

fratricidal rupture, could agree that Malebranche's 'generalism' was at the root of his central difficulties.

Pierre Bayle

Bayle, though a Calvinist, was briefly (*c.*1680–5) a Malebranchist as well;[290] and indeed nothing did more to spread the European fame of Malebranche's *Nature et grâce* than Bayle's glowing review of it (May 1684) in his universally diffused journal, *Nouvelles de la République des Lettres*. The 'hypothesis' that 'God acts through a general will which prescribes only a small number of simple and uniform laws', Bayle argues, is quite suitable for justifying 'several things which cause pain to minds of the second rank'.[291] (Is this slightly left-handed compliment an intimation of hostility to come?) When these 'minds' ask why 'nature produces so many monstrous things', or why 'in order of grace there are so many things which shock our reason', a Malebranchian can reply that they are 'consequences of the general laws which God has chosen', and that God loves his own wisdom 'infinitely more than all his works'. Though one may not agree with everything in Malebranche's *Nature et grâce*, Bayle insists, one is still 'forced to admit that no one has ever, perhaps, formed so well-linked a system in so little time'—a system which manifests the 'vast' and 'penetrating' 'genius' of its author.[292]

But Bayle's decisive work in this vein is the thoroughly Malebranchian *Pensées diverses sur la comète* (1682), whose general aim is to overturn 'superstition' by demonstrating that the comet which alarmed Europe in December 1680 was produced by Malebranchian 'general laws', that it was not a 'sign' of *Providence particulière* or a portent of doom. If God wants to instruct the world through something 'miraculous', Bayle argues, he sends 'persons' (Christ, for example) who shine 'with the brilliance of excellent virtues' that only the 'voluntarily blind' can ignore; he does not merely send a flying rock which signifies 'at most the anger of heaven'. If all the martyrs and prophets have not overcome 'idolatry', Bayle observes tartly, why should one expect much from

---

[290] For an appreciation of Bayle's knowledge of Malebranche's philosophy, see Labrousse, *Pierre Bayle*, ii. 187 ff.

[291] Bayle, *Compte rendu du traité de la nature et de la grâce*, from *Nouvelles de la République des Lettres* (May 1684), in *Œuvres complètes de Malebranche*, viii–ix. 1153.

[292] Ibid. 1153–6.

'a mute flame, which naturally inspires only a feeling of apprehension?'[293]

Those who have read Malebranche's *Nature et grâce*, Bayle goes on, will have understood that 'the events which are born of the execution of general laws of nature, are not the object of a *volonté particulière* of God'. And this Malebranchian 'generality', in Bayle's view, is usable in 'resolving a thousand difficulties which are raised against divine Providence'.

If we are permitted to judge the actions of God, we can say that he does not will all particular events because of the perfection they contain, but simply because they are linked to general laws which he has chosen to be the rule of his operations. . . . One can even imagine that the simplicity and uniformity of this way of acting, joined with an infinite fecundicity, seemed preferable to him, to another way of acting [which was] more complicated but more regular, even though some superfluous events had to result from this.[294]

So closely does Bayle adhere to Malebranche, at this point in his career, that he even copies Malebranche's treatment of morality as a kind of analogue to law-governed nature: just as it would be 'ridiculous' to claim that God ought to depart from laws of nature 'when a rock falls on a fragile vase which is the delight of its owner', Bayle argues, so also it is 'ridiculous to claim' that God should abandon generality 'to stop an evil man from enriching himself by despoiling an *homme de bien*'. Indeed Bayle outstrips Malebranche in the purity of his Malebranchism by urging that it is as 'unjust' to wish that 'an evil man become sick' through a divine *volonté particulière* as it is unreasonable to hope that 'a rock which falls on a vase will not break it'.[295] And in the same chapter of the *Pensées diverses* Bayle extracts a moral from his tale of the fragile vase and the evil man by urging that if 'a mere governor of a city will be laughed at, if he changes his rules and his orders as many times as it pleases anyone to murmur against him', this is even more true of God, 'whose laws concern so universal a good'. Can God 'derogate from his laws, because today they fail to please someone, tomorrow someone else?' Can one, Bayle asks, 'form false ideas of a *Providence générale*?'[296]

This hyper-Malebranchism Bayle carries over into a chapter of the

---

[293] Bayle, *Pensées diverses, écrites à un docteur de Sorbonne* (4th edn., Rotterdam: Chez Reinier Leers, 1704), ii. 452–3.
[294] Ibid. 462–3.   [295] Ibid. 458.   [296] Ibid. 457.

Pensées diverses called 'that there is nothing worthier of the greatness of God than to maintain general laws'. Some people say, Bayle begins, that God *ought* to intervene particularly in nature to stop the birth of 'monsters' that might later be worshipped by 'idolators'; but these people do not reflect that 'there could be nothing more unworthy of a *cause générale*, which sets all others in motion by a simple and uniform law, than to violate that law at every moment, in order to prevent murmurings and superstitions'.[297]

After the revocation of the Edict of Nantes in 1685, and following the death of his brother (a Calvinist pastor) in a French prison,[298] Bayle published an uncharacteristically violent anti-Catholic polemic entitled *Ce que c'est que la France toute catholique sous le règne de Louis le Grand*; and, as a commentator has noted, one of the most interesting features of *La France toute catholique* is 'the bitter use Bayle makes of Malebranche's theology', particularly his generalism.[299] (Perhaps Bayle had begun to feel that some 'particular' evils— including his own personal disasters of 1685—could not be explained away as 'consequences' of 'uniform' laws.) The revocation of the Edict, followed by fresh persecution of non-Catholics, Bayle argues, is

the best lesson in Malebranchism that could be given; for if it were worthy of God to act often through *volontés particulières* and through miracles, would he have suffered that a Church as corrupted as yours should grow to the point that it has—a Church which, through the enormity of its maxims and the baseness of some of its dogmas has merited the horror and contempt of all the world?[300]

'Let us say, then,' Bayle concludes savagely, 'with this Oratorian Father, that God, loving his wisdom better than anything else, prefers that his conduct bear the character of a wise agent . . . than that it remedy . . . the evils that happened in the world.'[301] Bayle does not yet, despite his ferocious sarcasm, call Malebranchism a 'pious fraud'—one of the favourite epithets of his *Dictionnaire historique et critique*; but he is clearly moving toward his later view that 'general will' does not *really* explain the evils of the world.[302]

---

[297] Ibid. 455–6.
[298] See Elisabeth Labrousse, 'Introduction' to Bayle, *Ce que c'est que la France toute catholique* (Paris: Vrin, 1973), 7 ff.
[299] C. Brush, *Montaigne and Bayle* (The Hague: Martinus Nijhoff, 1966), 239.
[300] Bayle, *La France toute catholique*, ed. Labrousse, 62.   [301] Ibid.
[302] See above all *Entretiens de Maxime et de Thémiste* (below).

Whatever may have been Bayle's doubts about the adequacy of Malebranchism by the time he wrote *La France toute catholique*, he continued to use Malebranche's distinction between *le particulier* (as something bad) and *le général* (as something good) in an important work from *c*.1686, the *Commentaire philosophique sur ces paroles de l'Évangile selon S. Luc, chap. XIV, vers 23, 'Et le Maître dit au Serviteur: "Va par les chemins et par les hayes, et contrains-les d'entrer, afin que ma maison soit remplie"'*. The central point of the *Commentaire* was to show that Scripture should be interpreted, not through 'literal sense' but through 'natural light'; that if a literal reading seemed to make Scripture advocate crimes (such as 'constraining' French Protestants to 'enter' the Catholic Church), then the literal interpretation must be rejected in favour of an 'equitable' reading.[303]

Now it is precisely in connection with 'equity' and *lumière naturelle* that Bayle takes up the familiar general–particular distinction. 'Without exception,' he begins, 'one must submit all moral laws to this natural idea of equity', which 'enlightens every man coming into the world.' But, Bayle goes on, in the language of *Recherche de la vérité*, 'since passion and prejudices only too often obscure the ideas of natural equity', he could wish that a man who wants to know those ideas well 'consider them *en général*, and leaving his *interêt particulier* out of account, as well as the customs of his country'. For it may happen that 'a sharp passion' will persuade a man that something 'very useful' and 'very pleasant' to himself is 'in conformity to reason', or that he may be swayed by 'the force of custom'.[304] Bayle ends by praising 'that universal and original light which emanates from God in order to show all men the general principles of equity'—general principles which are the 'touchstone' of all *lois particulières* ('not even excepting those which God has revealed to us in an extraordinary way').[305]

If, then, Bayle insists, a 'casuist' tells us that Scripture has particularly revealed to him that 'it is good and holy to curse one's enemies' or to persecute the faithful, we must shun him and turn our eyes toward 'natural religion fortified and perfected by the Gospel'. Then we shall hear 'that interior truth which speaks to our spirit without saying a word, but which speaks quite intelligibly to those

---

[303] Bayle, *Commentaire philosophique*, in *Œuvres diverses de M. Bayle* (The Hague: Compagnie des Librairies, 1737), ii. 379.
[304] Ibid. 379.   [305] Ibid.

who pay attention', while the 'pretended' Scripture of the casuist will be unmasked as a 'bilious vapour of temperament'. Even a 'particular fact' produced by God through 'special Providence' is not 'the light which leads us', and does not derogate from 'the positive law which is universally promulgated for all men in the Gospel', which requires all men to be meek and forgiving; still less, Bayle continues, does 'particular' Providence derogate from 'the natural and eternal law which supplies all men with the idea of honourability'. And Bayle ends the opening part of the *Commentaire philosophique* with the wholly Malebranchian thought that 'universal reason, which illuminates all minds', will never be denied to those who are 'attentive' and who do not permit 'corporeal objects to fill up the capacity of their soul' nor 'passions' to 'excite' their hearts.[306]

By the 1690s Bayle's doubts about Malebranchism began to overcome his vestigial respect for the doctrine; and in the *Réponse aux questions d'un provincial* he indicates exactly why his views changed, and who did the changing. At the time of his review of *Nature et grâce* and of the *Pensées diverses sur la comète*, Bayle relates, he had been 'among those who believed' that Malebranche had resolved many difficulties through 'general will' and 'general law'. Without now denying that 'the system of Père Malebranche' is 'the work of a superior genius, and one of the greatest efforts of the human spirit', Bayle avows that he can no longer embrace Malebranchian generality, 'after having read the books of M. Arnauld against this system, and after having considered well the vast and immense idea of the sovereignly perfect being'.[307] The 'idea' of an *être parfait* no longer conveys to Bayle what it seemed to convey to Malebranche: the true idea of God 'teaches', Bayle argues, that 'there is nothing easier for God than to follow a simple, fecund, and regular plan, which is, at the same time, suitable for all creatures'. It is only 'a limited intelligence'—Malebranche's own phrase, now turned against him—which takes more pride in its own 'ability' than in its 'love for the public good'.[308]

A prince who causes a city to be built may, through a false taste for grandeur, prefer that it have an air of magnificence, and an architecture of

---

[306] Bayle, *Commentaire philosophique*, in *Œuvres diverses de M. Bayle* (The Hague: Compagnie des Librairies, 1737), ii. 379.

[307] Bayle, *Réponse aux questions d'un provincial*, in *Œuvres diverses de M. Bayle*, iii. 812, 815.

[308] Ibid. 825.

bold and singular character, though at the same time very inconvenient for its inhabitants, than that, with less magnificence, it allow them to enjoy all sorts of conveniences. But if this prince has a true greatness of soul, that is, a strong disposition to make his subjects happy, he will prefer convenient but less magnificent architecture, to magnificent but less convenient architecture.[309]

From this architectural fable—which is not sufficiently well designed to be fatal to Malebranche—Bayle concludes that however 'well-intentioned' may be 'our legislators' on earth, they can still never 'invent rules which are convenient for all individuals [*particuliers*]'; the 'limitation' of these legislators' 'enlightenment' forces them to fall back on general laws which, 'everything considered', are 'more useful than damaging'.[310] Here generality is something *settled for*, but which (as in Aristotle) is not invariably 'equitable'.[311] But God does not suffer from this problem, since he is 'infinite in power and in intelligence'.[312] *Why* he does not 'suffer', why the theodicy problems which drive Malebranche to the 'general will' vanish simply by noticing divine power and intelligence, is not made clear, at least in this work; the probable answer is that, for Bayle, philosophy finally cannot solve theodicy problems satisfactorily, so that in the end one must rely on faith, not reason, in explaining (or rather believing in) the justice of God's operation. As Bayle himself says in the *Dictionnaire historique et critique*, a man is 'happily disposed toward faith when he knows how defective reason is. This is why Pascal and others have said that in order to convert the libertines they should make them realize the weakness of reason and teach them to distrust it.'[313] This fideism, Bayle's final (and apparently sincere) position, is radically at variance with Malebranche's insistence in the *Traité de morale* that 'faith passes away, but intelligence exists eternally'.[314] In the end, a fideism like Bayle's cannot coexist with a rationalism like Malebranche's.

Despite the fideism of the *Dictionnaire*, and Bayle's increasing doubts about a link between 'generality' and justice, there is an important passage in this work—the article dealing with Sarah, wife

---

[309] Bayle, *Réponse aux questions d'un provincial*, in *Œuvres diverses de M. Bayle*, iii. 826.

[310] Ibid.   [311] Aristotle, *Ethics*, 5. 1137[b] ff.

[312] Bayle, *Réponse aux questions d'un provincial*, 826.

[313] Bayle, *Historical and Critical Dictionary*, ed. R. Popkin (Indianapolis: Library of Liberal Arts, 1965), 206 (from the article 'Pyrrho').

[314] Malebranche, *Traité de morale*, 34.

of the prophet Abraham—in which that Malebranchian link is precisely maintained. In 'Sarah' Bayle considers the ways in which various Christian theologians have tried either to excuse or to condemn Sarah's conduct (recounted in Genesis) in countenancing Abraham's impregnation of her servant Agar after Sarah's sterility led to the impossibility of her bearing a child for Abraham. Bayle argues that St Augustine's effort to justify Abraham's adultery (and Sarah's connivance) in *The City of God* is not 'une bonne apologie', and that the attempts of St Ambrose are no better. All of the efforts of the early Fathers of the Church to excuse Abraham and Sarah, Bayle goes on, are implausible and even unworthy: 'The liberty which Calvin took in strongly censuring this action of Sarah and of her husband, is incomparably more useful to Christian morality, than the care which the Fathers took to justify Abraham and his wife.'[315] Bayle then, using a Malebranchian general–particular distinction, indicates just what is unjustifiable, not only in the conduct of Abraham and Sarah, but still more in the efforts of Augustine and Ambrose. Those Fathers, through their apologies, sacrificed 'les interêts généraux de la moralité' to 'the reputation of a particular person [*un particulier*]'.[316] And to show more plainly that morality is a 'general interest', while an individual reputation is only particular, Bayle goes on to remark that even the patriarch Abraham, yielding to lust, was as susceptible to 'the snares of Satan' as are 'manifestly criminal persons', and that Augustine's justificatory efforts involve a morality 'more lax' than that of the Jesuits Bauni and Escobar—those accommodating latitudinarians so ferociously attacked by Pascal in the *Lettres provinciales*.[317] (It was surely no accident that Bayle pitched upon the very figures that Pascal—whether justly or not—had saddled with permanently horrible reputations.[318]) In Bayle's 'Sarah', then, the *interêt général de la moralité* is pitted against Satanic snares, manifest criminality, and Jesuitical laxity; and these should not be admitted, according to Bayle, just to justify *un particulier*, even one who happened to be a prophet.

---

[315] Bayle, *Dictionnaire historique et critique* (Rotterdam: 1720), iii. 2540.
[316] Ibid.
[317] Pascal, *Les Provinciales*, ed. Louis Cognet (Paris: Garnier Frères, 1965), 72 ff., above all the *Cinquième lettre*.
[318] Ibid., pp. li ff. of Cognet's 'Introduction'.

King David comes in for a similarly harsh treatment in the *Dictionnaire*, couched once again in the language of *généralité* and *particularité*. Following a vivid description of some of King David's crimes—including several massacres and the killing of Uriah—Bayle observes that 'the profound respect that one ought to have for this great king' should not blind one to the 'blemishes' that disfigured his life; otherwise, Bayle fears, some will fancy that 'it suffices, in order for an action to be just, that it have been done by certain people whom we venerate'. But nothing could be 'more fatal . . . to Christian morality' than this countenancing of crimes carried out by great men: 'it is important for true religion that the life of the orthodox be judged by general ideas of rightness and of order [*par les idées générales de la droiture et de l'ordre*]'.[319] And Bayle concludes with virtually the same words that he applies to Sarah and Abraham:

There is no middle ground: either these actions [of King David] are worthless, or actions similar to them are not evil. Now, since one must choose one or the other of these two possibilities, is it not better to place the interests of morality above the glory of an individual [*la gloire d'un particulier*]?[320]

From 'Sarah', of course, one recalls that the 'interest of morality' is precisely *general*: one must not try to derive *la morale naturelle* from the (frequently bad) 'conduct' of someone who does 'great wrong to the eternal laws'.[321]

The article 'Sarah'—and its nearly identical companion-piece, 'King David'—is exceptional, in Bayle's late work, for its vestigial Malebranchism; more characteristic of his doubts about the worth of *généralité* is the piece on which he was working at the time of his death (1706), the *Entretiens de Maxime et de Thémiste*. The *Entretiens* are nominally a refutation of Isaac Jaquelot's *Examen de la théologie de Mr. Bayle* (1705); but Jaquelot's *Examen* is itself a doctrinaire restatement of Malebranche, gratuitously coupled with some non-Malebranchian ideas. Bayle's final work, then, is an oblique commentary, not on Malebranche *en soi*, but on comparatively unintelligent, second-hand *Malebranchisme*. Even so, Jaquelot's

---

[319] Cited in Elisabeth Labrousse, *Pierre Bayle* (Paris: Éditions Seghers, 1965), 136–7.

[320] Ibid. 137.   [321] Ibid.

Examen serves as the occasional cause of a more general enquiry into the worth of generality.[322]

If in early works such as the *Pensées diverses* Bayle had linked generality with justice and wisdom, in the *Entretiens* he was concerned to show that always operating generally might (wrongly) keep wise agents from departing from general laws and *volontés générales* even when goodness itself dictated such a departure. Jaquelot imagines, Bayle argues, that 'God could not have prevented the Fall of Adam without performing a miracle unworthy of his wisdom', without 'derogating' from general laws. But here, Bayle complains, 'the least philosopher' will properly point out that according to Scripture 'God performed a great number of miracles [which were] incomparably less useful and less necessary' than impeding the Fall of Adam—though it remains true that generality is worth *something* and that God therefore will not 'derogate from general laws unless it is a question of stopping a dreadful corruption of morals', and unless 'an infinity of miseries is going to inundate the human race'.[323] If this 'corruption' and 'inundation' will take place, however, *without* a particular divine intervention, Bayle is clear that *généralité* must yield:

The salvation of the people is the supreme law, *salus populi suprema lex esto*. It would be sinning against the laws of government not to be willing to derogate from the old laws, when the people's safety is at stake. Thus one shocks natural enlightenment if one supposes that, when it is a question of the safety of the human race, God would not have willed to derogate from general laws.[324]

And one 'wills' to derogate from 'general' laws, obviously, by a *volonté particulière*.

In later sections of the *Entretiens* Bayle goes on to say that an insistence on the constant operation of general laws places (merely) aesthetic standards above moral ones. If a 'pagan philosopher' were to examine Jaquelot's notion of *généralité*, Bayle argues, he would be told that God 'only created the world in order to show his power and his infinite knowledge of architecture and of mechanics', that his attribute of being 'good' and 'the friend of virtue' had 'no part in the

---

[322] Bayle, *Entretiens de Maxime et de Thémiste*, in *Œuvres diverses de M. Bayle*, iv. 3 ff.
[323] Ibid. 57–8.   [324] Ibid. 58.

construction of his great work'. Bayle then imagines what the pagan philosopher might have said:

What a God is M. Jaquelot's God! He prides himself only on knowledge; he prefers to let the whole human race perish than to suffer that some atoms move faster or slower than general laws demand. He would not disorder the slightest thing in the symmetry of his work in order to stop vice from ruling men, and would [instead] expose the whole of human-kind to disorders and to countless and appalling miseries.[325]

Bayle goes on to argue that *lumière naturelle* supplies men with a very different notion of God: 'goodness' is his chief attribute, and if he had to choose 'between a physical irregularity and a moral irregularity, he would choose the former'. If the 'architecture of the universe' has some 'defect', Bayle says, that harms no creature; but 'if moral evil is introduced among men', that is an 'injury' which spreads over 'an infinity of subjects'. If Jaquelot places the uniform operation of general laws above human 'safety'—if he gives greater weight to the aesthetic than to the moral—Bayle insists, then he makes God's rule 'resemble extremely the project of an enemy'.[326] In the end, for the Bayle of the *Entretiens*, Jaquelot's God's refusal to depart from *généralité*, even to save the human race, means 'that God's power must have had the first place; that his infinite knowledge of architecture and of mechanics must have had the second; and that his goodness must have had the third'.[327]

To be more exact, Bayle argues, 'goodness' could not even have occupied the third rank, since God's preferring of constancy and uniformity to moral good 'bears all the characters of hatred or of indifference to the human race'.[328] Bayle's suggestion that one can learn this by letting the 'tumult' of 'imagination' subside and by consulting 'reason' is perfectly Malebranchian; but his attack on generality is perfectly anti-Malebranchian. And so Bayle finally sets Jaquelot, his Malebranche surrogate, to one side, and confronts the Oratorian himself one last time. Even Père Malebranche himself, 'the inventor of the system of general laws', Bayle says, allows that God *sometimes* departs from generality and acts 'through *volontés particulières*'; thus it is absurd for either Malebranche or Jaquelot to assert that God could not have saved all men without harming his

---

[325] Bayle, *Entretiens de Maxime et de Thémiste*, in *Œuvres diverses de M. Bayle*, iv. 62.
[326] Ibid. 63.   [327] Ibid.   [328] Ibid. 66.

own attributes. Here Bayle puts a final speech into the mouth of his imagined pagan philosopher:

What! . . . God did nothing but derogate from general laws during the six days of the Creation, in order to form rocks, plants, and animals. Could he not have derogated from them a little later in order to spare the human race the moral evil and the physical evil which reign over men, and which will reign eternally in hell? He derogated from these same laws on a thousand less important occasions; could he not derogate from them when it was a question of the salvation or the ruin of the human race, the most noble creature that he had produced in our world?[329]

And near the end of that portion of the *Entretiens* which bears on Malebranchism and *généralité*, Bayle concludes that a Malebranchian God would, through love of his own 'wisdom', have 'subjected himself to the slavery of letting vice rule': general laws would have 'prevailed over goodness and over the love of moral good'. The Malebranchian God has found his own *lois générales* to be 'so fine, so admirable, so worthy of him' that even though they generate 'all the crimes, all the heresies, in a word all the disorders of the human race', he none the less 'has undertaken the continual and perpetual execution of these laws'.[330] And Bayle adds, with characteristic bravery, that a 'superior'—even a divine one—can become 'criminal' not just by ordaining evil, but also through mere permission, through what he calls 'connivance': just as (to use his own analogy), a parent who foresees that his virgin daughters will be seduced at a ball, and who none the less lets them go, is as guilty as the seducer.[331]

IV

In the eighteenth-century 'reception' of the Cartesian *généralité* which Malebranche had made famous in *Nature et grâce*, no figure matters more than Jean-Jacques Rousseau. That is especially true in political philosophy, since Rousseau had insisted that 'the general will one has as a citizen' is 'always right':[332] does not the Spartan mother on the opening pages of *Émile* have a *volonté générale* to 'save' the *polis*, as God might have a general will to save 'all men'?[333] But

---

[329] Ibid.   [330] Ibid. 64.   [331] Ibid. 67.
[332] Rousseau, *Du contrat social*, ed. Vaughan, 50.
[333] Rousseau, *Émile* (Paris: Pléiade, 1959), 588.

Rousseau's 'secularization' of general will, his systematic conversion of it from a theological into a 'civic' notion, is not what matters here; what is astonishing is the amount of attention that Rousseau gives to Malebranchian *généralité* in his own religious writings, as well as in the *Confessions*.

To be sure, one cannot imagine Rousseau as a member of the Oratorian order, or as 'seeing all things in God'—any more than one can imagine Malebranche's *Confessions*. None the less the relation between Malebranche and Rousseau, while a little unexpected, is important and revealing: if a figure as radically civic as the *citoyen de Genève* was deeply affected by *Malebranchisme*, that shows the pervasiveness of a form of thought which spread well beyond the confines of theology.

One could see plainly enough, even without considering the *Confessions*, that Rousseau had read the most important seventeenth-century French theologians—above all Malebranche and Fénelon—simply by looking at the 'Profession of Faith of the Savoyard Vicar' (from *Émile*), at the *Letter to Voltaire on Providence*, at the third and fifth of the *Lettres écrites de la montagne* (1764), and (above all) at Book VI of *La Nouvelle Héloïse*. All of these are replete with Malebranchian reminiscences.

Here the most important evidence is to be found in letters 6 and 7 from Book VI of Rousseau's novel. In the sixth letter Julie de Wolmar, advising her former lover Saint-Preux on religious matters, warns him to 'take care' that 'human pride' not 'mix' any 'low ideas' of God with 'the sublime ideas of the great being which you formulate for yourself'. Stressing human dependence on a divine father—'slaves by our weakness, we are free through prayers'—she makes it clear that the 'low ideas' which she fears are precisely Malebranchian, and cautions Saint-Preux against believing that the simple 'means which help our weakness' are also 'suitable to the divine power', and that God 'has need of art, like us, to generalize things in order to treat them more easily'. It seems to Saint-Preux, Julie goes on, that 'it would be an embarrassment' for God to have to 'look after' each particular person; perhaps Saint-Preux fears that a 'divided and continual attention' would 'fatigue' God, and that this is the reason for his believing it 'finer' that God 'do everything by general laws', doubtless because these would 'cost' him less 'care'. 'O great philosophers!' Julie ends mockingly, 'how obliged God is to you for having furnished him with these convenient methods and to have saved him so much work!'[334]

To this 'raillery' (as Émile Brehier has called it), Saint-Preux responds *en bon Malebranchiste*[335]: all 'analogies', he tells Julie, 'are in favour of these general laws which you seem to reject'. Reason itself, he continues, together with 'the soundest ideas' we can form of the 'supreme being', are 'very favourable' to (Malebranchian) generality: for while God's omnipotence, indeed, 'has no need of method to abridge work', none the less it is 'worthy of his wisdom' to prefer 'the simplest means'.[336]

Following an eloquent anti-Spinozist excursus on freedom—'a reasoner proves to me in vain that I am not free, because an inner feeling, stronger than all his arguments, refutes them ceaselessly'[337]— Saint-Preux returns to Malebranchian themes in connection with a discussion of grace. And on this subject, his generalism is more rigorous than Malebranche's own: precisely on Malebranchian grounds, for Saint-Preux, one must deny the reality of *any* particular, special grace. 'I do not believe', Saint-Preux insists, that God 'gives to one [person] sooner than to another' any 'extraordinary help' at all. Grace conferred particularly and unequally would constitute 'acceptation of persons', and would be 'injurious to divine justice'.[338] (For Rousseau, 'particular events are nothing in the eyes of the master of the universe', whose providence is *universelle* or *générale*.)[339]

Even if the 'hard and discouraging doctrine' of particularly conferred grace were 'deduced from Scripture itself', Saint-Preux goes on to say, 'is it not my first duty to honour God?'[340] (On this point, exactly as in Malebranche, the *idea* of what God would do takes precedence over 'Scripture': justice matters more than anthropology.) Whatever 'respect' one owes to the 'sacred text', Saint-Preux insists, one owes still more to its 'author': 'I would

---

[334] Rousseau, *Julie ou La Nouvelle Héloïse*, ed. René Pomeau (Paris: Garnier Frères, 1960), 660. For a splendid commentary, see Jean Starobinski, *Jean-Jacques Rousseau: La Transparence et l'obstacle* (Paris: Gallimard, 1971), 102 ff.

[335] Cited in Émile Bréhier, 'Les Lectures Malebranchistes de Jean-Jacques Rousseau', 113–14.

[336] Rousseau, *La Nouvelle Héloïse*, 671.   [337] Ibid.   [338] Ibid. 672.

[339] Rousseau, *Letter to Voltaire on Providence* (1756), in *Religious Writings*, ed. R. Grimsley (Oxford: Clarendon Press, 1970), 44.

[340] Rousseau, *La Nouvelle Héloïse*, 672.

rather believe the Bible falsified or unintelligible, than God unjust or evil-doing.' If the notion of 'grace' means anything, for Saint-Preux, it refers simply to the non-supernatural gifts which God has given equally to all: 'He has given us reason to know the good, conscience to love it, and liberty to choose it. It is in these sublime gifts that divine grace consists.' And he adds, pointedly, that 'we have all received them'.[341]

Rousseau's hostility to any Jansenist notion of non-universal grace, of divine 'favouritism', carries over into the *Lettres écrites de la montagne*—and in a way which shows that Rousseau knew perfectly that arguments over 'particular' grace had had (mainly unfortunate) social effects in the seventeenth century. In the *Cinquième Lettre*, Rousseau argues that his religious writings have been illegally condemned by the Genevan authorities, and appeals to the authority of the neo-Pascalian moralist Vauvenargues ('whoever is more severe than the laws is a tyrant').[342] He knows, Rousseau says, of only one comparable instance of legal oppression in Genevan history: 'this was in the great quarrel of 1669 over particular grace'.[343] Following the inability of *les Professeurs* to decide the truth about divine grace, Rousseau urges, the Council of Two Hundred rendered a judgement: 'the important question at issue was to know whether Jesus had died only for the salvation of the elect, or whether he had also died for the salvation of the damned.' After 'many sessions' and 'ripe deliberations', Rousseau adds sarcastically, the 'magnificent' Council of Two Hundred 'declared that Jesus had died only for the salvation of the elect'. But this, for Rousseau, was a merely political decision, in the worst sense of 'political': 'Jesus would have died for the damned, if Professor Tronchin had had more credit than his adversary'. Rousseau brands the whole affair as 'fort ridicule', and adds that civil authorities should 'appease quarrels without pronouncing on doctrine'.[344] In the (unpublished) original manuscript of *Montagne*, Rousseau at this point offers an analogy which only makes clearer his knowledge of seventeenth-century theological disputes: 'What ridicule would the Parlement of Paris not have drawn on itself if it had wanted to decide, on its own

---

[341] Ibid. 671.

[342] Vauvenargues, *Introduction à la connaissance de l'esprit humain*, in *Œuvres complètes*, ed. H. Bonnier (Paris: Hachette, 1968), i. 241.

[343] Rousseau, *Lettres écrites de la montagne* (1764 edn.), 170 n.

[344] Ibid. 171 n.

authority [*de son chef*], whether the five propositions were or were not in the book [*Augustinus*] of Jansenius!' He adds that since the Jansenists 'disputed' even Rome's right to judge the *Augustinus*, 'how could they have recognized [this right] in a secular tribunal'?[345] The published version of the *Cinquième Lettre*, together with the unpublished passage on Jansenism, make it plain that Rousseau knew perfectly the provenance[346] of the controversy over *volonté générale*: if he knew 'the five propositions', he knew that the last of them dealt with the scriptural assertion that 'god wills that all men be saved'.[347])

In any case, and whatever may have been the facts of the great quarrel of 1669, the whole controversy over *la grace particulière* is, in Rousseau's final judgement, one of those 'questions that interest nobody and that no one whosoever ever understands'; that being so, it should be 'always left to the theologians'.[348] This is what one would expect Rousseau to say, given his view in *La Nouvelle Héloïse* that 'all' have received the only *real* grace; and in *Montagne* he actually says it. (It is an irony worth noticing that Rousseau, in appealing to the authority of the neo-Pascalian Vauvenargues, does so in condemning as 'quite ridiculous' the very controversy over *grâce particulière* which Pascal himself had treated wholly seriously in the *Écrits sur la grâce*.[349] But Rousseau's citing of Vauvenargues at least shows that Rousseau knew the thought of this eighteenth-century Pascalian; and this would establish an important link between Pascal and Rousseau—both of whom worried about *généralité* as much as did Malebranche.)

If, for Saint-Preux in *La Nouvelle Héloïse*, God is a Malebranchian who operates through *lois générales* and avoids an unjust 'acceptation of persons', of what use is prayer—which asks precisely for *grâce particulière*? Here Saint-Preux, though careful in his language, is strict: 'in seeking grace, one renounces reason . . . who are we to want to force God to perform a miracle' on our behalf? Prayer, indeed, has the good effect of 'elevating' us to God and of 'raising us above ourselves'; but this does not mean that our prayers will be

[345] Rousseau, 'Manuscript autographe' of the *Lettres écrites de la montagne*, ed. J. S. Spink, in *Annales de la Société Jean-Jacques Rousseau*, 21 (1932), 13 n.

[346] Jean Pierre Gaberel, *Histoire de l'église de Génève* (Geneva: Jullien Frères, 1862), 121–3.

[347] Ibid.

[348] Rousseau, *Lettres écrites de la montagne* (1764–edn.), 171.

[349] Pascal, *Écrits sur la grâce*, 133 ff.

answered by God: 'it is not he who changes us; it is we who change by raising ourselves to him.'[350]

These quasi-Malebranchian passages—which seem to confirm Bossuet's fear that, if Malebranchian *généralité* is carried far enough, grace vanishes altogether—got Rousseau into great difficulty with the French censorship; and in a remarkable letter to the censor Malesherbes (March 1761), Rousseau says that if he has made Saint-Preux a 'Molinist'—mainly by affirming freedom and minimizing grace to the vanishing point—he has done so in order to avoid making him a 'Manichean': if equal and general human liberty is *not* the cause of evil, then an evil spirit, equal to God, must be. But, Rousseau adds, if Saint-Preux 'wants to be a heretic on grace, that is his affair'. As for the censor's charge that Saint-Preux is the leader of 'a revolt against the authority of Scripture', Rousseau says, he would sooner call it a 'submission to the authority of God and of reason': for God and reason, he continues, must 'go before' the Bible, and serve as its 'foundation'.[351] And that is a perfectly Malebranchian sentiment. This letter, together with other passages from *La Nouvelle Héloïse* treating Fénelon and 'quietism', make it clear that Rousseau's knowledge of the history of French theology was rather extensive, and also that, at the same time, God's 'case' must be judged by the concept of general justice, which cannot countenance any *particularisme* at all. For Saint-Preux, as for Malebranche, one must never trade an 'idea' for an 'anthropology'.

Part of Saint-Preux's objection to prayer turns on the notion that no one is entitled to demand a 'miracle' on his own behalf; and this serves to remind that Rousseau was just as out of sympathy with miracles as Malebranche had been. Rousseau's treatment of miracles, indeed—in the *Profession de foi du vicaire savoyard* and in the *Lettres écrites de la montagne*—is so Malebranchian that it is sometimes almost a transcription of *Nature et grâce*.

In the third *Lettre*, Rousseau defines the miraculous in Malebranche's very language: 'a miracle is, in a particular fact, an immediate act of the divine power, a real and visible exception to her laws.'[352] Here, of course, Malebranchisms are piled up: 'particular',

---

[350] Rousseau, *La Nouvelle Héloïse*, 673.

[351] Rousseau, letter to Malesherbes (Mar. 1761), in *Lettres philosophiques*, ed. Henri Gouhier (Paris: Vrin, 1974), 58–9.

[352] Rousseau, *Lettres écrites de la montagne*, iii, cited in *Religious Writings*, ed. Grimsley, 356.

'order', 'nature', 'laws'. Once one knows what a miracle is—or rather would be—there are two remaining questions, Rousseau urges. The first is, can God perform miracles? That, for Rousseau, is certainly no problem: 'this question, treated seriously, would be impious if it were not absurd'. The only interesting question, Rousseau affirms, is, 'Does God will to perform any miracles?'[353] Does he actually do what he obviously could do? Here Rousseau is quite clear: the (allegedly) miraculous adds nothing to 'the glory of God', and indeed only favours human 'pride' (Malebranche had said 'conceit').[354] In any case, Rousseau goes on, we shall never really *know* certainly whether there are any miracles, thanks to the definition of the miraculous itself:

Since a miracle is an exception to the laws of nature, in order to judge it one would have to know these laws. . . . Thus he who announces that such-and-such an act is miraculous declares that he knows all the laws of nature, and that he know that this act is an exception to them.

But where is this mortal who knows all the laws of nature? Newton did not pride himself on knowing them. . . . All that one can say of him who prides himself on performing miracles, is that he does quite extraordinary things: but who is denying that quite extraordinary things happen? I have seen some of these things myself, and I have even done some of them.[355]

And as an example of the 'quite extraordinary things' that he himself has done, Rousseau says that when he was secretary to the French ambassador in Venice (1743) he performed a number of 'new' and 'strange' magic-tricks involving the mysterious appearance of writing on 'blank' paper; finally he adds, as a deliberate provocation, that 'I contented myself with being a sorcerer because I was modest, but if I had had the ambition of being a prophet, who could have stopped me from being one?'[356] With a defiantly personal 'confessional' touch, then, Rousseau appropriates Malebranche's notion that human conceit (allied with magic) is at the root of most 'miraculous' happenings. (Rousseau's argument is, ironically, Antoine

[353] Ibid.

[354] Malebranche, *Méditations chrétiennes et métaphysiques*, 88–9: 'Que les hommes sont vains, et ridicules de s'imaginer, que Dieu troublera sans raison l'ordre et la simplicité de ses voies pour s'accomoder à leur fantaisie . . . [le] commun des hommes . . . plain d'un orgueil insupportable, et de l'amour d'eux-memes, s'attendent que Dieu pense à leurs affaires.'

[355] Rousseau, *Lettres écrites de la montagne*, cited in *Religious Writings*, ed. Grimsley, 357.

[356] Ibid. 358 n.

Arnauld's inverted: both appeal to the *limitations* of human knowledge, Rousseau to defend a Malebranchian nature ruled by general laws, Arnauld to defend God's particular providence.[357])

Rousseau's (more or less Malebranchian) distaste for miracles is at its clearest—in the *Lettres écrites de la montagne*—in his attempt to reduce the miraculous elements of Christ's mission to near-nothingness. Rousseau begins by insisting that Christ himself started his earthly work, 'not by miracles but by preaching' in the Temple at the age of 12. (What mattered to Christ, according to Rousseau, was not miracles but *la Parole*; Malebranche had said *le Verbe*, but the thought is the same.[358]) When, according to Rousseau, Christ 'finally' undertook a few miracles, it was 'most often' (*le plus souvent*: Malebranche's term) on 'des occasions particulières' such as the wedding-feast at Cana—and even here Christ's purpose was not at all to 'manifest his power', but simply to 'prolong the gaiety of the feast'. And this last observation is closely connected to Rousseau's view that what makes Christ 'lovable' is that he 'had a sensitive heart' and was an 'homme de bonne société'.[359] Rousseau adds pointedly that it is especially 'Jansenists' who try to make Christ and Christianity 'tiresomely austere'; and in a footnote he tells an amusing story of a 'Jansenist *curé*' who said of Christ's participation in the wedding-feast at Cana that 'Ce n'est pas ce qu'il fit de mieux'.[360] Complaining that Jansenism makes Christianity a 'terrible and displeasing' religion that subverts the 'agreeable' and 'sweet' 'véritable loi de Jésus-Christ', Rousseau finishes the third *Letter from the Mountain* by lumping Jansenism with partisanship for the miraculous: for he ends the letter with a general assault on 'fanatics' who have 'disfigured' and 'dishonoured' Christianity.[361]

Miraculous deviations from *généralité* are treated with equal reverence in Rousseau's single most important religious statement, the *Profession de foi du vicaire savoyard*. Following countless Malebranchian insistences that 'God's goodness is the love of order' and that it is through 'order' that he 'links each part of the world',[362] Rousseau has the vicar say withering things about the 'miraculous' missions of self-appointed divine agents. 'Let us suppose that divine majesty deigns to abase itself far enough to make a man the organ of

---

[357] Arnauld, *Réflexions philosophiques et théologiques*, in *Œuvres*, xxxix. 177.

[358] Rousseau, *Lettres écrites de la montagne* (1764 edn.), 85.

[359] Ibid. 131.　　　　　　　　　[360] Ibid. 131 n.　　　　　　　　　[361] Ibid. 131–2.

[362] Rousseau, *Émile*, cited in *Religious Writings*, ed. Grimsley, 152.

its sacred *volontés*: is it reasonable, is it just, to demand that the whole human race obey the voice of this minister?'[363]

Rousseau has the vicar continue in a Malebranchian language which has been given a slightly nasty edge: 'Is there any equity', the vicar asks, in having to accept, as evidence of a miraculous 'mission', nothing better than 'quelques petits miracles particuliers', performed before 'a few obscure people' known to the rest of the world only by 'hearsay'? If one had to accept as authentically miraculous the 'prodigies' which *les simples* (Malebranche's term) find astonishing, there would soon be 'more prodigies than natural events'. It is not 'quelques petits miracles particuliers', the vicar insists, but 'the unalterable order of nature which best reveals the Supreme Being'; if there were 'many exceptions' to order, law, and generality one would no longer know 'what to think'. 'For myself,' the vicar concludes, 'I believe too much in God to believe in so many miracles [which are] so little worthy of him.'[364] (Again a Malebranchian distinction: it is not a question of what God can do, but of what is 'worthy' of him.)

The same partisanship for an orderly, 'general' nature, coupled with the same hostility to *miracles particuliers*, recurs in Rousseau's main defence of *Émile* (including the *Profession de foi*) after its condemnation—the *Lettre à Christophe de Beaumont*. In some fragments of this letter (fragments left out of the final version because they were dangerously sarcastic), Rousseau says that those who depict God as a miracle-worker must imagine that he 'amuses himself' with nature-defying 'sleight of hand' because he is 'at a loose end' for something to do; and he adds a further sarcasm in which (quite pure) Malebranchism takes an uncharitable turn: miracle-lovers, Rousseau says, represent God '. . . as a bad workman [*un mauvais ouvrier*] who is forced at every moment to retouch his machine for want of knowing how to make it run from the very beginning'.[365] And in an adjoining sentence which colours the whole passage, Rousseau insists that 'there are liars who say "believe", and imbeciles who believe that they believe'.[366]

When, then, Rousseau says in the *Confessions* that he supplemented the social education he was receiving from Mme de Warens at Les

[363] Ibid. 173.   [364] Ibid.

[365] Rousseau, *Lettre à Christophe de Beaumont*, in *Œuvres complètes* (Pléiade edn.), 1023–4 ('fragments de la lettre').

[366] Ibid. 1023.

Charmettes with a very different sort of education—'I began with
some book of philosophy, such as the Port-Royal *Logic*, the *Essay* of
Locke, Malebranche, Leibniz, Descartes, etc.'[367]—one can well
believe that the 'book' of Malebranche that he pitched upon may
have been the *Traité de la nature et de la grâce*; without this Saint-
Preux's defence of *généralité* in *La Nouvelle Héloïse*, and the
arguments against *grâce particulière* in the *Lettres écrites de la
montagne*, have no traceable provenance. And if Rousseau's early
poem, *Le Verger des Charmettes*, is indeed bad verse, it at least reveals
good reading—good reading that establishes a rapport between the
seventeenth century and Rousseau:

> Tantot avec Leibniz, Malebranche et Newton,
> Je monte ma raison sur un sublime ton,
> J'examine les lois des corps et des pensées,
> Avec Locke je fais l'histoire des idées.[368]

If Rousseau's 'reason' attains 'sublimity' partly through Malebranche's aid, it is still receiving Oratorian assistance in *Le
Persifleur*—written (for Diderot) the year before Rousseau became
Rousseau by publishing the *Discourse on the Arts and Sciences* (1750).
Le Persifleur—a prospectus for a literary magazine that never
materialized—is cast in a *galant*, studiedly mercurial manner; but
Rousseau takes care to advise potential readers of 'The Banterer' that
he will sometimes alternate *une saillie extravagante* with *la plus
profonde métaphysique*: that of 'Plato, Locke or Mallebranche
[*sic*]'.[369] Rousseau may have mispelled 'Malebranche'; it is clear that
he did not misread him. And it is of the greatest significance that
Rousseau is willing to rank Malebranche with his own usual
candidates for greatest ancient and greatest modern philosopher.

But it is not just Rousseau's religious writings that reflect seventeenth-
century philosophy, and particularly Malebranchism. To be sure,
one doesn't usually think of Rousseau as a writer on science—with
the exception of his late botanical studies. But when Rousseau does,
exceptionally, write on a scientific subject—as in the *Institutions
chymiques* of *c*.1747—he uses the notions of *généralité* and *particularité* as

---

[367] Rousseau, *Les Confessions*, ed. B. Gagnebin and M. Raymond, in *Œuvres
complètes* (Pléiade edn.), i. 237.

[368] Cited in Bréhier, 'Les Lectures malebranchistes de Jean-Jacques Rousseau', 85.

[369] Rousseau, 'Le Persifleur', in *Les Conféssions* (Pléiade edn.), 1111.

much in the realm of nature as in that of 'grace': as in Malebranche, generality and simplicity have equal weight for Rousseau in *la physique* and in *la morale*.[370]

This is especially clear in the fine set-piece called 'Of the Mechanism of Nature', with which Rousseau opens Book II of the *Institutions chymiques*. Beginning with an analogy between nature and the opera ('in our opera-theaters . . . each gives his attention to a particular object; rarely is there someone who appreciates the whole'), Rousseau goes on to complain that even scientists become so obsessed with particularities ('des Papillons, des Mouches') that nature in the large escapes them altogether:

> But if each part, which has only a particular function [*une fonction particulière*] and a relative perfection, is capable of delighting with astonishment and admiration those who take the trouble to consider it correctly, how [much finer] must it be for those who know the relations of all the parts and who thereby judge the general harmony [*l'harmonie générale*] and the operation of the whole mechanism[?][371]

In this early Rousseauean passage, plainly, it is a fault to let *particularité* obscure one's view of the rapports of the parts in a *harmonie générale*—a perfectly Malebranchian thought.

Malebranchism is, if anything, even more evident in Rousseau's remarks about the God who must have produced this *harmonie générale*. Setting out with the thought that 'an intelligent being is the active principle of all things', Rousseau goes on to urge that while it is true that such a being 'could no doubt have produced and preserved the universe by the immediate concourse of his power and will alone'—that is, through a multiplicity of *volontés particulières*—it was none the less 'more worthy of his wisdom to establish general laws [*des loix générales*] . . . whose effect is alone sufficient for the preservation of the world and all that it contains'.[372] (This, as is evident, is simply Malebranche's *Nature et grâce* recapitulated; equally evidently, the notion that general laws are 'worthy' of God's 'wisdom' anticipates Saint-Preux's defence of Malebranchian *généralité* in *La Nouvelle Héloïse*.[373])

It is true enough that when it comes to *knowing* (adequately) the 'general laws' of nature, Rousseau is instantly more cautious—as he

---

[370] Rousseau, *Institutions chymiques*, in *Annales de la Société Jean-Jacques Rousseau*, 13 (1920–1), 44 ff.
[371] Ibid. 45.   [372] Ibid.   [373] Rousseau, *La Nouvelle Héloïse*, 671.

was to be, later, in *Lettres écrites de la montagne*, which insist that miracle-recognizers must know perfectly what is 'natural' and what supernatural.[374] 'It would be necessary to know the structure of the universe better than we do,' Rousseau admits, 'in order to determine which are the first and most general of these laws [of nature]; perhaps they are all reducible to a single one.'[375] But if general natural laws are reducible to one only, in Rousseau's view, it is hard to see how that can be simple Cartesian motion: 'we see well enough that movement is the universal agent . . . but when Descartes claimed to draw from this one principle the generation of the universe, he built a system singular for its ridiculousness' and which 'armed' doctrinaire materialists with absurd ideas of self-moved matter.[376] Movement alone, however, Rousseau goes on to complain, will never be able to produce 'the least of all the plants, nor the most vile insect': anticipating the argument of Kant's *Critique of Judgement*, he insists that 'the construction of an organized body through laws of movement [alone] is a chimera that one is forced to leave those who content themselves with words'.[377] Despite these fascinating intimations of Kant, the crucial point of the *Institutions chymiques* is still that *harmonie générale* is the *vérité* to be *recherché*, even if one doesn't (yet) *know* that general harmony perfectly. Malebranche would never have countenanced Rousseau's harsh words about Descartes, but he would have recognized the rest of the opening of Book II of the *Institutions chymiques*. And that is because Malebranche and Rousseau both search after generality in nature and in grace.

V

Given the philosophical importance and the historical weight of Malebranche's *Traité de la nature et de la grâce*, it is perhaps surprising that no English translation of the work has appeared for almost three hundred years: the versions of Thomas Taylor (1694) and of Richard Sault (1695) were the first and last.[378] But what is still more surprising is the fact that between the last edition supervised

---

[374] Rousseau, *Institutions chymiques*, 47.   [375] Ibid.   [376] Ibid.
[377] For a comparison of Rousseau's and Kant's use of teleology in biology, see the editor's *Kant's Political Philosophy* (Totowa, NJ: Rowman and Littlefield, 1983), 72–3.
[378] See Ginette Dreyfus's Introduction to Malebranche, *Traité de la nature et de la grâce* (1712 text), pp. xiii–xiv.

by Malebranche himself (1712) and the edition of Ginette Dreyfus in the *Œuvres complètes de Malebranche* (1958), only one printing of *Nature et grâce* took place even in France itself—and that in 1837, from a defective text.[379] Here one can only agree with Dreyfus's eloquent complaint in her Introduction to the 1958 version:

> One will be astonished, one will be scandalized by the fact that, for so long, it had been almost impossible to obtain a work which is of so great an interest from so many points of view: literary, since its concise beauty awakened the admiration of a Sainte-Beuve; philosophical, since it contains the first exposition of the system of occasionalism, [and] since Leibniz dwelt on it while writing his *Discourse on Metaphysics* and never ceased to return to it, up and including the *Theodicy*; theological, since it brought about a quarrel with Jansenism; historical, since it unleashed across Europe a series of polemics between the greatest philosophical and theological practitioners of the time: Bossuet, Fénelon, Arnauld, Bayle, Leibniz.[380]

One need only add the name Rousseau to that distinguished list, to have an even fuller sense of the large role played by Malebranche's *Nature et grâce* in modern European thought.

---

[379] Ibid. p. vii.   [380] Ibid.

Treatise on Nature and Grace

Nicolas Malebranche

Excerpt of a Letter

I do not understand anything, Sir, in the judgement of your friends concerning the work which I am sending you. The author of this *Treatise* does not rest his argument on the authority of St Augustine: thus he abandons this holy Doctor. Do you think that this is a just conclusion? Do the defenders of transubstantiation abandon the Council of Trent, because they make no use of its authority in order to convince the Calvinists? Do those who write against the Socinians abandon all the Fathers and all the Councils, because they use only Scripture and reason against their adversaries? But, Sir, why do they stop with St Augustine only? The author of the *Treatise* cites therein no Father and no Council: does he then abandon, according to your friends' principles, all the Fathers and all the Councils? Certainly men who are authors are much to be pitied, if they concern themselves with the judgements of men: for what can be more unreasonable and more unjust than that of your friends—who, none the less, pass for equitable and sincere people? The author, as you will see, Sir, avows that his main plan is to make God lovable to men, and to justify the wisdom of his conduct in the minds of certain philosophers who push metaphysics too far, and who, in order to have a powerful and sovereign God, make him unjust, cruel, and bizarre. He believes himself obliged to speak reasonably in order to convince these people, who, as you know, pride themselves on understanding this language perfectly. And since it is a matter of making understood the truths which are taught by Scripture, he often makes use of terms from that same Scripture; for it was necessary that the mind compare that which Scripture teaches us with that which reason reveals, in order to strengthen and maintain oneself in the faith by seeing truth. But, Sir, in this work, he ought not to rest his thought on the authority of the Fathers for several reasons.

Firstly, because the greater part of those to whom he speaks would not have deferred to it very much—not only because they do not feel for the Fathers all the respect which is due them, but also because they know well enough that one can say whatever one likes to people, when one cuts arguments up into pieces. There is no book in which there are more passages from St Augustine than in the *Augustinus* of Jansenius; and none the less no one is too convinced that the Augustine of this Bishop very much resembles the true one.

Secondly, the work ought to be short for many reasons; and if the author had wanted to prove through the Fathers what he claims about grace, he would perhaps have been obliged to produce several volumes, which would not have been read at all by those whom he had in mind. Jansenius, who claimed to explicate the thought of St Augustine, composed three tomes on this subject which make quite a large volume in folio; and he scarcely spoke of the other Fathers. It would have been necessary to refute the sentiments of this author, to speak of the Fathers whom he neglected, and to establish the true sense of St Augustine—such that one would have produced a work which it would not have been easy to read and to examine, as is the one which I send you.

Thirdly, the individual character of the author is to speak clearly and with order, and to spread enlightenment in attentive minds: which he would not have been able to do, if he had been obliged to insert in his discourses a mass of passages which often need to be explained, and which cause the thread and the connections of his thought to be lost.

In the fourth place, there are more people who submit themselves to reason or to Holy Scripture, than there are who yield to the authority of a Father. Thus the work will always be quite useful—though it cannot convince certain people who regard St Augustine or rather a pretended St Augustine as their sole master, as their reason and the rule of their faith.

For the rest, the author is quite persuaded that it has already been made clear that his sentiments about the efficacy of grace are in conformity to those of St Augustine. It is well enough known that several people are still going to bring up to date some works which will fully justify him in this matter. Finally he seems to me to be well resolved to satisfy the wishes of certain theologians, after having contented the philosophers—provided of course that minds are disposed to listen to him, and that there is some necessity to speak on a matter which has already been the cause of so many disputes. For in the end, Sir, I know the author personally: he prefers peace to all things; he has written, as you will see, in a way that can irritate only those who are of a regrettable and ill-tempered humour; he speaks as if there had never been any quarrel concerning the subject which he treats; and I know that if he had not been hard-pressed by his friends to reveal his sentiments about grace in a few words, he would have remained in silence, following the resolution which he had made. But having known by experience that his principles could serve to disabuse those who have some love for the truth, he believed himself obligated to put them down on paper, and to get them into a state in which they could be published some day—which has now arrived a little sooner than was thought.

Notice

I pray those into whose hands this writing may fall to believe that I have undertaken it principally to meet the difficulties of some philosophers who did not have (it seems to me) all the sentiments which religion teaches us we ought to have concerning the goodness of God, and who did not sufficiently recognize at all the obligations which we have towards Jesus Christ. I wish that it only be regarded as an essay, that it be judged only after being examined without prejudice, and that one should not let oneself be overtaken by those feelings of fear and of defiance which are naturally excited in us by everything that bears some mark of novelty. Since I have written for philosophers who pride themselves on great precision and on rigorous exactness, I have been obliged to avoid general terms which are ordinarily used; for I can satisfy them only by using terms which awake distinct and particular ideas in their minds, so far as the subject may permit it. I believe that equitable people will judge that I have no other plan whatsoever, than to prove in all possible ways the truths that faith teaches us, and that I am not in the slightest bold enough to place in doubt that which passes for certain in the Church, and which religion obliges us to believe. But it has always been permitted to give new proofs of ancient truths, to make God lovable to men and to make it understood that there is nothing harsh and unjust in the conduct he follows in the establishment of his Church.

This work is divided into three discourses. In the first, I represent God as doing all the good to his creatures which his wisdom permits him. In the second I will show how the Son of God, as wisdom incarnate and as head of the Church, diffuses in its members the graces which he could not grant them as eternal wisdom, [and] which they do not receive from his Father. And I thus strive to make understood the obligations and the relations which we have to Jesus Christ. Finally in the third [discourse] I explain what liberty is, and how grace acts in us without injuring it. Since there are people who are scarcely equitable, who will draw unfortunate consequences from the very principles most favourable to religion, I pray that no one condemn me on their word, and that, before judging me, they do me the justice of hearing me. Certainly I ought not to be obliged to make this plea.

Discourse I

On the Necessity of General Laws of Nature and of Grace

First Part
On the Necessity of General Laws of Nature

I

God, being able to act only for his own glory, and being able to find it only in himself, cannot have had any other plan in the creation of the world than the establishment of his Church.

II

Jesus Christ, who is the head of it, is the beginning of the ways of the Lord: he is the first-born of created beings; and while he was born among men in the fullness of time, it is he who is their exemplar in the eternal plan of his Father. It is in his image that all men have been created—those who have preceded his temporal birth as well as ourselves. In a word, it is in him that all subsists; for it is only he who can make the work of God perfectly worthy of its author.

III

There must be some relation between the world and the action by which it is produced. Now the action by which the world is drawn from nothingness, is the action of a God; his worth is infinite; and the world, however perfect it may be, is not infinitely lovable, and cannot render to God an honour worthy of him. Thus, separate Jesus

Christ from the rest of created beings and see if he who can act only for his own glory, and whose wisdom has no limits, can form the plan to produce anything outside himself.[1]

But if you join Jesus Christ to his Church, and the Church to the rest of the world, from which it is drawn, you will then raise to the glory of God a temple so august and so holy, that you will perhaps be surprised that the foundations of it were laid so late.

IV

However, if you take note that the glory which comes to God from his work is not at all essential to him; if you remain in agreement that the world cannot be a necessary emanation from the divinity, you will see quite well that it was not necessary that it be eternal, though it ought never to end. Eternity is the mark of independence; thus it was necessary that the world begin. The destruction of substances is a mark of inconstancy in him who has produced them; thus they will never come to an end.

V

If it is true, then, that the world had to begin, and that the Incarnation of Jesus Christ could not have been as ancient as the eternal generation of the divine person, it was necessary that an eternity precede time. Do not mind, then, that God delayed the production of his work; he loves too much the glory he receives from it through Jesus Christ. One can say in a very true sense that he made it as soon as he was able to make it. For while with respect to us he might have created it ten thousand years before the beginning of the centuries, ten thousand years having no relation to eternity, he could not have done it either sooner or later, since it was necessary that an eternity precede it.

---

[1] The text of the final sentence of section III reads: 'Ainsi, separez Jésus-Christ du reste des créatures, et voyez si celui qui ne peut agir que pour sa gloire, et dont la sagesse n'a point de bornes, pourra prendre le dessein de rien produire au dehors.' Malebranche's argument is that *without* Christ, God can have no motive to produce a finite world; therefore 'de rien produire' must be rendered as 'to produce anything'— if the philosophical point is to be preserved.

VI

It is manifest that *early* and *late* are properties of time: and if one supposed that God had created the world sooner than he did, by as many millions of years as there are grains of sand on the shores of the seas, could one not also ask whence it comes that God, who so loves the glory which he receives from the establishment of his Church, did not begin it several centuries sooner? Thus it suffices to say that an eternity had to precede the Incarnation of the Word, to make it understood that this great mystery was accomplished neither too early nor too late. Thus it was necessary that God create the universe for the Church, the Church for Jesus Christ, and Jesus Christ in order to find in him a victim, and a sovereign priest worthy of the divine majesty. No one will doubt this order in the plans of God, if one takes care to notice that there can be no other end of his actions than himself. And if one realizes that eternity is not proper to created beings, one will remain in agreement that they have been produced when it was necessary that they be. These truths presupposed, let us strive to reveal something in the conduct which God holds to in the execution of his great plan.

VII

If I were not persuaded that all men are reasonable only because they are enlightened by eternal wisdom, I would be, no doubt, quite presumptuous to speak of the plans of God, and to want to reveal some of his ways in the production of his work. But since it is certain that the eternal Word is the universal reason of minds, and that by the light which it spreads ceaselessly in us we can all have some commerce with God, one should find nothing to object to in the fact that I consult that light which, though consubstantial with God himself, does not fail to respond to all those who know how to interrogate it with serious attention.

VIII

I grant, none the less, that faith teaches many truths which one cannot discover by the natural union of the mind with reason. Eternal truth does not answer all our questions; for we sometimes ask more than we can receive. But this should not serve as a pretext to cover our laziness and our lack of application.

IX

The general run of men soon grow weary of the natural prayer which the mind, by its attention, ought to give to the truth within, in order to receive light and intelligence from it. And, tired as they are from this feeble effort, they speak of it with contempt; they discourage each other, and conceal their weakness and their ignorance under deceiving appearances of false humility.

X

But their example should not inspire in us that agreeable virtue which cherishes laziness and negligence in minds, and which consoles them in their ignorance of the truths which are most necessary to them. One must pray ceaselessly of him who enlightens all men, that he will bestow his light upon us, that he will recompense our faith with the gift of understanding, and above all that he will keep us from mistaking for the evident truth which accompanies his answers, the mere probability and the confused feelings which hurl proud minds into the darkness of error.

XI

When one claims to speak of God with some exactitude, one must not consult oneself, nor speak like the common run of men. One must mentally elevate oneself above all created beings, and consult, with great carefulness and respect, the vast and immense idea of the infinitely perfect being: and since this idea represents the true God to us, one who is quite different from that imagined by most men, one ought not to speak of this matter according to popular language. Everyone is permitted to say, with Scripture, that God *repented* of having created man, that he became *angered* against his people, that he delivered Israel from captivity by the *strength of his arm*. But these expressions, or similar ones, are not permitted to theologians, when they have to speak exactly. Thus, when it is remarked hereafter that my expressions are not ordinary, one ought to be surprised about that. Rather one will have to notice carefully whether they are clear, and whether they accord perfectly with the idea that all men have of the infinitely perfect Being.

XII

This idea of the infinitely perfect Being contains two attributes which are absolutely necessary in order to create the world—a wisdom that has no limits, and a power that nothing is capable of resisting. The wisdom of God reveals to him an infinity of ideas of different works, and all the possible ways of executing his plans; and his power so far makes him the master of all things, and so far independent of the help of everything whatsoever, that it suffices that he will in order that his wills be executed. For one must above all take notice that God has no need of instruments in order to act, that his wills are necessarily efficacious: in a word, that as his wisdom is his own intelligence, his power differs not at all from his will. From that infinite number of ways by which God was able to execute his plan, let us see which is the one which he had to prefer to all the others; and let us begin with the creation of the visible world—from which and in which he forms the invisible world, which is the eternal object of his love.

XIII

An excellent workman should proportion his action to his work; he does not accomplish by quite complex means that which he can execute by simpler ones, he does not act without an end, and never makes useless efforts. From this one must conclude that God, discovering in the infinite treasures of his wisdom an infinity of possible worlds (as the necessary consequences of the laws of motion which he can establish), determines himself to create that world which could have been produced and preserved by the simplest laws, and which ought to be the most perfect, with respect to the simplicity of the ways necessary to its production or to its conservation.

XIV

God could, no doubt, make a world more perfect than the one in which we live. He could, for example, make it such that rain, which serves to make the earth fruitful, fall more regularly on cultivated ground than in the sea, where it is unnecessary. But in order to make this more perfect world, it would have been necessary that he have changed the simplicity of his ways, and that he have multiplied the laws of the communication of motion, through which our world exists: and then there would no longer be that proportion between the action of God and his work, which is necessary in order to determine an infinitely wise being to act; or at least there would not have been the same proportion between the activity of God and this so-perfect world, as between the laws of nature and the world in which we live; for our world, however imperfect one wishes to imagine it, is based on laws of motion which are so simple and so natural that it is perfectly worthy of the infinite wisdom of its author.

XV

Indeed I am persuaded that the laws of motion which are necessary to the production and the preservation of the earth, and of all the stars that are in the heavens, are reducible to these two: the first, that moved bodies tend to continue their motion in a straight line; the second, that when two bodies collide, their motion is distributed in both in proportion to their size, such that they must afterwards move at an equal speed. These two laws are the cause of all the motions which cause that variety of forms which we admire in nature.

XVI

I grant, none the less, that it does not seem that the second law is ever observable in the experience one can have on this subject: but that is so because we see only what happens in visible bodies, and because we do not think at all of the invisible ones which surround them—which by the efficacy of the same law, giving elasticity to visible bodies, oblige those same visible bodies to rebound, and not to observe that same law between themselves. I ought not to explain this further.

XVII

Now these two laws are so simple, so natural, and (at the same time) so fruitful, that even if one were to have no other reasons for judging that it is they which are observed in nature, one would still have every reason to believe that they are established by him who always acts in the simplest ways—in whose action there is nothing that is not law-governed [*reglé*], and who proportions it so wisely to his work that he brings about an infinity of marvels through a very small number of wills.

XVIII

It fares not with the general cause as with particular ones, with infinite wisdom as with limited intelligence. God having foreseen everything that had to follow from natural laws even before their establishment, he ought not to have established them if he was going to overturn them. The laws of nature are constant and immutable; they are general for all times and for all places. Two colliding bodies of such-and-such a size and of such-and-such a speed will rebound now in the same way that they rebounded heretofore. If rain falls on certain lands, and if the sun roasts others; if weather favourable for crops is followed by hail that destroys them; if a child comes into the world with a malformed and useless head growing from his breast, and makes him wretched; it is not that God has willed these things by particular wills; it is because he has established laws for the communication of motion, of which these effects are necessary consequences: laws so simple and at the same time so fruitful that they serve to produce everything beautiful that we see in the world, and even to repair in a little time the most general mortality and sterility.

XIX

He who, having built a house, throws one wing of it down in order to rebuild it, reveals his ignorance; he who plants a vine, and pulls it up as soon as it has taken root, shows his levity; because he that wills and no longer wills lacks either enlightenment or firmness of mind. But one cannot say that God acts through caprice or through ignorance, when a child comes into the world with superfluous members which keep it from living or when a hailstone causes an almost ripe fruit to fall. The reason for this is, that if God causes a fruit to fall through hail before it is ripe, it is not that he wills and no longer wills; for God acts not at all by particular wills, like particular causes. He has not established the laws of the communication of motion with the design of producing monsters, or of making fruits fall before their maturity; he willed these laws because of their fruitfulness, and not of their sterility. Thus that which he willed, he still wills, and the world in general for which he established these laws will subsist eternally.

XX

Here one must take note that the essential rule of the will of God is order; and that if man (for example) had not sinned (a supposition which would have changed the plans), then, order not permitting that he be punished, the natural laws of the communication of motion would never have been able to make him unhappy: for, the law of order which wills that the just person suffer nothing despite himself being essential to God, the arbitrary law of the communication of motion must necessarily be subjected to it.

XXI

There are, still, some rare occasions on which these general laws of motion ought to cease to produce their effect. But it is not the case that God changes his laws, or corrects himself; it is because of the order of grace, which that of nature must serve, that miracles happen in certain circumstances. Besides, it is proper that men know that God is so much the master of nature that, if he submits himself to the laws which he has established, it is rather because he wills the good, than by an absolute necessity.

XXII

If then it is true that the general cause ought not to produce his work by particular wills, and that God had to establish certain laws of the communication of motion which are constant and invariable, through whose efficacy he foresaw that the world could subsist such as we see it, one can say in a very true sense that God wishes that all his creatures be perfect; that he wills not at all that children perish in the womb of their mothers; that he does not love monsters; that he did not make the laws of nature to engender them; and that if he had been able (by equally simple ways) to make and to preserve a more perfect world, he would never have established any laws, of which so great a number of monsters are necessary consequences; but that it would have been unworthy of his wisdom to multiply his wills in order to stop certain particular disorders, which even constitute a kind of beauty in the universe.

XXIII

God has given to each seed a germ which contains in miniature the plant and the fruit, another germ which depends on the former, and which encloses the root of the plant—which root has a new root whose imperceptible branches spread themselves in the two lobes, or in the meal of this seed. Does he not sufficiently mark in this way that he wills, in a very true sense, that all seeds produce their like? For why would he have given to some grains of corn, which he willed to be sterile, all the parts proper to make them fruitful? However, since rain is necessary to make them grow, and it falls to earth only through general laws, which do not distribute it precisely on well-cultivated lands, and at the most suitable times, not all these grains profit [from rain]; or if they profit, hail or some other mischievous accident, which is a necessary consequence of those same laws of nature, stops them from nourishing their ears. Now since it is God who has established these laws, one could say that he willed that certain seeds be fruitful, rather than some others—if one did not otherwise know that, the general cause not being able to act at all by particular wills, nor an infinitely wise being by complex means, God ought not to have taken any other measures than those which he has taken to govern the rains according to the seasons and to places, or according to the desires of workers. So much is not needed for the order of nature. Let us explain a little more fully that of grace; and above all let us take note that it is the same wisdom and the same will, in a word the same God, who has established both of these orders.

Second Part

On the Necessity of General Laws of Grace

XXIV

God, loving himself by the necessity of his being, and wanting to procure for himself an infinite glory, an honour perfectly worthy of himself, consults his wisdom concerning the accomplishment of his desires. This divine wisdom, filled with love for him from whom it receives its being through an eternal and ineffable generation, seeing nothing in all possible creatures (whose intelligible ideas it contains) that is worthy of the majesty of its Father, offers itself to establish an eternal cult in his honour and as sovereign priest, to offer him a victim who, by the dignity of his person, is capable of contenting him. Divine wisdom represents to him an infinity of plans for the temple that it wants to erect to his glory, and at the same time all the ways of carrying them out. First of all, the plan which appears to be the greatest and the most magnificent, the most just and the most extensive, is the one all of whose parts have the greatest relation to the person who constitutes the whole glory and sanctity of it; and the wisest method of executing this plan is that of establishing certain laws which are very simple and fruitful to guide it towards its perfection. That is what reason seems to answer to all those who consult it attentively, and following the principles that faith teaches us. Let us examine the circumstances of this great plan, and we will afterwards strive to reveal the ways of executing it.

XXV

Holy Scripture teaches us that it is Jesus Christ who must make all the beauty, the sanctity, and the magnificence of this great work. For if Holy Scripture compares it to a city, it is Jesus Christ who makes all the lustre; the sun and the moon do not illuminate it, it is the brightness of God and the light of the lamb. If it represents it as a living body, of which all the parts have a marvellous connection between them, it is Jesus Christ who is the head of it; it is from him that spirit and life are distributed to all the members that compose it.

If it speaks of it as a temple, it is Jesus Christ who is the cornerstone of it, on whom the whole edifice is raised: it is he who is its sovereign priest; it is he who is its victim; all the faithful are priests only because they participate in his priesthood; they are only victims because they have a part in his sanctity. It is only in him and by him that they ceaselessly offer themselves to the majesty of God. Finally it is only by the relation that they have to him that they contribute to the beauty of this august temple; which has always been and which will eternally be the object of the pleasure of God himself.

XXVI

Reason also teaches us these same truths. For what relation can there be between created beings, however perfect one supposes them to be, and the action by which they have been produced? Every creature being limited, how can it be worth the action of a God, whose price is infinite? Can God receive something from a mere creature that determines him to act? But let it be the case that God made man in the hope of being honoured by him: whence comes it that the number who dishonour him is the greater? Does not God sufficiently declare thereby that he spurns the pretended glory that he receives from his work, if one separates this work from his well-loved Son, that it is only through Jesus Christ that he resolved to produce it, and that without him it would not exist for a moment?

XXVII

A man forms a plan to undertake a work because he has need of it, or because he wants to see the effect that this work will produce, or finally because he learns, through the testing of his powers, what he is capable of producing. But God has no need of his creatures. He does not in the slightest resemble men, who receive new impressions from the presence of objects. His ideas are eternal and immutable: he saw the world before he had formed it, as he sees it now. Finally, knowing that his wills are efficacious, he knew perfectly, without making any test of his powers, everything that he is capable of producing. Thus Scripture and reason teach us that it is because of Jesus Christ that the world exists, and that it is by the dignity of this divine person that it receives a beauty which makes it pleasing in the sight of God.

XXVIII

It follows, it seems to me, from this principle, that Jesus Christ is the model on whom we are made, that we have been formed in his image and in his likeness, and that we possess nothing beautiful, except in so far as we are his expressions and images; that he is the end of the law, and the terminus of the ceremonies and of the sacrifices of the Jews; that it was necessary in order to determine this succession of generations that preceded his birth, that they have certain relations with him, by which they were made more pleasing to God than all others. Thus Jesus Christ having to be the head and the bridegroom of the Church, it was necessary, in order to prefigure him, that all men come from one alone, and that their propagation begin in the way reported by Moses and explained by St Paul. In a word it follows from this principle that the present world must be the image of the future world, and that, so far as the simplicity of general laws may permit, all those who must inhabit it have been or will be the images and the likenesses of the sole son of God, since Abel, in whom he was sacrificed, down to the last member who will form his Church.

XXIX

We judge the perfection of a work through its conformity with the idea of it, which eternal wisdom gives us: for there is nothing good or lovable, except through relationship to the beauty that is essential, necessary, and independent. Now this intelligible beauty, having made itself felt, becomes (even in this state) the rule of beauty and of perfection. Thus all corporeal creatures must receive from it their beauty and their brilliance. All minds must have the same thoughts and the same inclinations as the soul of Jesus, if they would be pleasing to those who find nothing beautiful nor anything pleasing but that which is conformed to wisdom and to truth. Since one is thus obliged to believe that the work of God is in perfect conformity to eternal wisdom, one has every reason to think that this same work has infinite relations with him who is the head, its principle, its model, and its end. But who will be able to explain all these relationships?

XXX

That which makes the beauty of a temple is the order and the variety of the ornaments which come together in it. Thus, to render the living temple of the majesty of God worthy of him who must inhabit it, and proportioned to the wisdom and to the infinite love of its author, there are no beauties that ought not to be found there. But it is not the same with this temple raised to the glory of God as with material temples. That which constitutes the beauty of the spiritual edifice of the Church is the infinite diversity of the graces which he who is the head of it distributes to all the parts that compose it: it is the order and the admirable relations which he places between them: these are the different degrees of glory which shine from all sides.

XXXI

It follows from this principle that, to establish that variety of recompenses which makes the beauty of the heavenly Jerusalem, it was necessary that men be subject on earth not only to the afflictions which purify them, but also to the feelings of concupiscence which make them win so many victories by giving them over to so great a number of diverse struggles.

XXXII

The blessed in heaven will no doubt have a sanctity and a variety of gifts that answer perfectly to the variety of their good works. Those continual sacrifices by which the old man destroys and annihilates himself, will cover the spiritual substance of the new man with graces and with beauties. And if it was necessary that Jesus Christ himself suffer all sorts of afflictions, before entering into possession of his glory, the sin of the first man, who caused to enter into the world the evils which accompany life, and the death which follows it, was necessary in order that men, after having been tested on earth, be legitimately raised to this glory whose variety and order will make the beauty of the future world.

XXXIII

It is true that concupiscence, such as we feel it, is not necessary in order to merit: Jesus Christ, whose merits are infinite, was not at all subject to it. But though he was the absolute master of his body, he was willing to admit in himself the most vexatious motions and feelings, in order to merit thereby all the glory which had been prepared for him. Of all feelings, the most repugnant to a soul which wants and which deserves to be happy is pain; and he willed to suffer very cruel ones. Pleasure makes actually happy the one who actually enjoys it, and he willed to deprive himself of it. Thus he offered up, like us, an infinity of sacrifices through a body like ours which he took on. But these sacrifices were different from those of the greatest saints, because he voluntarily induced in himself all those painful sensations which in the rest of men are necessary consequences of sin; and thus, these sacrifices being voluntary in every sense, they were purer and more meritorious.

XXXIV

If I had a clear idea of those blessed spirits who have no body, I could perhaps respond clearly to a difficulty which arises in considering them. For it can be objected either that there is very little variety in the merits or in the rewards of the angels, or perhaps that it was not at all appropriate for God to unite bodies with such spirits, who are now so dependent upon them. I grant that I do not see a great diversity in the rewards which ought to correspond to the merits of purely intelligible substances, especially if they have merited their reward through a single act of love. Not being united to a body which could be the occasion for God to give them (according to certain very simple and very general laws) a train of different feelings or thoughts, I see no diversity at all in their struggles or in their victories. But perhaps another order has been established, which is unknown to me: thus I ought not to speak of it. It is sufficient that I establish a principle by which one can understand that God had to create bodies and unite spirits to them, in order that, by the quite simple laws of the union of these two substances, he could give us, in a general, constant, and uniform way, that great variety of feelings and of motions, which is the principle of the diversity of our merits and of our rewards.

XXXV

Finally it was necessary that God alone have all the glory of the beauty and of the perfection of the future world. This work, which infinitely surpasses all others, ought to be a work of pure mercy. It was necessary that creatures might not glory in having any other part in it than that which the grace of Jesus Christ had given them. In a word it was appropriate that God let all men be enveloped by sin, in order to show all of them mercy in Jesus Christ.

XXXVI

Thus the first man, being able to persevere in original justice by the power of his charity, it was not necessary that God fix him to his duty by preventing pleasures: having no concupiscence to vanquish, God did not have to prevent his free will by the delectation of his grace. Finally, having everything in general which was necessary to him in order to merit his reward, God, who does nothing useless, had to leave him to himself although he foresaw the Fall—because he wanted to raise him up in Jesus Christ, confound free will, and make his mercy shine. Let us now strive to reveal the means by which God executes the eternal plan of the sanctification of the Church.

XXXVII

Although in the establishment of the future world God acts by means quite different from those by which he preserves the present world, it ought not, however, to be imagined that this difference is such, that the laws of grace do not bear the character of the cause who has established them. Since it is the same God who is the author of the order of grace and of that of nature, it is necessary that these two orders be in agreement with respect to everything they contain, which marks the wisdom and the power of their author. Thus, since God is a general cause whose wisdom has no limits, it is necessary for the reasons which I stated before, that in the order of grace as well as in that of nature, he act as a general cause; and that having as his end his glory in the construction of his Church, he establish the simplest and the most general laws, which have by their effect the greatest amount of wisdom and of fruitfulness.

XXXVIII

The more enlightened an agent is, the more extensive are his volitions. A very limited mind undertakes new plans at every moment; and when he wants to execute one of them, he uses several means, of which some are always useless. In a word, a limited mind does not sufficiently compare the means with the end, the power and the action with the effect that they must produce.

On the contrary a broad and penetrating mind compares and weighs all things: it never forms plans except with the knowledge that it has the means to execute them. The simpler machines are, and the more various their effects, the more spiritual they are, and worthy of being esteemed. A great number of laws in a state often shows little penetration and breadth of mind in those who have established them: it is often the mere experience of need, rather than wise foresight, which has ordained them. God, whose wisdom has no limits, must then make use of means which are very simple and very fruitful in the formation of the future world, as in the preservation of the present world. He ought not to multiply his wills, which are the executive laws of his plans, any further than necessity obliges. He must act through general wills, and thus establish a constant and lawful order, according to which he has foreseen, through the infinite extent of his wisdom, that a work as admirable as his is, ought to come into existence. Let us see the consequences of this principle and the application that can be made of it in order to explain some difficulties which seem to be embarrassing enough.

XXXIX

Holy Scripture teaches us on the one hand that God wills that all men be saved, and that they come to a knowledge of the truth; and on the other, that he does everything that he wills: and none the less faith is not given to everyone; and the number of those that perish is much greater than that of the predestined. How can one reconcile this with his power?

XL

God foresaw from all eternity both original sin, and the infinite number of persons that this sin would sweep into hell. None the less he created the first man in a condition from which he knew he would fall; he even established between this man and his posterity relations which would communicate his sin to them, and render them all worthy of his aversion and his wrath. How can one reconcile this with his goodness?

XLI

God frequently diffuses graces, without having the effect for which his goodness obliges us to believe that he gives them. He increases piety in persons almost to the end of their life; and sin dominates them at death, and throws them into hell. He makes the rain of grace fall on hardened hearts, as well as on prepared grounds: men resist it, and make it useless for their salvation. In a word, God undoes and redoes without cease: it seems that he wills, and no longer wills. How can one reconcile this with his wisdom?

There, it seems to me, one sees great difficulties for the whole economy of religion, the idea that we have of a good, wise, powerful God, constant in his plans, lawful in his actions. A thousand places in Scripture again furnish many other difficulties concerning what we see happening every day in the order of grace: and while quite able people have responded to them, it seems to me that one can only resolve them clearly through the principle which I have just established.

XLII

As for me, I have always believed that God truly wills that men be saved. Reason and Scripture have always stopped me from doubting it. And although authors whom I honour with a profound respect have published, in past centuries, different explanations of this truth, I have always had difficulty in accepting those which seem to me to set, without any necessity, limits to the extent of God's goodness and mercy. Thus, consulting the idea that all men have of God, I have offered the sentiment which I expound today to the censure of all those who are willing to examine it with attention, and judge it with equity.

XLIII

God being obliged to act always in a way worthy of him, through simple, general, constant, and uniform means—in a word means conformed to the idea that we have of a general cause whose wisdom has no limits—he had to establish certain laws in the order of grace, as I have proved him to have done in the order of nature. Now these laws, because of their simplicity, necessarily have unhappy consequences with respect to us: but these consequences do not make it necessary for God to change these laws into more complicated ones. For these laws have a greater proportion of wisdom and of fruitfulness to the work that they produce, than all those which he could establish for the same plan, since he always acts in the wisest and most perfect way. It is true that God could remedy these unhappy consequences through an infinite number of particular wills: but order will not have it so. The effect which would be produced by each of his particular wills would not be worth the action which would produce it. And in consequence God is not to be blamed for not disturbing the order and the simplicity of his laws by miracles which would be quite convenient to our needs, but quite opposed to the wisdom of God, whom it is not permitted to tempt.

XLIV

Thus as one has no right to be annoyed that the rain falls in the sea where it is useless, and that it does not fall on seeded grounds where it is necessary—because the laws of the communication of notion are quite simple, quite fruitful, and perfectly worthy of the wisdom of their author, and because according to these laws it is not possible that rain be distributed on the earth rather than in the seas—so too one ought not to complain of the apparent irregularity according to which grace is given to men. It is the regularity with which God acts, it is the simplicity of the laws which he observes, it is the wisdom and the uniformity of his conduct, which is the cause of that apparent irregularity. It is necessary, according to the laws of grace, that God has ordained, on behalf of his elect and for the building of his Church, that this heavenly rain sometimes fall on hardened hearts, as well as on prepared grounds. If, then, grace falls uselessly, it is not the case that God acts without design. It is still less the case that God acts with the aim of making men more guilty through the abuse of his favours. Rather the simplicity of general laws does not permit that this grace, which is inefficacious in this corrupted heart, fall in another heart where it would be efficacious. This grace not being given at all by a particular will, but in consequence of the immutability of the general order of grace, it suffices that that order produce a work proportioned to the simplicity of his laws, in order that it be worthy of the wisdom of its author. For finally the order of grace would be less perfect, less admirable, less lovable, if it were more complex.

XLV

If God gave grace by particular wills, no doubt he would not take it into his head, in order to convert a sinner who has four degrees of concupiscence, to give him three degrees of spiritual delectation, supposing that those degrees were not sufficient to convert him; he would refrain from bestowing his liberality until the sinner should no longer be in the presence of the object that tempts him, or rather he would give that same grace (or three degrees of power) to one in whom concupiscence would be less lively. For to what purpose is it to give three degrees of spiritual delectation to one for whom four degrees are necessary, and to refuse them to him to whom they would be sufficient to convert him? Does this agree with the idea that we have of the wisdom and of the goodness of God? Is this to love men, is it to will to same them all, is it to do for them everything that can be done? God, however, cries through his prophet: 'Citizens of Jerusalem, peoples of Judah, judge between me and my vineyard. What could have been done more to my vineyard, that I have not done in it: wherefore, when I looked that it should bring forth grapes, brought it forth wild grapes?'[2] What wisdom is there in giving, by particular wills, so many useless graces to sinners, supposing that God wills their conversion, as Scripture teaches us, and supposing that he had not at all the unhappy plan to make them more guilty and more criminal through his gifts?

XLVI

But if grace is bestowed on men by laws which are very simple and very general, all these great difficulties vanish. The order of grace which God has established having a greater relation of wisdom and of fruitfulness to the work which it produces than any other, God had to choose it for the establishment of his Church. Thus one can affirm that God truly wills the salvation of all men: that he does for them all

---

[2] Isaiah 5: 3–4.

he can do, acting as he ought to act; that if there were some order of grace equally simple and more fruitful, equally worthy of his wisdom and more useful to men, he would have chosen it; and that he therefore saves as many persons as he can save, acting according to the adorable laws which his wisdom prescribes to him.

XLVII

Let men, then, love and adore not only the good will of God, by which the elect are sanctified, but also the secret judgements of his justice, through which there is so great a number of rejected ones. It is the same order of wisdom, it is the same laws of grace, which produce effects which are so different. God is equally adorable and lovable in all he does: his conduct is always full of wisdom and of goodness. Woe to the impious who condemn it without knowing anything about it, and who want the immutable order of divine wisdom to accommodate itself to their passions and their interests.

XLVIII

Wise and diligent workers plough, fertilize, and sow their lands with much labour and expense. They carefully observe the most suitable seasons for different kinds of cultivation, and do not tax God with the success of their labours. They leave their work to the order of nature, knowing well that it is useless to tempt God, and to claim that, on our behalf, he changes the order which his wisdom prescribes to him.

XLIX

Jesus Christ has come to teach us to imitate their conduct. Since he has an immense love for us, and wills to save us all, so far as the simplicity of the general laws of nature will permit, he has forgotten nothing to make us enter into the paths that lead to heaven. That which is most opposed to the efficacy of grace, is pleasures of sense and feelings of pride: for there is nothing which corrupts the mind so much, and which hardens the heart more. But did not Jesus Christ sacrifice and destroy, in his person, all grandeurs and sensible pleasures? Has not his life been for us a continual example of humility and of penitence? How was he born? How did he die? How did he speak among men? Everyone knows. To what is his doctrine reducible; which way do his counsels tend? Is it not to humility and to penitence, to a general privation of everything which flatters the senses, of everything which corrupts the purity of the imagination, of everything which sustains and which fortifies the concupiscence of pride? What he said, what he did, what he suffered has thus been to prepare us to receive the celestial rain of grace through his doctrine, through his example, through his merits, and to make it efficacious. Not being able or not having to change the laws of nature, tempt God, or trouble the order of the simplicity of his ways, he has done for men everything that can inspire the most extensive, the most industrious, and the most ardent charity.

L

I fear not at all to say that the charity of Jesus Christ is immense and incomprehensible, after what Scripture has said. And although all men do not receive its effects, it would be rash to want to set bounds to it. He died for all men, even for those who perish every day. Why do not sinners enter into the order of grace? Why do they not follow the counsels of Jesus Christ? Why do they not prepare themselves to receive rain from heaven? They cannot merit it, but they can augment its efficacy with respect to themselves. Can they not, through self-love, through the fear of hell, or (if one likes) by general graces, avoid many occasions of sin—deprive themselves of pleasures (at least of those they have not already tasted) by which they will not be enslaved in consequence? Thus they can remove some impediments to the efficacy of grace, and prepare the ground of their heart, such that it becomes fruitful when God pours his rain according to the general laws which he has prescribed to himself. But they want God to save them without their troubling themselves—like idle and thoughtless workers who, without bestowing ordinary labour on their field, claim that God should distribute sufficiently fruitful and abundant rains to spare them all work. A false and vain confidence! God makes it rain on fallow lands as well as on those that are cultivated. But let the proud and the voluptuous know that the rain of grace will fall much less on them than on other men; and that none the less they place themselves in a condition in which it would be needed in abundance to convert them.

LI

Since God does not ordinarily distribute his grace except by general laws, one sees clearly the necessity of the counsels of Jesus Christ. One sees that these counsels must be followed, in order that God may save us by the simplest means, and that, giving us few graces, he works greatly in us. One sees clearly that he must for his part work ceaselessly, that he must cultivate his ground before the heat of concupiscence shall have dried and hardened it, or at least when the rain shall have taken away the dryness and the hardness; that one must observe with care the moments in which the passions leave us some liberty, in order to draw some advantages therefrom; that one must clear away, as much as is in one's power, everything that can suffocate the seed of the Word; and that one must not imagine foolishly that one will repent, when one has made one's fortune in the world, or when one is ready to leave it. For besides the fact that it does not depend on the workers to cause rain according to their needs, when a field has long lain fallow, the brambles and the thorns have pushed their roots so deep that those who have never accustomed themselves to work have neither the power nor the desire to cultivate it.

LII

But if God acted in the order of grace by particular wills, if he efficaciously brought about, in all men, all their good actions and all good works with a particular plan, I do not see how one could justify the fact that he acts by the simplest laws, when I consider all those detours by which men arrive where God leads them—for I do not doubt at all that God gives to one man more than a hundred good thoughts in a single day. No more do I understand how one can reconcile his wisdom and his goodness with all those inefficacious graces which are resisted by the malice of men; for, God being good and wise, must he not proportion helps to needs, if he gives them with a particular plan of comforting?

LIII

God makes the weed grow with the wheat until the day of harvest; he makes it rain on the just and on the unjust: because grace, falling on men by general laws, is often given to him who will make no use of it—whereas if others had received it, they would have been converted by it. If Jesus Christ had preached to the Syrians and to the Sidonians, as well as to the inhabitants of Bethsaida and of Chorazin, they would have done penance in sackcloth and ashes; if the rain which falls on the deserts were distributed on prepared grounds, it would have made them fruitful. But all that which is regulated by general laws is not in agreement with particular plans: in order that these laws be wisely established it suffices that, being extremely simple, they lead to perfection the great work for which God had to establish them.

But although I do not think that God has, for each of his elect, an infinity of particular plans, nor that he gives them each day a great number of good thoughts and of good motions by particular wills, I do not deny, however, that they are all predestined by a good will of God with respect to them, for which they ought to have an eternal gratitude. Here is how I explain these things.

LIV

God discovers in the infinite treasures of his wisdom an infinity of possible works, and at the same time the most perfect way of producing each of them. He considers, among others, his Church, Jesus Christ who is its head, and all the persons who must compose it in consequence of the establishment of certain general laws. Finally, in view of Jesus Christ and of all his members, he establishes the laws for his own glory. This being so, is it not evident that Jesus Christ, who is the principle of all the glory which comes to God from his work, is the first of the predestined; that all the elect are also truly loved and predestined gratuitously in Jesus Christ, because they can honour God in Jesus Christ; that finally, they all have an infinite obligation to God, who without considering their merit has established the general laws of grace, which must sanctify them and lead them to the glory that they will possess eternally?

LV

Someone will say, perhaps, that these laws are so simple and so fruitful that God had to prefer them to all others, and that, loving only his own glory, his Son had to be incarnated—that he has done nothing purely for his elect. I grant it: God has done nothing purely for his elect. For St Paul teaches me that he made his elect for Jesus Christ, and Jesus Christ for himself. If, to render God lovable to men, one has to make him act purely for them, or in a way which would not be the wisest, I would prefer to remain silent. Reason teaches me to make God lovable by making him infinitely perfect, and by representing him as so full of charity for his creatures, that he produces none of them with the plan of making them unhappy: for if all do not have the happiness to enjoy his presence, it is simply that, order willing that so great a good be merited, all do not merit it, for the reasons I have stated. Is it not to make God lovable, to represent him such that the reprobate themselves can only adore his conduct and repent of their negligence?

LVI

However, to content those who will have it that God has predestined each of his elect by a particular will, one can say, without doing harm to the system which we have just proposed, that God, before creating souls to unite them with bodies, foresaw everything that would have to happen to them according to the general laws of nature and of grace, and everything they would do in all possible circumstances. Thus, as I suppose, being able to create the soul of Paul or that of Peter, and to unite it to such a body as he foresaw should be that of a predestined person, he resolved from all eternity to create the soul of Paul through a good will which he had for him, and he predestined him through this choice for eternal life. Instead of which he creates the soul of Peter, and unites it with another body, not through a good will which he has for it, but through a kind of necessity, because of the union of souls to bodies, which he has quite wisely established; for as soon as bodies are formed, he is obliged to unite souls with them—which would have been useful to all of them before the advent of sin. Now the body of Peter being engendered by a pagan father, or by a father who takes no care to raise his children; or finally Peter finding himself engaged through his birth to places, to times, and to employments which bring him to evil, he will be infallibly among the number of the reprobate. However, Peter will be useful to the plans of God. For although he does not by himself enter into the body of the predestined, he will enter through some of his posterity. He will serve the beauty and the greatness of the

Church of Jesus Christ through the infinite relations which he will
have with the elect. For the rest, he will not be unhappy except in
proportion to the bad use he will have made of his liberty: for God
punishes with pain only voluntary disorders. That is all that I can say
to satisfy the inclination of some people; but I do not see clearly that
one should entirely rely on this.

LVII

Those who claim that God has particular plans and particular wills
for all the particular effects which are produced in consequence of
general laws ordinarily rely on the authority of Scripture to shore up
their feeling. Now since Scripture is made for everyone, for the
simple as well as for the learned, it is full of *anthropologies*. Not only
does it give to God a body, a throne, a chariot, a retinue, the passions
of joy, of sadness, of anger, of remorse, and the other movements of
the soul: it also attributes to him ways of acting which are ordinary in
men, in order to speak to the simple in a more sensible way. If Jesus
Christ was made man it was in part to satisfy the inclination of men
who love that which resembles themselves, and who apply themselves
to that which touches them. It is in order to persuade them by this
kind of true and real anthropology, of truths that they would not
have been able to understand in another way. Thus St Paul, to
accommodate himself to everyone, speaks of the sanctification and of
the predestination of the saints, as if God acted ceaselessly in them
by particular wills. And even Jesus Christ speaks of his Father as if
he applied himself, through comparable volitions, to clothe the lilies
of the field and to preserve the least hair on his disciples' heads.
Because, at bottom, the goodness of God towards his creatures being
very great, these expressions give a great idea of it, and make God
lovable even to the coarsest minds, which have the most self-love.
However, just as through the idea one has of God and through the
passages from Scripture which are in conformity to that idea one
corrects the sense of some other passages which attribute members
to God, or passions like our own, so too when one wants to speak
with exactitude of the way in which God acts in the order of grace or
of nature, one must explain the passages which make him act as a
man or as a particular cause through the idea one has of his wisdom
and of his goodness, and by the other passages of Scripture which are
in conformity to that idea. For finally if one can say or rather if one is

obliged to say (because of the idea that one has of God) that he does not make each drop of rain fall by particular wills, although the natural sense of some passages of Scripture authorizes this notion, there is even a necessity to think, notwithstanding certain authorities of the same Scripture, that God does not at all give to some sinners, by particular wills, all the good movements which are useless to them, and which would be useful to several others: because without this principle it does not seem to me possible to reconcile Holy Scripture well either with reason or with itself—as I think I have proved.

If I believed that what I have just said was not sufficient to convince persons capable of attention, that God acts not at all by particular wills, like particular causes or limited intelligences, I would enlarge my argument here to make it clear that there are few truths of which one can give more proofs: supposing that one remains in agreement that God alone governs the world, and that the 'nature' of the pagan philosophers is a chimera. For nothing, indeed, happens in the world which does not prove this principle, if one excepts miracles only—which, none the less, would not be miracles at all, different from the effects that one calls natural, if it were true that God acts ordinarily by particular wills, since miracles are only such because they do not happen according to general laws and prove the principle which I have established: but as for ordinary effects, they clearly and directly demonstrate general laws or wills. If, for example, one drops a rock on the head of passers-by, the rock will always fall at an equal speed, without discerning the piety, or the condition, or the good or bad dispositions of those who pass by. If one examines some other effect, one will see the same constancy in the action of the cause that produces it: but no effect proves that God acts by particular wills, though men often imagine that God at every moment performs miracles in their favour. Since this way in which they want God to act is conformed to ours, since it flatters the self-love which relates everything to itself, and since it accommodates itself quite well to our ignorance of the combination of occasional causes which produce extraordinary effects, it enters the mind naturally, when one does not sufficiently study nature, and one does not consult with sufficient attention the abstract idea of an infinite wisdom of a universal cause of an infinitely perfect being.

Discourse II

On the Laws of Grace in Particular, and on the Occasional Causes Which Govern Them and Which Determine Their Efficacy

First Part
On the Grace of Jesus Christ

I

Since God alone acts immediately and by himself in minds, and produces in them all the different modifications of which they are capable, it is only he who diffuses light in us, and inspires in us certain feelings which determine our different volitions. Thus it is only God who can, as true cause, produce grace in souls. For grace, or that which is the principle or the motive of all the lawful movements of our love, is either a light which teaches us, or a confused feeling which convinces us, that God is our good: since we never begin to love an object if we do not see clearly by the light of reason, or if we do not feel confusedly by the taste of pleasure, that this object is good—I mean to say capable of making us happier than we are.

II

But since all men are enveloped in original sin, and they are by their nature infinitely beneath God, it is only Jesus Christ who, by the dignity of his person and by the holiness of his sacrifice, can have access to his Father, reconcile us with him, and merit his favours for us. Thus it is Jesus Christ alone who can be the meritorious cause of grace. These truths are certain. But we are looking neither for the cause which produces grace through its efficacy, nor that which merits it through his sacrifice and his good works; we seek that which regulates and which determines the efficacy of the general cause, that which one can call fruitful, particular, occasional.

III

For in order that the general cause act by general laws or wills, and that his action be lawful, constant, and uniform, it is absolutely necessary that there be some occasional cause which determines the efficacy of these laws, and which serves to establish them. If the collision of bodies, or something similar, did not determine the efficacy of general laws of the communication of motion, it would be necessary that God move bodies by particular wills. The laws of the union of the soul and the body are only rendered efficacious by the changes which take place in one or the other of these two substances. For if God made the pain of a pricking felt by the soul without the body's being pricked, or without the same thing happening in the brain as if the body were pricked, he would not act by general laws of the union of the soul and the body, but by a particular will. If it rained on the earth in another way than through a necessary consequence of general laws of the communication of motion, the rain and the falling of each drop that composes it would be the effect of a particular will. Such that, if order did not require that it rain, this would be entirely unworthy of God. It is thus necessary that, in the order of grace, there be some occasional cause which serves to establish the laws and which determines their efficacy: and it is this cause which one must strive to discover.

IV

If one consults a little the idea of intelligible order, or considers the sensible order which appears in all the works of God, one discovers without difficulty that the occasional causes which determine the efficacy of general laws and which serve to establish them, must have a relation to the plan for which God established these laws.

Experience, for example, makes it clear that God has not taken, and reason convinces us that he ought not to have taken, the course of the planets as occasional causes of the union of our soul with our body. He ought not to will that our arm move in such-and-such a way, or that our soul suffer toothache, when the moon shall be joined to the sun, if this conjunction does not act on the body. The plan of God being to unite our soul to our body, he cannot according to this plan give the soul feelings of pain, except when some changes in the body contrary to it come about. Thus one need not look outside our soul or our body for the occasional cause of their union.

V

It follows from this that God, having the plan to form his Church through Jesus Christ, could not (according to this plan) look elsewhere than in Jesus Christ and in the creatures united by reason to Jesus Christ, for the occasional causes which serve to establish the general laws of grace, by which the spirit of Jesus Christ is diffused in his members, and communicates his life and his holiness to them. Thus the rain of grace is not diffused in our hearts according to the different situations of the stars, nor according to the meeting of certain bodies, nor even according to the different courses of animal spirits which give us movement and life. All bodies can excite in us only purely natural movements and feelings: for all that comes to the soul from the body is only for the body.

VI

However, since grace is not given to all those who wish for it, nor as soon as they wish for it, and since it is given to those who do not ask for it, it follows that even our desires are not at all the occasional causes of grace. For these sorts of causes always have their effect very promptly, and without them the effect is never produced. For example, the collision of bodies being the occasional cause of the change which takes place in their motion, if two bodies do not meet, their motion changes not at all, and if they change, one can be assured that the bodies have met. The general laws which diffuse grace in our hearts, thus find nothing in our wills which determine their efficacy—just as the general laws which govern the rains are not based on the dispositions of the places where it rains. For whether the grounds be fallow or whether they be cultivated, it rains indifferently in all places, both in the deserts and in the sea.

VII

We are thus reduced to saying that, just as Jesus Christ only can merit grace for us, so too he only can furnish the occasions of the general laws according to which it is given to men. For, since the principle or the foundation of general laws, or that which determines their efficacy, is necessarily either in us or in Jesus Christ, and since it is certain that it is not in us, for the reasons that I have just said, it is necessary that it be located in Jesus Christ.

VIII

In addition it was necessary that after the advent of sin, God have no further consideration for our wills. Being all in a state of disorder, we could no longer be an occasion for God to give us grace. We needed a mediator not only to give us access to God, but to be the occasional cause of the favours which we hope for from him.

IX

Since God had a plan to make his Son the head of his Church, it was appropriate that he make him the occasional or natural cause of the grace which sanctified it; for it is from the head that life and movement must be diffused in the members. And it was even with this same prospect that God permitted sin. For if man had remained in a state of innocence, since his wills would have been meritorious of grace and even of glory, God would have had to establish in man the occasional cause of his perfection and of his happiness—the inviolable law of order will have it so; such that Jesus Christ would not have been the head of the Church, or at least he would have been a head with whose influence all the members would have been able to dispense.

X

If our soul were in our body before it was formed, and if it were according to our diverse volitions that all the parts that compose it were arranged, by how many different feelings and different movements would it be touched, through all the effects that it would know as having to issue from those volitions—principally if it had a strong desire to form the most vigorous and best-made body that can be.

XI

Now Holy Scripture not only says that Jesus Christ is the head of the Church: it also teaches us that he begets it, that he forms it, that he gives it increase, that he suffers in it, that he merits in it, that he acts and influences in it ceaselessly. The zeal that Jesus Christ had for the glory of his Father, and the love that he bears his Church, inspire ceaselessly in him the desire to make it the most ample, the most magnificent, and the most perfect that can be. Thus, since the soul of Jesus Christ has not at all an infinite capacity, and he wants to place in the body of the Church an infinity of beauties and ornaments, one has every reason to believe that there is in this holy soul a continual chain of thoughts and desires, with respect to the mystical body which it forms without ceasing.

XII

Now it is these continual desires of the soul of Jesus Christ, which tend to sanctify his Church and to render it worthy of the majesty of his Father, which God has established as occasional causes of the efficacy of the general laws of grace. For faith teaches us that God has given to his Son an absolute power over men, by making him head of his Church; and this cannot be conceived, if the different wills of Jesus Christ are not followed by their effects. For it is obvious that I would not have the slightest power over my arm, if it moved without my willing it, and if, when I willed to move it, it remained as if dead, and without movement.

XIII

Jesus Christ has merited this sovereign power over men, and this quality of head of the Church, through the sacrifice which he offered on earth; and after the Resurrection he entered into full possession of this right. At present he is the sovereign priest of future goods, and by his different desire he prays ceaselessly to his Father on behalf of men. And since his desires are occasional causes, his prayers are always granted; his Father refuses him nothing, as Scripture teaches us. However, it is necessary that he pray and that he desire in order to obtain: because occasional, natural, physical causes (these three terms here signify the same thing) do not have, by themselves, the power to do anything, and because all creatures, and Jesus Christ himself considered as a man, are by themselves nothing but weakness and impotence.

XIV

Jesus Christ, then, having different thoughts successively, with respect to the different dispositions of which souls in general are capable, these different thoughts are accompanied by certain desires with respect to the sanctification of these souls. Now these desires, being occasional causes of grace, must diffuse it in persons in particular whose dispositions are like that of which the soul of Jesus presently thinks: and this grace must be all the more strong and abundant, as the desires of Jesus are greater and more lasting.

XV

When a person considers some part of his body which is not formed as it ought to be, he naturally has certain desires with respect to this part, and to the use he wants to make of it in order to live among men; and these desires are followed by certain insensible movements of the animal spirits which tend to put this part in the condition or in the disposition which we wish it to be. When the body is entirely formed, and the flesh is too firm, these movements can change nothing in the structure of the parts; they can only give them certain dispositions which are called bodily habits. But when the body is not entirely formed, and its flesh is extremely soft and delicate, the movements which accompany the desires of the soul not only place certain particular dispositions in the body: they can even change its construction. This appears often enough in infants who are in their mothers' wombs. For not only are they moved, like their mothers, by the same passions: they also receive on their bodies marks of these passions—marks from which their mothers are always exempt.

XVI

The mystical body of Jesus Christ is not yet a perfect man, and will only be such at the end of time; Jesus Christ forms it ceaselessly. For he is the head whose members receive growth through the efficacy of his influence, according to the measure which is fit for each of them, in order that each be formed and edified by charity. These are truths which St Paul has taught us. Now since the soul of Jesus Christ has no other action than the different movements of his heart, it is necessary that his desires be followed by the influence of grace which alone can form Jesus Christ in his members, and give them that beauty and that proportion which must be the eternal object of divine law.

XVII

The different movements of the soul of Jesus Christ being occasional causes of grace, one should not be surprised if it is sometimes given to great sinners, or to persons who wil not make the slightest use of it. For the soul of Jesus, thinking to raise a temple of a vast extent and of an infinite beauty, can wish that grace be given to the greatest sinners: and if at that moment Jesus Christ actually thinks of misers, for example, then misers will receive grace. Or again Jesus Christ having need, for the construction of his Church, of minds of a certain character (which comes about ordinarily only in those who suffer certain persecutions, whereof the passions of men are the natural principle): in a word Jesus Christ having need of minds of a certain character in order to bring about certain effects in his Church, he can in general apply to them, and by that application diffuse in them the grace that sanctifies them—just as the mind of an architect thinks in general of squared stones, for example, when those sorts of stones are presently necessary to his building.

XVIII

But since the soul of Jesus Christ is not a general cause, one has reason to think that it often has particular desires with respect to certain persons in particular. When we claim to speak of God, we ought not to consult ourselves, and make him act like us; one must consult the idea of the infinitely perfect Being, and make God act conformably to that idea. But when we speak of the action of the soul of Jesus, we can consult ourselves, we must make him act as particular causes act. We have, for example, reason to believe that the vocation of St Paul was the effect of the efficacy of a particular desire of Jesus Christ. We must even regard the desires of the soul of Jesus which have generally a relation to all minds of a certain character as particular desires, though they embrace several persons, because these desires change at every moment like those of particular causes. But the general laws by which God acts are always the same, because the wills of God must be firm and constant, since his wisdom is infinite.

XIX

The different desires of the soul of Jesus diffusing grace, one sees clearly how it is that it is not diffused equally in all men, and that it falls on the same persons more abundantly at one time than at another. For the soul of Jesus Christ not thinking at the same time of all men, it does not have at one time all the desires of which it is capable. Such that Jesus Christ does not act on his members in a particular way except by successive influences. In the same way our soul does not move, at one single time, all the muscles of our body: for the animal spirits are diffused unequally and successively in our members, according to the different impressions of objects, the different movements of our passions, and the different desires which we freely form within ourselves.

XX

It is true that all the just receive ceaselessly the influence of the head who gives them life, and that when they act in the spirit of Jesus Christ they merit and receive new graces, without its being necessary that the soul of Jesus Christ have some particular desires which are their occasional causes. For order, which will have it that all merit be rewarded, is not at all an arbitrary law in God; it is a necessary law, which depends not at all on any occasional cause. But although he who has done a meritorious action may be rewarded for it, without the soul of Jesus Christ presently having some desires with respect to him, none the less it is certain that he has not merited grace except by the dignity and the holiness of the spirit which Jesus Christ has communicated to him. For men are only pleasing to God and only do something good, in so far as they are united to his Son by charity.

XXI

One must also grant that those who observe the counsels of Jesus Christ out of the esteem they have for them, and through their fear of future punishment, solicit (as it were) by their obedience the charity of Jesus Christ to think of them, though they still act only out of self-love. But all their actions are not occasional causes: either of grace, since they are not invariably followed, or of the movements of the soul of Jesus Christ with respect to them, since those same movements never fail to diffuse grace. Thus it is only the desires of Jesus Christ which infallibly have their effect as occasional causes; because, God having established Jesus Christ as head of his Church, it is only through him that he must diffuse in his elect the grace which sanctifies them.

XXII

Now one can distinguish in the soul of Jesus Christ desires of two kinds: passing and particular present desires, whose efficacy lasts only for a short time, and stable and permanent desires, which consist in a firm and constant disposition of the soul of Jesus Christ with respect to certain effects, which tend to the execution of his plan in general.

If our soul, by its different movements, communicated to our body everything that is necessary to it to form it and to make it grow, one would be able to distinguish therein these two species of desire. For it would be by present and passing desires that it would diffuse in the muscles of the body the animal spirits which give it a certain disposition, with respect to the present thoughts of the mind. But it would be by stable and permanent desires that the soul would give to the heart and to the lungs the natural movements which serve in respiration and in the circulation of the blood. It would again be by comparable desires that it would digest food, and that it would distribute it to all the parts that have need of it—because that kind of action is necessary to the preservation of the body at every moment.

XXIII

It is by present, passing, and particular desires of the soul of Jesus, that grace is diffused in persons who are not prepared for it, and in a way that has something singular and extraordinary about it. But it is by permanent desires that it is given regularly to those who receive the sacraments with the necessary dispositions. For the grace which we receive through the sacraments is not at all given to us precisely because of the merit of our action, though we receive them in a state of grace; it is because of the merits of Jesus Christ, which are liberally applied to us in consequence of his permanent desires. We receive through the sacraments much more grace than our preparation merits; and it even suffices, for us to receive some influence from it, that we oppose no obstacle to it. But it is also to abuse what is most holy in religion to receive them unworthily.

XXIV

Among the present and passing desires of the soul of Jesus Christ, there are certainly some which are more lasting and more frequent than the others; and the knowledge of these desires is of great importance for morality. No doubt Jesus Christ thinks more often of those who observe his counsels than of other men. The feelings of charity which he has for the faithful are more frequent and more durable than those which he has for libertines and for the impious; and since all the faithful are not equally disposed to enter the Church of the predestined, the desires of the soul of Jesus are not, with respect to all of them, equally lively, frequent, and lasting.

Man desires with more ardour the fruits which are the most fitting for the nourishment of his body; he thinks more often of bread and of wine, than of meats which are difficult to digest. Jesus Christ, having a plan to form his Church, must then occupy himself more with those who can more easily enter into it, than with those who are extremely distant from it.

Holy Scripture, too, teaches us that the humble, the poor, and the penitent receive greater grace than other men; because those who have contempt for honours, riches, and pleasures are much more suitable for the Kingdom of God.

Those who, after the example of Jesus Christ, have learned to be mild and humble of heart, will find rest for their souls. The yoke of

Jesus Christ, which is intolerable to the proud, becomes mild and light to them by the help of grace. For God hears the prayers of the humble: he will console them, he will crown them with blessings; but he will debase the high mind of the proud. Blessed are the poor in spirit, for theirs is the kingdom of heaven. But woe to the rich, for they have their consolation in this world. How difficult it is, says Jesus Christ, for those who have much wealth to enter the kingdom of heaven. It is easier for a camel to pass through the eye of a needle. It cannot be done without a miracle.

For those who, like David, humble their souls by fasting, exchange their clothes for sackcloth, in a word scourge themselves, upon sight of their sins and of God's holiness—they become the worthy objects of the compassion of Jesus Christ. For God will never spurn a contrite and humble heart. One always disarms his anger when one takes the side of God against oneself, and when one avenges him.

XXV

Since the will of Jesus Christ is entirely conformed to order, of which all men naturally have some idea, one could also discover through reason that the soul of Jesus Christ has more thoughts and desires with respect to certain persons than with respect to others. For order requires that Jesus Christ diffuse more graces in those (for example) who are called to holy orders, or in those who have a vocation which of necessity engages them in the affairs of the world; in a word in those who are the principal parts in the body of the Church militant, rather than in those who have no regard to anybody, or who meddle in the ecclesiastical state, or who raise themselves above others through ambition or through interest. For if it is appropriate that Jesus Christ give graces to the former in proportion as they guide other persons, they do not deserve that he give them any grace which will sanctify them in a condition which they have chosen out of self-love. They may have the gift of prophecy without having that of charity, as Scripture teaches us.

XXVI

But though one can discover by the light of reason and by the authority of the sacred books, something of the different desires of the soul of Jesus, none the less that order and that sequence of desires which accompany the predestination of the saints, and which only tend to honour God in the establishment of his Church, is an impenetrable abyss to the human mind. For if St Paul had not taught us that God willed to let all men be enveloped in incredulity in order to exercise his mercy towards all, would we ever have thought that it was necessary that the Jews fall into blindness, not only so that the multitude of nations might enter into the Church, but so that they themselves might receive mercy at the end of time? The future world having to be a work of pure mercy, having to have an infinity of ornaments of which we have no idea; since the substance of minds is unknown to us, it is clear that we can discover almost nothing in the different desires of the soul of Jesus—these desires having a relation to plans of which we know nothing. Thus in the distribution of his graces which God makes, we must often say, with St Paul: *O the depth of the riches both of the wisdom and knowledge of God! How unsearchable are his judgements, and his ways past finding out! For who has known the plans of God, and who has been admitted to the secret of his counsels?*[3]

XXVII

We have proved that the different desires of the soul of Jesus are the occasional causes of grace, and we have tried to discover something about his desires. Let us now see of what kind of grace they are the occasional causes. For although Jesus Christ is the meritorious cause of all graces, it is not necessary that he be the occasional cause of the graces of enlightenment [*lumière*], and of certain external graces which prepare for the conversion of the heart and which cannot operate; for Jesus Christ is always an occasional or necessary cause according to the order established by God with respect to all the graces which effect salvation.

XXVIII

In order to understand distinctly which is the grace that Jesus Christ as head of the Church diffuses in his members, one must know what that concupiscence is, which the first man communicated to all his

---

[3] Romans 11: 33–4.

posterity. For the second Adam has come to remedy the disorders of
which the first was the cause: and there is such a relation between the
sinful and terrestrial Adam and the innocent and celestial Adam,
that St Paul views the former communicating sin to his children by
his disobedience, as the prefiguring of the second diffusing justice
and holiness in Christians by his obedience.

XXIX

Order requires that the mind dominate the body and that it not be
divided, despite itself, by all those sentiments and by all those
movements which attach it to sensible objects. The first man,
moreover, before his sin, was so far the master of his senses and of
his passions, that they were mute as soon as he so wished: nothing
was capable of turning him from his duty in spite of himself, and all
the pleasures which now precede reason, only warned him respectfully,
and in a prompt and easy way, of what he had to do for the
preservation of his life. But after his sin he lost, all of a sudden, the
power which he had over his body. Such that, no longer being able
to stop the movements or efface the marks that sensible objects
produced in the main part of his brain, his soul found itself, by the
order of nature and in punishment of his disobedience, miserably
subjected to the law of concupiscence—to that carnal law which
fights ceaselessly against the mind, which at every moment inspires
the love of sensible goods in it, and which dominates it through
passions so strong and so lively, and at the same time so gentle and so
pleasant, that it cannot and will not make even necessary efforts to
break the bonds that hold it captive. For the contagion of sin is
diffused in all the children of Adam by an infallible consequence of
the order of nature, as I have explained elsewhere.

XXX

The heart of man is always the slave of pleasure; and when reason
teaches us that it is not fitting to enjoy it, we avoid it only to
rediscover it in a form more mild and solid. We willingly sacrifice
our little pleasures to the greater; but the invincible impulsion which
we have for our happiness, does not permit us to deprive ourselves
for a lifetime of the sweetness that one tastes when one gives oneself
over to one's passions.

XXXI

It is certain that pleasure makes him who enjoys it happy, at least during the time that he enjoys it. Thus, men being made to be happy, pleasure always sets their will in motion, and puts it ceaselessly in motion towards the object which causes it or which seems to cause it. One must say the opposite about pain. Now concupiscence consists only in a continual chain of feelings and of movements which precede reason and which are not subject to it: of pleasures which, seeming to flow from the objects that surround us, inspire love in us; of pains which, making the practice of virtue hard and painful, give us a horror of it. It was, then, necessary that the second Adam, in order to remedy the disorders of the first, produce in us pleasures and horrors contrary to those of concupiscence— pleasure relating to true goods, and horrors or distastes relating to sensible goods. Thus the grace of which Jesus Christ is the occasional cause, and which he diffuses ceaselessly in us as head of the Church, is not the grace of enlightenment, though he has merited this grace for us, and though he can sometimes communicate it to us in a way that I shall state shortly; it is rather the grace of feeling. It is preventing delectation which produces and which sustains charity in our hearts, for pleasure naturally produces and sustains the love of the objects which cause it, or which seem to cause it. It is also the horror which sometimes spreads over sensible objects which gives us an aversion to them, and puts us in a condition to follow our enlightenment in the motions of our love.

XXXII

It was necessary to oppose the grace of feeling to concupiscence, pleasure to pleasure, horror to horror, so that the influence of Jesus Christ might be directly opposed to the influence of the first man. It was necessary that the remedy be contrary to the illness in order to cure it. For the grace of enlightenment cannot cure a heart wounded by pleasure: it is necessary either that this pleasure cease, or that another succeed it. Pleasure is the balance of the soul: it inclines naturally towards it; sensible pleasures pull it down to earth. It is necessary, for it to be able to determine itself, by itself, either that these pleasures dissipate, or that the delectation of grace raise it towards heaven, and put it nearly back in equilibrium. It is thus that the new man can combat the old man, that the influence of our leader resists the influence of our [earthly] father, that Jesus Christ surmounts in us all our domestic enemies.

Since man had no concupiscence before his sin, he did not have to be carried towards love of the true good through preventing delectation. He knew clearly that God was his good; it was not necessary that he feel it. He did not have to be drawn by pleasure to love him whom nothing kept from loving and whom he knew to be perfectly worthy of his love: but after sin the grace of delectation was necessary to him to counterbalance the continual efforts of concupiscence. Thus enlightenment is the grace of the Creator; delectation is the grace of the Redeemer. Enlightenment is communicated by Jesus Christ, as eternal wisdom; delectation is given by Jesus Christ as incarnated wisdom. Enlightenment was originally nothing but nature; delectation has always been pure grace. Enlightenment, after sin, is given to us only because of the merits of Jesus Christ; delectation is given us because of the merits and through the efficacy of the power of Jesus Christ. Finally enlightenment is diffused in our minds according to our different wills, and our different efforts, as I shall soon explain; but the delectation of grace is diffused in our hearts only through the different desires of the soul of Jesus Christ.

XXXIII

It is true that pleasure produces enlightenment, because the soul gives more attention to the objects from which it receives more pleasure. Since the greater part of men despises or neglects the truths of religion, because these abstract truths do not touch them, one can say that the delectation of grace instructs them—for, making them sensible of these great truths, they learn them more easily by the attention they bring to them. It is for that reason that St John says that the unction that one receives from Jesus Christ teaches all things, and that those who have received it have to need of anyone to instruct them.

XXXIV

None the less one must take note that this unction does not produce enlightenment by itself; it only excites our attention, which is the natural or occasional cause of our knowledge. We see too that those who have the most charity do not always have the most enlightenment. Since all men are not equally capable of attention, the same unction does not instruct equally all those who receive it. Thus, although enlightenment may be diffused in the soul through a supernatural *infusion*, and although charity often produces it, none the less one must often view this kind of grace as a natural effect— because charity itself ordinarily produces enlightenment in souls only in proportion as it brings the soul to desire the knowledge of that which it loves. For in the end the different desires of the soul are natural or occasional causes of the discoveries that we make, on any subject that may be. But it is necessary that I explain this at greater length in the second part of this discourse.

Second Part
On the Grace of the Creator

XXXV

I know only two principles which determine, directly and by themselves, the movements of our love: enlightenment and pleasure—enlightenment, which reveals our different goods to us; pleasure, which gives us a taste for them. But there is a great difference between enlightenment and pleasure. Enlightenment leaves us entirely to ourselves; it makes no attempt against our liberty; it does not efficaciously bring us to love; it does not produce in us any natural or necessary love; it only brings us to bring ourselves to love, by a free love, the objects which it reveals to us, or (what is the same thing) it brings us to direct towards particular goods the general impulsion of love which God pours ceaselessly into us. But pleasure determines our will efficaciously: it transports us, so to speak, towards the object which causes it or which seems to cause it; it produces in us a natural and necessary love; it diminishes our liberty; it divides our reason, and does not leave us entirely to ourselves. A moderate attention to the internal feeling which we have concerning what happens within us, will be able to convince us of these differences.

Thus, since man before sin was free with a perfect liberty; since he had no concupiscence at all which kept him from following his enlightenment in all the movements of his love; and since he knew clearly that God is infinitely worthy of being loved, he did not have to be determined at all by preventing delectation, as I have already said, or by other graces of feeling which would have diminished his merit, and which would have borne him to love as if by instinct that good which he ought to have loved only through reason. But since the advent of sin, the grace of feeling, in addition to enlightenment, has been necessary to him, to resist the movements of concupiscence. For, man wanting invincibly to be happy, it is not possible for him ceaselessly to sacrifice his pleasure to his enlightenment—his pleasure, which makes him presently happy and which exists in him even despite his whole resistance, to his enlightenment which exists only through painful application of the mind, which dissolves in the presence of the slightest present pleasure, and which finally promises solid happiness only after death (which seems to the imagination to be a veritable annihilation).

Enlightenment, then, is due to man to conduct him in the search for the good; it is of the natural order; it supposes neither the corruption nor the redemption of nature. But that pleasure which relates to the true good is pure grace. For naturally the true good ought to be loved only through reason. Thus the occasional causes of grace of feeling must be found in Jesus Christ, because he is the author of grace. But the occasional causes of enlightenment must ordinarily be met with in the order of nature, because enlightenment is the grace of the Creator. Let us strive to reveal these causes.

XXXVI

In the established order of nature I see only two causes which diffuse enlightenment in minds, and which thus determine the general laws of the grace of the Creator—one of which is in us, and depends in some way on us, the other which is met with in the relation that we have with all that surrounds us. The first is nothing else than the different movements of our wills. The second is the meeting of sensible objects which act on our mind in consequence of the laws of the union of our soul with our body.

XXXVII

The inner feeling which we have of ourselves teaches us that the love of enlightenment produces it, and that the attention of the mind is the natural prayer by which we obtain enlightenment from God: for all those who apply themselves to the truth discover it in proportion to their application. And if our prayer were not interrupted, if our attention was not troubled, if we had some idea of what we ask, we would never fail to receive, in so far as we are capable of receiving. But our prayers are ceaselessly interrupted, unless they are self-interested: our senses and our imagination throw all our heads into trouble and confusion; and although the truth which we consult responds to our requests, the confused sound of our passions keeps us from hearing its answers, or makes us speedily forget them.

XXXVIII

If one considers that man, before sin, was animated by charity, that he had within himself all that was necessary to him in order to persevere in justice, and that he had to merit his reward through his perseverance and through his application, one will understand easily that the different desires of his heart should be established as occasional causes of the enlightenment which is diffused in his mind: otherwise his distraction would not be voluntary at all, nor his attention meritorious. Now nature, though corrupted, is not destroyed; God has not ceased to will what he has willed; the same laws subsist. Thus our different wills are still today the occasional or natural causes of the presence of ideas in our mind. But, because the union of the soul with the body has changed into dependence through a necessary consequence of sin, and of the immutability of the will of God, such as I have explained elsewhere, our body now troubles our ideas and speaks so loudly in favour of its respective goods, that the mind only rarely consults, and only listens distractedly to, internal truth.

XXXIX

Experience still teaches us at every moment that the dealings we have with enlightened persons are capable of instructing us, by exciting our attention—that sermons, reading, conversation, a thousand incidents of all sorts, can awaken ideas in us, and even inspire us with good sentiments. The death of a friend is no doubt capable of making us think of death, unless some great passion occupies us. And when a preacher who has great natural talent undertakes to demonstrate a quite simple truth, and to convince others of it, one must agree that he can persuade his hearers, and even stir their conscience, give them fear and hope, and excite in them several other passions which will put them in a state of less resistance to the efficacy of the grace of Jesus Christ.

Men being made to live in society with each other, it was necessary that they be able to communicate their thoughts and their actions naturally. It was necessary that they be united through the mind as they were by the body, and that speaking by the voice to their ears and through Scripture to their eyes, they diffuse enlightenment and intelligence in attentive minds.

XL

Now enlightenment, however it be produced in us—be it that our particular desires or that fortuitous meetings are the occasional causes of it—can be called grace mainly when it is strongly related to salvation: though it is only a consequence of the order of nature because, since the advent of sin, God owes us nothing, and because anything good we may have has been merited for us by Jesus Christ; for our being itself exists only through Jesus Christ. But this kind of grace, although merited by Jesus Christ, is not the grace of Jesus Christ. It is the grace of the Creator. Because Jesus Christ is not ordinarily the occasional cause of it, and because one must look for the cause in the order of nature.

XLI

There are still many other natural effects which one could, with reason, view as graces. For example, two persons have at the same time two quite different desires depending on curiosity. The one wants to go to the opera, and the other wants to hear a preacher who is cutting a figure in the world. If they satisfy their curiosity, he who goes to the opera will find such objects as (according to the present disposition of his mind) will excite in him passions which will damn him. The other, on the contrary, will find in the preacher so much enlightenment and so much power, that the grace of conversion, being given to him at that moment, will be quite efficacious. That supposed, let a shower of rain arise, or some other accident which keeps them at home. This rain is no doubt a natural effect, since it depends on natural laws of the communication of motion. However, one can say that it is grace, with respect to him whose damnation it prevents, and that it is a punishment with respect to him whose conversion it stops.

XLII

Since grace is conjoined with nature, all the movements of our soul and of our body have some relation to salvation. Someone is saved for having, in a state of grace, taken a step which happily has made him fracture his head. And someone is damned for having, at a certain time, unhappily avoided the ruins of a house ready to overwhelm him. We know not at all what is advantageous to us: but we know well that there is nothing so indifferent in itself, that it has not some relation to our salvation, because of the mixture and the combination of effects which depend on the general laws of nature, with those which depend on the general laws of grace.

XLIII

Since, then, enlightenment reveals the true good, the means to obtain it, our duties towards God, in a word the paths that we must follow; since it even suffices with respect to those who are animated by charity, to make them do the good, to make them merit new graces, to make them vanquish certain temptations, as I have explained elsewhere: I believe that one can legitimately give it the name of grace, though Jesus Christ is only its meritorious cause. And since external graces which do not act immediately in the mind, none the less enter into the order of the predestination of the saints, I regard them still as true graces. In a word I believe that one can give the name of grace to all natural effects, when they have a relation to salvation, when they serve the grace of Jesus Christ, and when they remove certain impediments to its efficacy. If, however, one does not consent to this, I have no wish to dispute over words.

XLIV

All these kinds of graces—if one wants to leave them that name—being the graces of the Creator, the general laws of these graces are the general laws of nature. For one must take note that sin has not destroyed nature, although it has corrupted it. The general laws of the communication of motion are always the same; and those of the union of the soul and the body are not changed, except in this alone, that what was only a union with respect to our mind, has been changed into dependence for the reasons which I have stated elsewhere. For we are now dependent on the body to which we were only united.

XLV

Now the laws of nature are always quite simple and quite general. For God does not act at all by particular wills, unless order requires a miracle. I have sufficiently proved this truth in the first discourse. Thus when a stone falls on the head of a good man and deprives him of his life, it falls in consequence of the laws of motion: it is not because this man is just, and that God wants presently to reward him. When a similar accident destroys a sinner, it is not because God wants presently to punish him. For God, on the contrary, wills to save all men—but he must not change the simplicity of his laws to suspend the punishment of a criminal. In the same way, when enlightenment spreads in our soul, it is because we have desires which are its occasional or natural cause—it is because we listen to some enlightened person, and our brain is disposed to receive the impressions of him who speaks to us. It is not that God has, with respect to us, a particular will; rather he follows the general laws of nature which he has imposed on himself. I see nothing mysterious in the distribution of these kinds of graces, and I do not stop to point out the consequences which flow from these truths.

XLVI

One must take note that Jesus Christ, who is only the meritorious cause of the goods which God gives us according to the order of nature, is sometimes the occasional cause of the grace of enlightenment, as well as of that of feeling. I believe, none the less, that this is very rare, since indeed it is not necessary. Jesus Christ does as much as is possible to make nature serve grace. For besides the fact that reason teaches us that order will have it so, because this way is the simplest, this sufficiently appears in the conduct which he held to on earth, and through the order which he established and which he still preserves in the Church. Jesus Christ has used the word to enlighten the world, and has even sent his disciples, two by two, to prepare the nations to receive it. He has established apostles, prophets, evangelists, doctors, bishops, priests, to work on the edifice of the Church. Was this not to make nature serve grace, and to diffuse the light of faith in minds by the simplest and most natural means? Indeed Jesus Christ, on earth, did not have to enlighten men by particular wills, because he was able to instruct them, as inner truth and as eternal wisdom, by the quite simple and quite fruitful laws of nature.

XLVII

What seems to be more hidden in the order that God has followed in order to establish his Church is no doubt the time, the place, and the other circumstances of the Incarnation of his son, and of the preaching of the saviour. For why was it necessary that Jesus Christ be made man four thousand years after the creation of the world—he for whom the world had been created? Why did he have to be born among the Jews—he who had to reprove that unhappy nation? Why choose to be the son of David, when the house of David had no more glory, and not choose to be the son of the [Roman] emperors, who commanded all the world—he who had come to convert and to enlighten the whole world? Why should he choose as his apostles and as his disciples persons who were coarse and ignorant; preach to the citizens of the Bethsaida and of Chorazin who remained in their unbelief, and leave in that state Tyre and Sidon, which would have been converted, if they had been granted the same grace; stop St Paul from announcing the word of God in Asia, and order him to pass into Macedonia? A thousand other circumstances which accompanied the preaching of the saviour are no doubt mysteries for which it is not possible to give clear and evident reasons. That also is not my plan. I only want to establish principles which can throw some light on these difficulties and on others like them, or which at least will make it understood that one can conclude nothing against what I have said to this point about the order of nature and grace.

XLVIII

It is certain that natural effects combine and mix in an infinity of ways with the effects of grace, and that the order of nature augments or diminishes the efficacy or the effects of the order of grace— according to the different ways in which these two orders mix with each other. Death, which according to the general laws of nature comes at a certain time to a good or to a bad prince, to a good or to a bad bishop, causes a great deal of good or evil in the Church: because similar accidents bring about a very great variety in the sequence of effects which depend upon the order of grace. Now God wills to save all men by the simplest means. Thus one can and even must say, in general, that he has chosen the time, the place, the ways which, in the fullness of time, and according to the general laws of nature and of grace, must (all things being equal) cause to enter into the Church a greater number of predestined persons. God does everything for his glory. Thus of all the possible combinations of nature and grace, he has chosen, through the infinite extent of his knowledge, that which should form the most perfect Church, the most worthy of his greatness and his wisdom.

XLIX

It seems to me that this already suffices as a response to all the difficulties which can be raised about the circumstances of our mysteries. For if one says that Jesus Christ should have been born of a Roman emperor, and have performed his miracles in the capital of the world, so that the Gospel might have spread with greater ease in the most distant countries, one need only boldly reply that, whatever men may think of it, this combination of nature with grace would not have been as worthy of the wisdom of God as that which he chose. I grant that religion was more easily diffused in earlier times: but its establishment would not have been so divine, or so extraordinary, and in consequence its establishment would not have been an invincible proof of its solidity and truth. Thus according to this combination, religion would now be either destroyed, or less diffused throughout the world. Moreover, when one says that God acts by the simplest means, one always supposes equality in all the rest, and principally in the glory that must come to God from his work. Now the Church would not have been so perfect, nor so worthy of the greatness and the holiness of God, if it had been formed so easily. For the beauty of the heavenly Jerusalem consisting in the different rewards due to the different struggles of Christians, it was necessary that the martyrs spill their blood, as well as Jesus Christ, to enter into possession of the glory which they possess. In a word, this principle—that of all the infinite combinations of orders of nature and grace, God has chosen that which must produce the effect which is most worthy of his greatness and his wisdom—suffices in general to meet the objections that can be raised about the circumstances of our mysteries. Just as, to justify the orders of nature and grace in themselves, it suffices to know that God, being infinitely wise, forms his plans only through an admirable relation between wisdom and fruitfulness, discovered in the ways capable of bringing it to pass, as I have explained in the first discourse.

L

Since most men judge of God in relation to themselves, they imagine that he first forms a plan, then consults his wisdom about the means of executing it. For our wills go before our reason at every moment, and our plans are almost never perfectly reasonable. But God does not conduct himself like men. This is how he acts, if I have well understood the idea of the infinitely perfect Being. God knows, through the infinite light of his wisdom, all the possible works, and at the same time all the ways of producing each of them. He sees all the relations of means to their ends. He compares all things in a view which is eternal, immutable, necessary; and by the comparison he makes between the relations of wisdom and of fruitfulness, which he discovers between the plans and the means of executing them, he freely forms a plan. But the plan being formed, he necessarily chooses the general means which are the worthiest of his wisdom, his greatness, and his goodness; for as he forms his plan only through the knowledge he has of the means of executing it, the choice of plan includes the choice of means.

LI

When I say that God freely forms his plan, I do not mean that he can choose another which would be less worthy of his wisdom, rejecting that which is more worthy of him. For, supposing that God wills to produce a work outside himself which is worthy of him, he is not at all indifferent in his choice; he must produce the most perfect that is possible with respect to the simplicity of the means by which he acts. He owes it to himself to follow the rules of his wisdom, he must always act in the wisest and most perfect way. But I say that God forms his plan freely, because he invincibly and necessarily loves only his own substance. Neither the Incarnation of the Word, nor for stronger reasons the creation of the world, is a necessary emanation from his nature. God suffices fully to himself—for the infinitely perfect Being can be conceived alone, and without any necessary relation to a single one of his creatures.

LII

Since God loves himself necessarily, he also necessarily follows the rules of his wisdom. But since created beings make no part of his being, he so suffices unto himself that nothing obliges him to create them—he is quite indifferent or quite free with respect to them. And it is for that reason that he made the world in time: for this circumstance makes it clear that creatures are not at all necessary emanations from the divinity, and that they are essentially dependent on a free will of the Creator.

LIII

Here, none the less, is an objection which at once strikes the mind: if it were true that God necessarily follows the rules of his wisdom, the world would not have been created in time. For either the world is worthy of God, or it is unworthy. If it is better that the world be drawn from nothingness, it ought to be eternal; and if it is better that it remain in nothingness, it should never be drawn out of it. Thus God is not at all obliged to adhere to the rules which his wisdom prescribes to him, since the world has been created in time.

But the answer to this objection is not very difficult. It is better that the world be than that it not be: but it would be better that it not be at all than that it be eternal. It is necessary that the creation bear the essential character of dependency. If minds were eternal, they would have some reason to consider themselves as gods or as necessary beings, or at least as capable of contributing to the greatness or to the felicity of God, imagining that he could not have done without producing them; they could even compare themselves in some way to divine persons, believing themselves to be produced, like them, through a necessary emanation. Thus God had, according to the rules of his wisdom, to leave on creatures the mark of their dependence—assuring them none the less that he has not made them to destroy them, and that, being constant in his plans, they will exist eternally.

LIV

One can still raise the difficulty in this way. God necessarily follows the rules of his wisdom, he necessarily does that which is best. Now it was at least better that the world be created in time, than not to be at all; certainly it was appropriate, according to the rules of God's wisdom, that the world be produced in the circumstances according to which God produced it. Thus the creation of the world in time is absolutely necessary: God is not free with respect to it; he could not keep himself from producing it in time.

In order to resolve this difficulty one must take note that although God follows the rules which his wisdom prescribes to him, he does not necessarily do, none the less, that which is best: for being the master of his action, he can choose to do nothing. To act, and not to follow exactly the rules of wisdom, is a defect. Thus, supposing that God acts, he acts necessarily in the wisest way that can be conceived. But to be free in the production of the world is a sign of abundance, of plenitude, of self-sufficiency. It is better that the world be than that it not be, for the Incarnation of Jesus Christ makes the work of God worthy of its author. I agree. But since God is essentially happy and perfect, since he alone is good in his own sight, or the cause of his perfection and his happiness, he invincibly loves only his own substance; and everything which is outside of God must be produced by an action which is, in truth, eternal and immutable, but which draws its necessity only from the supposition of divine decrees.

LV

Here is yet another principle of which I have spoken, which may throw some light on the difficulties that can be raised concerning the circumstances of the Incarnation of Jesus Christ and of the creation of the world. Reason and the authority of Holy Scripture teach us that the first and the main plan of God is the establishment of his Church in Jesus Christ. The present world is not created to remain such as it is; lying and error, the injustices and the disorders which we see, make us understand well enough that it must end. The future world in which truth and justice will live, is that land which God has set on solid foundations, and which, being the object of divine love, will last eternally. God has only created this visible world in order to form, little by little, that invisible city of which St John teaches us so many marvels; and since Jesus Christ will be its principal beauty, God has always had Jesus Christ in view in the production of his work. He has done everything for man, and with respect to man, as Scripture teaches us: but this man, according to St Paul, for whom God has done everything, is Jesus Christ. This is to teach men that they are created, and subsist, only in Jesus Christ. It is to tie them strictly to Jesus Christ, it is to bring them to make themselves like unto Jesus Christ, that God has represented Jesus Christ and his Church in the most important of his creatures. For it is necessary that God find Jesus Christ in the whole of his work, in order that that work be the object of his love, and worthy of the action by which he produces it.

LVI

If one considers the way in which Holy Scripture tells us that the first man was created, how his wife was formed from his flesh and from his bones, his love for her, and the very circumstances of their sin, one will doubtless judge that God was thinking of the second Adam when he formed the first; that he was considering the father of future time in creating the father of the present world; and that of the first man and the first woman, he willed to make express prefiguring of Jesus Christ and of his Church. St Paul does not permit us to doubt of this truth, when he assures us that we are formed from the bones and the blood of Jesus Christ, that we are his members, and that the marriage of Adam and Eve is the representation of Jesus Christ and of his Church.

LVII

God could perhaps form men and animals by means as simple as ordinary generation. But since this way prefigured Jesus Christ and his Church; since it bore the character of the first of God's plans, as it represented, so to speak, the well-loved son of the father, this son in whom the whole work of the creation subsists, God had to prefer it to all the others—in order that we also learn, thereby, that just as intelligible beauties consist in the relation they have with eternal wisdom, so sensible beauties must (in a way which is scarcely known to us) have some relation to truth incarnate.

LVIII

There are no doubt many relations between the most important creatures and Jesus Christ—who is their model and their end. For everything is full of Jesus Christ, everything expresses and represents him, so far as the simplicity of the laws of nature may permit. But I would not dare to enter into detail on this point. For, besides the fact that I fear being mistaken, and that I am not sufficiently familiar with nature or with grace, with the present world or the future world, to discover their relations, I know that men's imagination is so scoffing and so delicate that one cannot, by reason, lead them to God, and still less to Jesus Christ, without tiring them, or without exciting their raillery! The majority of Christians are accustomed to a philosophy which prefers to have recourse to fictions as extravagant as those of the poets, than to have recourse to God; and there are some who know Jesus Christ so little, that one would pass for a visionary in their minds if, saying the same things as St Paul, one did not cite his words. For it is this great name which pulls them up, rather than a view of the truth. The authority of Scripture keeps them from blaspheming against that which they do not know; but, since they consult it very little, it cannot enlighten them very much.

LIX

It is certain that the Jewish people was the prefiguring of the Church, and that the holiest and most remarkable among the kings, the prophets, and the patriarchs of this people represented the true Messiah, our Lord Jesus Christ. One cannot deny this truth without sapping the foundations of the Christian religion, and without making the most learned of the Apostles pass for the most ignorant of men. Jesus Christ not yet being, he had at least to be prefigured. For he had to be waited for, he had to be desired, he had to diffuse, through his images, some kind of beauty in the universe to make it pleasing to his Father. Thus it was necessary that he be in some way as old as the world; it was was necessary that he die forthwith after sin in the person of Abel: *Agnus occisus ab origine mundi; principius et finis; Alpha et Omega; heri et nodi; est, erat, venturus est:*[4] these are the qualities which St John gives to the saviour of men.

LX

Now, supposing that Jesus Christ had to be prefigured, it was necessary that he be such principally by his ancestors, and that their history, dictated by the Holy Spirit, be preserved in all the ages, in order that one be able even at present, to compare Jesus Christ with his prefigurings, and recognize him as the true Messiah. Of all the nations of the earth, God loving most that which had the most connection with his son, the Jews had to be the fathers of Jesus Christ according to the flesh, since they had been the most lively and the express prefigurings of his son.

LXI

But if one pushes the difficulty to the point of asking for the reason for the choice that God made of the Jews, to be the principal prefigurings of Jesus Christ, I believe that I can and must assure first that, God always acting by the simplest means, and discovering in the infinite treasures of his wisdom all the combinations of nature with grace, he has chosen that which must render the Church the most ample, the most perfect, the most worthy of his greatness and of his holiness, as I have already said. In the second place I think that I must answer that God, foreseeing that everything which had to happen to the Jewish people by a necessary consequence of natural laws would have more relation to the plan that he had to prefigure

[4] Revelation 13: 8.

Jesus Christ, and his Church, than everything that was to happen to other nations, it was more appropriate that he choose this people than any other. For in the end predestination through the law is not like predestination through grace; and while there is nothing in nature that can oblige God to diffuse his grace equally over a whole people, it seems to me that nature can merit the law in the sense that I understand here.

LXII

It is true that everything which happened to the Jews, which prefigured Jesus Christ, was not a necessary consequence of the order of nature; miracles were necessary to make the Jews the living and express prefigurings of the Church. But nature at least furnished the basis and the material; perhaps it furnished the main traits in several situations; miracles did the rest. But no other nation would have been so suitable for so just and finished a plan.

LXIII

It seems to me that one is obligated to think that, God having a wisdom which foresees all the consequences of all the possible orders and of all their combinations, he never performs miracles, when nature is sufficient, and that he thus had to choose that combination of natural effects which, sparing him miracles (so to speak), none the less faithfully realizes his plans.

For example, it is necessary that all sin be punished; but it is not always in this world. Supposing, none the less, that it was appropriate for the glory of Jesus Christ and for the establishment of religion, that the Jews be punished before the whole world for the crime they had committed in putting the Saviour to death, it was appropriate that Jesus Christ come into the world at about the reign of Herod—supposing that according to the necessary outcome of the order of nature, this people had to be divided at about this time, that civil war and continual seditions had to enfeeble it, and that finally the Romans had to ruin it and dissipate it after the total destruction of their city and of their temple. It is true that it seems that there was something extraordinary in the desolation of the Jews. But since it is wiser of God to produce such surprising effects by the quite simple and quite general laws of nature than by particular wills, which are always miraculous, I do not know whether one ought on this occasion to have recourse to miracles; as for myself, I do not dispute it here. It is a point on which it is not easy, or even necessary, to be clear. I only give this example to make some application of my principles and to make them more easily comprehensible.

It seems to me that everything I have said up till now about nature and grace suffices to satisfy all equitable and moderate persons concerning an infinite number of difficulties which only trouble the minds of those who want to judge God by themselves. For if one faithfully consults the idea of the infinitely perfect Being, of a general cause, of an infinite wisdom, and if one agrees to the principles which I have established in conformity to this idea, I think that one will not be at all surprised or shocked by the conduct of God, and that, instead of condemning it or murmuring against it, one will not be able to keep oneself from admiring and adoring it.

Discourse III

On Grace
On the Way in Which It Acts in Us

First Part
On Liberty

I

There is nothing so unformed as the substance of minds, if one separates it from God; for what is a mind without intelligence and without reason, without movement and without love? However, it is the word and the wisdom of God which is the universal reason of all minds; and it is the love through which God loves himself which gives the soul its whole movement towards the good. The mind can only know the truth through a natural and necessary union with the truth itself; it can only be reasonable through reason; in the end it can only be (in one sense) mind and intelligence because its own substance is enlightened, penetrated, perfected by the light of God himself. I have explained these truths elsewhere. In the same way the substance of the soul is only capable of loving the good through the natural and necessary union of the sovereign good with eternal and substantial love: it advances towards the good only in so far as God transports it; it wills only through the movement which God ceaselessly impresses upon it; it loves only through charity, it wills only through the love of the good of which God makes it a part, though it abuses it. For finally, since God only makes and preserves minds for himself, he carries them towards himself as much as he conserves their being; he communicates the love of the good to them, so far as they are capable of receiving it. Now this natural and continual movement of the soul towards the good in general, towards indeterminate good, towards God, is what I here call *will*: because it is this movement which makes the substance of the soul capable of loving different goods.

II

This natural movement of the soul towards the good in general is invincible, for it does not depend on us to will to be happy. We love necessarily that which we know clearly and which we feel vividly to be the true good. All minds love God by the necessity of their nature, and if they love something other than God by the free choice of their will, it is not that they fail to seek after God, or the cause of their happiness; rather they deceive themselves. It is that, feeling confusedly that the bodies which surround them make them happy, they view them as goods, and by an ordinary and natural sequence they love them and unite with them.

III

But the love of all these particular goods is not at all naturally invincible. Man, considered such as God made him, can keep himself from loving the goods which do not fill up his whole capacity for loving. Since there is a good which encloses all the others, man can sacrifice to the love of this good all other loves: for God having made minds only for himself, he cannot bring them invincibly to love anything other than himself, and without relation to himself. In the end the inner feeling which we have of ourselves teaches us that we can reject a fruit, though we are inclined to take it. Now this power of loving or not loving particular goods, the *non-invincibility* which is met with in the movement which brings minds to love that which does not seem to them in every sense to enclose all goods— this power, this *non-invincibility*, is what I call *liberty*. Thus in putting the definition in place of the definandum, this expression, *our will is free*, signifies that the natural movement of the soul towards the good in general, is not invincible with respect to the good in particular. One frequently associates with the word 'free' the idea of voluntariness: but in what follows I shall use this word only

in the sense which I have just indicated, because it is the most
natural and the most ordinary.

IV

The word good is equivocal: it can signify either the pleasure which
makes one formally happy, or the cause of pleasure, real or apparent.
In this discourse I shall always take the word good in the second
sense; because pleasure indeed is impressed in the soul, in order that
it love the cause that makes it happy, in order that it transport itself
towards it through the motion of its love, and that it unite itself
strictly with it to be continually happy. When the soul loves only its
own pleasure, it in effect loves nothing distinct from itself; for
pleasure is only a condition or a modification of the soul which
renders it presently happy and contented. Now since the soul cannot
be, for itself, the cause of its happiness, it is unjust, it is ungrateful,
it is blind, if it loves its pleasure, without offering the love and the
respect which is due to the true cause which produces it in it. Since it
is only God who can act in the soul immediately and by himself, and
make it feel pleasure through the present efficacy of his all-powerful
will, it is only he who is truly good. None the less I call by the name
good, the creatures which are the apparent causes of the pleasures
which we feel on their occasioning them. For I do not want to
distance myself from the ordinary way of speaking, except in so far
as this is necessary to me to explain myself clearly. All the creatures,
though good in themselves or perfect with respect to the plans of
God, are not at all good with respect to us; they are not our good,
they are not at all the true cause of our pleasure or of our happiness.

V

The natural movement which God imprints ceaselessly in the soul to
bring it to love him, or (to employ a term which abridges several
ideas and which need not be equivocal or confused after the
definition of it which I have just given) the *will* is determined
towards particular goods, either by clear and evident knowledge, or
by a confused feeling which shows us these goods. If the mind does
not see or taste some particular good, the movement of the soul
remains indeterminate; it tends towards the good in general. But this

movement receives a particular determination as soon as the mind has the idea or the feeling of some particular good. For the soul being incessantly pushed towards indeterminate good, it must move as soon as the good appears to it.

VI

Now when the good which is presented to the mind and to the senses does not fill up these two faculties, when it is recognized under the idea of a particular good, of a good which does not enclose all goods at all, and when it is relished through a feeling which does not fill up the whole capacity of the soul, it can still desire the sight and the enjoyment of some other good: it can suspend the judgement of its love; it can refrain from resting in present enjoyment; it can, through its desires, seek out some new object. And since its desires are the occasional causes of its enlightenment, it can—through the natural and necessary union of all minds with him who encloses all the ideas of all goods—discover the true good, and in the true good many other particular goods different from that which it saw and relished before. Thus having some knowledge of the emptiness and the vanity of sensible goods, paying attention to the secret reproaches of reason, to the regrets of conscience, to the complaints and the threats of the true good—which will not have it that one sacrifice it to apparent and imaginary goods—it can, through the movement which God imprints ceaselessly in it to carry it towards good in general, towards the sovereign good, that is to say towards him, halt its course towards any good that may be. It can resist sensible attractions, seek out and find other objects, compare them with each other, and with the ineffaceable idea of the sovereign good, and love none of them through a determined love. And if this sovereign good is relished a little, it can prefer it to particular goods—though the sweetness which they seem to diffuse in the soul be quite strong and quite pleasant. These truths need to be explained at greater length.

VII

The soul is pushed ceaselessly towards the good in general: it desires to possess all goods; it never wants to limit its love; there is no good which seems to it such that it refuses to love it. Thus when it actually enjoys a particular good, it still has a tendency to go farther: it still desires something else through the natural and invincible impulsion which God puts in it; and in order to change its love or to share it, it suffices to present another good to it than that which it enjoys, and to make it feel the sweetness of it. Now the soul can ordinarily seek and discover new goods. It can even approach and enjoy them. For finally its desires are natural or occasional causes of its objects of knowledge; objects reveal themselves to it and come near to it in proportion as it wishes to know them. An ambitious person who considers the brilliance of some dignity can also think of the servitude, of the constraints of the real evils that accompany human greatness. It can take account of everything, weigh everything, compare everything, if passion does not blind it. For I grant that there are moments in which passion completely deprives the mind of its liberty; and it always diminishes it. Thus, since a dignity (however great it may seem) does not pass in the mind of a man who is perfectly free and perfectly reasonable, for universal and infinite good, and since the will extends itself generally to all goods, this perfectly free and perfectly reasonable man can seek and find other ones, because he can desire them—for it is his desires that reveal and present themselves to him. He can afterwards examine them, and compare them with the ones which he enjoys. But because he can meet only with particular goods on earth, he can and must, here below, examine and seek ceaselessly without resting. Or rather, in order that he not undertake change at every moment, he should generally neglect all those goods which pass away and desire only immutable and eternal goods.

VIII

However, since men want not to seek but to enjoy, since the effort of examination is now very painful, and repose and enjoyment are always very pleasant, the soul ordinarily rests as soon as it has found some good: it stops at it to enjoy it; it deceives itself because, in deceiving itself and in judging that it has found what it is seeking, its desire turns into pleasure, and pleasure makes it happier than desire. But its happiness cannot last very long. Its pleasure being ill-founded, unjust, deceptive, it troubles and disquiets it forthwith, because it wills to be truly and solidly happy. Thus natural love of the good awakens it, and produces new desires in it. These confused desires represent new objects. Since it loves pleasure, it runs after those which diffuse it, or which seem to diffuse it; and since it loves repose, it stops with them. It does not first examine at all the defects of the present good, when prepossessed with its sweetness; rather it considers it on its best side; it attaches itself to that which charms it; it thinks only of enjoying it. But the more it enjoys it, the more it loves it, the more it draws near to it, the more it considers it. Now the more it considers it, the more it discovers defects in it: and since it always wants to be truly happy, it cannot deceive itself forever. When it is thirsty, famished, weary with seeking, it becomes drunk and filled with the first good that it meets with; but it soon becomes disgusted with a nourishment which man is not made for. Thus love of the true good still excites in it new desires for new goods. And ceaselessly undertaking change, all its life and all its happiness on earth consists only in a continual revolution of thoughts, of desires, of pleasures. Such is a soul which makes no use of its liberty, which lets itself be led aimlessly by the motion which transports it, and by the fortuitous meeting with objects which determine it. But this condition is that of a man who has so weak a mind that he takes the false for the true at every moment, and who has so corrupted a heart that he sells himself and delivers himself blindly to whatever touches him, to the good which makes him actually feel the sweetest and most agreeable pleasures.

IX

But a man who is perfectly free, such as we conceive Adam immediately after his creation, knows perfectly that it is only God who is his good, or the true cause of the pleasures which he enjoys. Although he feels sweetness at the approach of the bodies which surround him, he does not love them; he loves only God, and if God forbids him to unite with bodies, he is ready to abandon them, whatever pleasure he finds in them. He wants to stop only with the enjoyment of the sovereign good: he wills to sacrifice all others to it; and whatever desire he may have to be happy or to enjoy pleasures, no pleasure is stronger than his enlightenment. It is not that pleasures may not blind him, trouble his reason, and fill up his capacity for thought: for, the mind being finite, all pleasure is capable of dividing and distracting it. Rather it is the case that, pleasures being subjected to his volitions, he does not let himself be intoxicated by them. Because the sole invincible pleasure is that of the blessed, or that which the first man would have found in God, if God had willed to anticipate and prevent his fall: not only because this pleasure fills up all the faculties of the soul, without troubling reason, or bringing it to the love of a false good, but also because nothing is opposed to the enjoyment of this pleasure—neither the desire for perfection nor that for felicity. For when one loves God, one is perfect; when one enjoys him, one is happy; and when one loves him with pleasure, one is happy and perfect all at once. Thus the most perfect liberty is that of minds which can at every moment surmount the greatest pleasures: it is that of minds in respect to which no movement towards particular goods is ever invincible; it is that of man before sin, before concupiscence troubled his spirit and corrupted his heart. And the most imperfect liberty is that of a mind with respect to which every movement towards a particular good, however small it seems, is invincible in all kinds of circumstances.

X

Now between these two kinds of liberty there are more and less perfect sorts, to an infinity of degrees; this is what is not sufficiently taken note of. It is ordinarily imagined that liberty is equal in all men, and that it is a faculty which is essential to minds, the nature of which always remains the same, though its action varies according to different objects. For men suppose, without reflection, a perfect equality in all those things in which they do not sensibly notice any inequality. Men indulge their mind, and deliver it from all effort, when they give all things an abstract form, whose essence consists in a kind of indivisibility. But men are deceived; liberty is not at all a faculty such as is imagined. There are not two persons equally free with respect to the same objects. Children are less so than men, who have the entire use of their reason; and there are not even two men whose reason is equally enlightened, equally firm and assured with respect to the same objects. Those who have violent passions, and who are not accustomed to resisting them at all, are less free than those who have generously combated them, and who are naturally moderate; and there are not two men equally moderate, equally sensitive to the same objects, and who have equally fought for the preservation of their liberty. There are even persons so sold into sin that they resist it less, and think less of resisting it, when they are awake, than men of good will when they are asleep—because according to the word of truth, he who sins becomes the slave of it: *qui facit peccatum servus est peccati.*

XI

It is true that according to the institution of nature, all men are equally free; for God does not invincibly push minds to love any particular good whatever. But concupiscence corrupts the heart and the reason; and man having lost the power to efface the marks of sensible pleasures and to arrest the movements of concupiscence, this liberty, equal in all men if they had not sinned, has become unequal according to the differing degrees of their enlightenment, and according as concupiscence acts differently in them. For concupiscence itself, which is equal in all men, in that they have all lost the power which they had over their bodies, is unequal in a thousand ways because of the differences which are met with in the structure of the body, in the abundance and motion of minds, and in the relations and the liaisons, almost infinite, which are set up in the dealings of the world.

XII

To understand still more distinctly the inequality which is met with in the liberty of different persons, one must take note that every man who is perfectly reasonable, perfectly free, and who wants to be truly happy, can and must in the presence of any object whatsoever which makes him feel pleasure, suspend his love, and examine with care whether this object is the true good, or whether the movement which bears him towards this object agrees exactly with that which carries him towards the true good. Otherwise he would love by instinct and not by reason; and if he could not suspend the judgement of his love before an examination, he would not be perfectly free. If he recognized clearly that this object which makes him feel pleasure is truly good with respect to him; and if this obviousness, joined with feeling, is such that he can no longer suspend his judgement, though then perfectly free, he is no longer so with respect to this good—he loves it invincibly, because pleasure is in accord with enlightenment. But since it is only God who can act in us or who is our good, since the movement which carries us towards creatures does not accord with that which carries us towards God, every perfectly reasonable man, as perfectly free, can and must keep himself from judging that sensible objects are goods. He can and must suspend the judgement which governs, or which ought to govern, his love; for he can never see obviously that sensible goods are true goods, since one can never see obviously what does not exist.

XIII

This power of suspending the judgement which actually governs love, this power which is the principle of our liberty, and through which pleasures are not always invincible, is very diminished since the advent of sin, though it is not annihilated. And in order to actually have this power, during the time that an object tempts us, it is necessary, in addition to some love of order, to have presence of mind, or to be sensitive to the regrets of conscience—for a child, or a man asleep, does not actually have this power at all. But all men are not equally enlightened; the mind of sinners is filled with shadows. All consciences are not equally tender; the heart of sinners is hardened. The love of order, and actual graces, are unequal in all men. Thus all men are not equally free: they do not all have an equal power to suspend their judgement; pleasure determines and carries away some sooner than others. There is one who can suspend his judgement or stop his consent, when a present object makes him feel a very lively and very sensible pleasure; and another person has so small a mind and so corrupted a heart that, with respect to him, the slightest pleasure is invincible, and the slightest evil intolerable. Since he does not have the habit of fighting against sensible attractions, he is so disposed that he does not even think of resisting them. Thus he does not then have the power of suspending his consent, since he does not even have the power to reflect upon it; in respect to this object he resembles a man who is asleep or who has lost his mind.

XIV

The more the reason is weakened, the more the soul becomes sense-governed, and judges promptly and falsely concerning sensible goods and evils. When a man is dozing, if a leaf pricks him or even tickles him, he wakes up with a start, frightened, as if a snake had bitten him. He perceives this small evil, and judges it, as if it were among the greatest evils; it seems intolerable to him. His reason being weakened by dozing, he cannot suspend his judgement; the smallest goods and the smallest evils are almost always invincible with respect to him. It is the senses which act in him, and the senses judge promptly; that must be so for many reasons. When the reason is less enfeebled, small pleasures are not invincible, nor small evils intolerable; one does not always go where one finds the most pleasure. For there are pleasures so small that they are contemptible to the reason, which always has some love of order. One is not so greatly frightened by the presence of small evils: one resolves, for example, to be bled, and one endures it, one does not judge so promptly, one examines; and the stronger the reason is, the more it can suspend its consent despite sensible attractions and frights. Now there is nothing more certain than that, although all men share in the same reason, they do not share equally, and that all are not equally sensible, at least with respect to the same objects; that they are not equally well-born, equally well-raised, equally helped by the grace of Jesus Christ, and that thus they are not all equally free, or capable of suspending the judgement of their love with respect to the same objects.

XV

Now one must take notice that the principal duty of minds is to preserve and to augment their liberty; because it is through the good use they can make of it that they can merit their happiness, if they are aided by the grace of Jesus Christ, and diminish at least their unhappiness if they are left to themselves. What weakens our liberty, or what makes most pleasures invincible with respect to us, is that the light of our reason is obscured, and that we have lost the power that we ought to have over our body. One must, then, educate one's reason through continual meditations; one must consider one's duties in order to fulfil them, and one's weaknesses in order to have recourse to him who is our whole power. And since we have lost the power to block the impressions which are made on the body by the presence of objects, which finally corrupt the mind and the heart, we ought to flee those objects; we ought to make use of the power that remains to us. We must be ceaselessly watchful of the purity of our imagination, and even work with all our powers to efface the marks which false goods impress there—since these marks excite in us desires which divide our mind and diminish our liberty. It is in this way that a man whose liberty is almost annihilated, with respect to whom pleasures, however small they may be, are invincible, can acquire such a power and liberty that he will yield nothing to greater souls—other helps being supposed equal. For, at least during the time that these pleasures do not solicit him to do evil, he can seek to avoid them: he can fortify himself through some reason which is capable of counterbalancing through future pleasures, the pleasures which he is not enjoying presently at all. For, since there is no one who does not have some love of order, there is no man who cannot vanquish a weak and slight pleasure through a strong and solid reason. Finally there is no one who, at least through the ordinary aid of grace, cannot vanquish certain pleasures, or avoid the others. Now these pleasures, earlier invincible or much sought after, being vanquished or avoided, one can prepare oneself to combat others, at least before they tempt. For the sweetness which one tastes after the victory, animates one to fight: the joy of good conscience and the grace of Jesus Christ give courage; and the fear of defeat is not useless, since it makes us fly to him through whom one can do everything—it makes one wisely avoid dangerous occasions. Thus one always gains through this exercise; for if one finally succumbs one thereby becomes more humble, more wise, more circumspect, and sometimes one is even more ardent in combat, and in a better condition to win or to resist.

XVI

As in the study of the sciences, those who do not submit themselves to the false glimmerings of appearances, and who accustom themselves to suspend their judgement until the light of reason appears, rarely fall into error, by contrast the majority of men are deceived at every moment by their hasty judgements. In the same way, in the governance of morals, those who accustom themselves to sacrificing their pleasures to the love of order and who ceaselessly mortify their senses and their passions—principally in those things which seem to be of least consequence, which everyone can do—will acquire (even in important matters) a great deal of facility in suspending the judgement which governs their love. Pleasure does not surprise them, like other men, or at least does not drag them along without their thinking about it. It seems, on the contrary, that in making them feel, it warns them to be wary of themselves, and to consult reason or the rules of the gospel. They have a conscience which is more tender and more delicate than those who, according to the language of Scripture, drink sin like water; they are mindful of the secret reproaches of reason, and of the salutary warnings of the truth within—such that the habit that one forms of resisting weak and light pleasures furnishes an opening for vanquishing the stronger ones, or at least of enduring some pain and some shame when one is defeated, which soon brings about disgust and horror. Liberty thus increasing little by little, and being perfected by the use made of it, and by the help of grace, one can finally put onself in a condition to fulfil even the most difficult commandments: because through ordinary graces which are diffused at every moment in Christians, one can overcome temptations, one can ordinarily avoid the greater ones; and by the help of the grace of Jesus Christ there is none that one cannot vanquish.

XVII

It is true that when a sinner is so disposed that a pleasure overtakes him, he is not only not in a condition to think of resisting it, it is true (I say) that this sinner can actually no longer fulfil the commandment which ordains that he not enjoy it: for this pleasure is invincible with respect to him. Also, supposing that person is in this state of impotence through a natural necessity, his sin not being free at all, he would not make himself more culpable—I mean worthier of being punished by pain—than if he were disordered during sleep. If this impotency were even a necessary consequence of free disorders which preceded his conversion, it would not be imputed to him, by reason of his charity. But having had to, and having been able to, accustom himself to resist pleasure, to fight for the preservation and for the augmentation of his liberty, even a sin committed by a kind of necessity makes him culpable and worthy of being punished; if it is not because of this sin, it is at least because of the negligence which is at the root of it. The commandment of God is not absolutely impossible at all; the sinner himself must and can, for the reasons I have just stated, put himself in a state to observe it. For men must and can work ceaselessly to augment and perfect their liberty—not only through the aid of the grace of Jesus Christ, but even through their natural powers, or by ordinary graces; for finally one can make nature serve grace in a thousand connections.

Second Part
On Grace

XVIII

The inequality which is met with in the liberty of different persons being clearly conceived, it will not be, it seems to me, too difficult to understand how grace acts in us—if one attaches to the word grace ideas which are distinct and particular, and if one takes note of the difference which there is between the grace of the Creator and the grace of the Redeemer. I have already said, in the preceding discourse, that there is this difference between enlightenment and pleasure: that enlightenment leaves us entirely to ourselves, and that pleasure makes efforts against our liberty. For light is outside us; it does not touch or modify our soul at all; it does not push us towards the objects which it reveals, it only brings us to bring ourselves to the place where we consent freely and by reason to the impulsion that God gives us towards the good. Knowledge of our duty, the clear idea of order separated from all feeling, a view of the good which is dry, abstract, quite pure, and quite intelligible—that is to say without taste, or foretaste—leaves the soul in a state of perfect liberty. But pleasure is in the soul: it touches it, and modifies it. Thus it diminishes our liberty, it makes us love the good through a love of instinct and of being carried away rather than through a love of choice and of reason. It transports us, as it were, towards sensible objects. It is not the case, none the less, that pleasure is the same thing as love or the movement of the soul towards the good; rather it causes it, or determines it towards the object which makes us happy. Since one can only demonstrate truths of which one has clear ideas, and since we have none about what goes on within us, it is not possible for me to demonstrate what I maintain as one demonstrates the consequences which depend on common notions. It is necessary then that each consult the internal feeling that he has of what happens within himself, if he wants to convince himself of the difference that subsists between enlightenment and pleasure, and that he observe with care that ordinarily enlightenment is accompanied by pleasure—from which none the less it must separate itself in order to judge it soundly. I will not explain this further here.

XIX

If, then, it is true that pleasure naturally produces love, and that it is like a weight which makes the soul incline towards the good which causes it, it is clear that the grace of Jesus Christ, or the grace of feeling, is efficacious by itself. For while preventive delectation, when it is weak, does not entirely convert the heart of those who have passions which are too lively, none the less it always has its effect, inasmuch as it always inclines them towards God. It is always efficacious in some way; but it does not always produce the whole effect which it could cause, because concupiscence opposes it.

XX

For example: there is, in one of the bowls of a scale, a weight of ten pounds. One places in the other bowl a weight of only six pounds. This second weight will truly weigh something: for if one added as much again, or if one took enough out of the other bowl, or if finally one suspended the scale closer to the bowl which is the more weighted, this weight of six pounds would tip the scale. But while this weight truly weighs, it is clear that its effect always depends on the weights which resist it. Thus the grace of feeling is always efficacious by itself: it always diminishes the effect of concupiscence, because pleasure naturally brings about love for the cause which produces it, or which seems to produce it. But although this grace is always efficacious by itself, it depends, or rather the effect depends, on the actual dispositions of him to whom it is given. The weight of concupiscence resists it: and sensible pleasures, which draw us to the creatures that seem to produce it in us, hinder the pleasures of grace from uniting us strictly to him who alone is capable of acting in us and of making us happy.

XXI

But the case is not the same with respect to the grace of enlightenment or the grace of the Creator: it is not at all efficacious by itself; it does not transport the soul; it gives it no movement at all; it leaves it perfectly to itself. But although it is not at all efficacious by itself, it does not fail to be followed by many effects, when it is great, and animated by some grace of feeling which gives it life and power, or again when it comes against no opposing pleasure which greatly resists it. There is the difference which exists between the grace of the Creator and the grace of the Redeemer, between enlightenment and pleasure, between the grace which does not presuppose concupiscence at all, and the grace which is given to us to counterbalance the pleasures and concupiscence. The one is sufficient to the man who is perfectly true, and fortified by charity; the other is efficacious in the weak man for whom pleasure is necessary to be attracted to the love of the true good.

XXII

But the power and the efficacy of grace must always be compared with the action of concupiscence, with the light of reason, and above all with the degree of freedom of the person to whom it is given. And one must not imagine that God diffuses it by particular wills, with the design that it produce in us certain effects, and nothing more. For when one says that grace always produces in the heart the effect for which God has given it, one is mistaken, if one supposes that God acts like men, through particular views. God distributes his grace with the general desire that it sanctify all those who receive it. He sees well enough, however, that it will not have, in certain persons, the whole effect which it will have in others, not only because of inequality of power on the side of grace, but also because of the inequality of resistance on the side of concupiscence.

XXIII

Since concupiscence has not entirely destroyed liberty in man, the grace of Jesus Christ, however efficacious it may be, is not absolutely invincible. One can defeat a sensible pleasure when it is weak: one can suspend the judgement of one's love, when one is not carried along by some passion which is too violent; and when one succumbs to the allure of this false pleasure, one is guilty because of the bad use of one's liberty. In the same way the delectation of grace is not ordinarily invincible. One can fail to follow the good feelings which it inspires—which distance us from the false goods which we love. This grace does not fill up the soul in such a way that it carries it towards the true good without choice, without discernment, without free consent. Thus when one abandons oneself to one's feeling, and when one advances, so to speak, farther than it invincibly pushes us; when one sacrifices the pleasure of concupiscence which diminishes its efficacy, one is meritorious through the good use one makes of one's liberty.

XXIV

It is true that the delectation of grace, considered in itself and without relation to the pleasures of concupiscence which are contrary to it, is always invincible. Because, this holy pleasure being conformed to the light of reason, nothing can stop its effect in a perfectly free man. When the mind sees clearly by the light of reason that God is its good, and when it feels it vividly by the taste of pleasure, it is not possible for it to keep itself from loving it. For the mind wants to be happy, and nothing then keeps it from following the pleasant feelings of its love; it suffers no remorse which opposes its present happiness; and it is not held back by pleasures contrary to that which it enjoys. The delectation of grace is thus invincible. Also the love which it produces is not at all meritorious, if it is not greater than it. I mean that the love which is only the purely natural or necessary effect of the delectation of grace, contains nothing meritorious, though this love is good in itself. For when one advances only as far as one is pushed, or rather when one advances only in so far as one is paid in hand, one has no right to rewards. When one loves God only in so far as one is drawn to him, or because one is drawn, one does not love him at all through reason, but by instinct; one does not love him on earth as he wants and as he ought to be loved. But one merits, when one loves God by choice, by reason, by the knowledge one has that he is lovable. One merits when one advances, so to speak, towards the good, after pleasure has determined the movement of love.

XXV

This reason alone demonstrates either that the first man was not brought to the love of God through the blind instinct of pleasure, or at least that this pleasure was not so lively as that which he felt at the sight of his natural perfections, or in the actual use of sensible goods. For it is evident that this pleasure would have made him impeccable. This pleasure would have put him in a state like that of the blessed— who no longer merit, but not because they are no longer in a wayfaring state. For one always merits in proportion as one does actions which are meritorious in themselves; and God being just, it is necessary that one be rewarded for them. But they no longer merit, because the pleasure which they find in God is equal to their love, because they are thoroughly imbued with it, and because being freed from all sorts of pain and from every movement of concupiscence, they no longer have anything to sacrifice to God.

XXVI

For that which makes us impeccable is not precisely that which makes us incapable of meriting. Jesus Christ was impeccable, and none the less he merited his glory, and that of the Church of which he is the head. Since he was perfectly free, he loved his Father, not through the instinct of pleasure, but by choice and by reason; he loved because he saw intuitively how lovable he was. For the most perfect liberty is that of a mind which has all possible enlightenment, and which is not determined by the slightest pleasure, because all pleasure, preventing or otherwise, naturally produces some love; and if one does not resist pleasure, it efficaciously determines the natural movement of the soul towards the pleasing object. But enlightenment, however great one conceives it, leaves the mind perfectly free—supposing that this enlightenment is considered alone and without any pleasure.

XXVII

Since Jesus Christ is nothing else than the Word or reason incarnate, certainly he ought not to love the good by a blind love, by a love of instinct, by a love of feeling; he ought to love it through reason. He ought not to love an infinitely lovable good, and which he knows to be perfectly worthy of his love, as one loves goods which are not lovable at all, and which cannot be known as worthy of love; he ought not to love his Father by a love in any respect like that by which one loves the vilest of creatures, whose bodies one loves. His love, in order to be pure, or at least in order to be perfectly meritorious, ought not at all to be produced by preventive pleasures. For pleasure can and must be the reward of a legitimate love, as indeed it is now among the saints, and in Jesus Christ himself. But it cannot be the principle of merit; it ought not to precede reason, if it is not weakened. Now reason in Jesus Christ was not weakened in the slightest; sovereign reason sustained created reason. Jesus Christ not being subject to the motions of concupiscence, he had no need of preventive delectation, to counterbalance the sensible pleasures which overtake us. It may even be that he willed not to taste the pleasure of joy, or the pleasure which naturally followed from the knowledge he had of his virtue or of his perfections, in order that his sacrifice might be more holy, more pure, and more disinterested. Finally it may be that, besides the privation of all these pleasures, preventing and otherwise, he suffered within himself from terrifying droughts, which souls filled with charity cannot express better than as being abandoned by God—according to these words of Jesus Christ on the cross, *My God, my God, why have you abandoned me.* But if one will absolutely have it that Jesus Christ was pushed by pleasures, even preventing ones, to love his Father, it is necessary to say, according to the principles which I have just established, either that he loved him with more ardour than felt pleasure, since the natural love which produces the instinct of pleasure is not at all meritorious; or at least one must say that he merited through sensible pains, through the continual sacrifice which he freely and voluntarily offered to God. For it was necessary that he suffer in order to enter into possession of his glory, as Scripture teaches us.

XXVIII

If the delectation of grace, without relation to any contrary pleasure, infallibly carries along the consent of the will, the case is not the same with the pleasure of concupiscence. These pleasures considered in themselves and without any relation to other actual pleasures are not always invincible. The light of reason condemns these pleasures: the regrets of conscience give one a horror of them; one can ordinarily suspend one's consent. Thus the grace of Jesus Christ is stronger than concupiscence. One can call it victorious grace, because it is always the mistress of the heart, when it is equal to that of concupiscence. For when the balance of our heart is perfectly in equilibrium through the equal weights of contrary pleasures, the pleasure which is the most solid and the most reasonable always carries the day, because light favours its efficacy, and because the regrets of conscience are opposed to the action of false pleasure.

XXIX

One must conclude from weighing everything I have just said, that one always merits when one loves the true good through reason; and that one merits not at all when one only loves it through instinct. One always merits when one loves the true good through reason, because order will have it that the true good be loved in that way, and that enlightenment all alone does not transport us at all, when one only loves the true good through instinct, or in so far as pleasure transports or invincibly determines the mind—because order will have it that the true good, or the good of the mind, be loved by reason, be loved by a free love, by a love of choice and of discernment, and that the love which pleasure alone produces is a blind love which is natural and necessary. I grant that when one goes farther than one is pushed by pleasure, one merits. But in this one acts by reason, and in the way that order wills that one act—for that part of love which exceeds pleasure is a pure and reasonable love.

XXX

In the same way one must conclude that one always demerits, when one loves a false good by the instinct of pleasure—provided none the less that one does not love the false good more than one is invincibly brought to love it. For when one naturally has so little liberty and mental capacity that pleasure transports us in an invincible way, then—though one is ungoverned and one's love is bad and against order—one does not demerit at all. In order to demerit, I mean to merit being punished, one must run after false goods with more ardour or go farther than pleasure invincibly carries us. For it must be observed that there is a good deal of difference between a good action, and a meritorious action, between a disordered action and a demeritorious one. The love of the blessed is good, and it is not meritorious; the love of a just person is often disordered in sleep, and it is not at all demeritorious. All that is in conformity to order is good, and everything that is contrary to it is bad; but there is nothing meritorious or demeritorious except the good or bad use of freedom, save in that in which we are the factors. Now one makes a good use of one's liberty when one follows one's light—when one advances, so to speak, freely and by oneself, towards the true good, whether one has been previously determined to it by preventive delectation or by the light of reason; when one sacrifices sensible pleasures to one's duty, and surmounts pain through the love of order. By contrast one makes a bad use of one's liberty when one makes pleasure one's reason; when one sacrifices one's duty to one's passions, one's perfection to one's present happiness, the love of order to the love of self—and when one does all of this at a time in which one can truly keep oneself from doing it. I shall explain all of this more clearly.

XXXI

When two objects are presented to the human mind, and it determines itself with respect to them, I grant that it never fails to determine itself on that side wherein it finds the most reason and pleasure—on that side wherein, everything considered, it finds the most good. For the soul not being able to will or to love except through love of the good, since its will is only love of the good, and the natural movement of the soul towards the good, it loves infallibly that which is most in conformity to that which it loves invincibly. But it is certain that when sensible pleasures, or something of the sort, do not trouble the mind, one can always suspend the judgement of one's love and not determine oneself principally with respect to false goods. For the soul can have no evidence that false goods are true goods, nor that the love of these false goods is in perfect accord with the motion which carries us towards the true good. Thus when a man loves false goods at the time when his senses and his passions do not wholly trouble his reason, he demerits: because in this case he can and should suspend the judgement of his love. For if he suspends it for a while in order to consider what he must soon do, the false good would appear very nearly such as it is, the pleasure which it seems to diffuse in the soul would vanish, the idea of some other good would be presented to his mind, the regrets of conscience and perhaps even the delectation of grace would change all the dispositions of his mind and of his heart. For the state of a traveller has nothing fixed: a thousand different objects present themselves ceaselessly to his mind; and the life of men on earth is only a continual sequence of thoughts and of desires.

XXXII

At first sight it seems that with respect to the true good one cannot suspend the judgement of one's love. For one can only suspend one's judgement when the evidence is not complete. Now one can see with perfect evidence that God is the true good, and even that it is only he who can be good with respect to us; one knows that he is infinitely more lovable than we are able to conceive. But one must take note that although one can no longer suspend the judgement of one's reason with respect to speculative truths, when the evidence is complete, one can still suspend the judgement of one's love with respect to goods, whatever evidence there may be in our ideas. For when feeling combats reason, when taste opposes light, when one finds sensibly bitter and disagreeable that which reason represents to us clearly as sweet and pleasant, one can suspend judgement in order to choose whether one will follow one's reason or one's senses. One can act, and often one acts against one's light: because when one pays attention to feeling the light goes out, if one makes no effort to hold on to it; because one pays more attention to feeling than to enlightenment, because feeling is always more lively and more pleasant than the most evident light.

XXXIII

It is pleasure which actually makes minds happy. Thus one ought to enjoy pleasure, when one loves the true good. A mind thinks of God; it approaches him through its love, and tastes no sweetness. On the contrary God sometimes fills it with bitterness and dryness: he abandons it, he repulses it, as it were, not in order that it cease to love him, but in order that its love be more humble, more pure, and more meritorious; finally he orders it to endure certain things which make it actually unhappy; but if it draws near to bodies it finds that it becomes happy in proportion as it unites itself to them. Certainly this is perplexing, whatever enlightenment one may have—for one invincibly wills to be happy. Thus one greatly merits if, following one's light, one renounces oneself, notwithstanding the droughts which desolate us; if one sacrifices one's actual happiness to love of the true good; if living by faith and relying on the promises of God, one remains inviolately attached to one's duty. Thus one sees well that Jesus Christ was able to merit his glory, although he knew the true good with the greatest evidence: because, having a great love for his Father, he completely submitted himself to his orders, without being carried along by preventive pleasures; because, staying with his light, he suffered great pains, and sacrificed to his charity all the liveliest and most sensible pleasures. For he took a body, like us, in order to have a victim that he could offer to God, and in order that, receiving ceaselessly through his body as occasional or natural cause a great number of different feelings, he could consume himself in a holocaust, in honour of the true good, through the suffering of pain and through the privation of sensible pleasures.

XXXIV

In order not to leave in some people an imperfect idea of the grace of Jesus Christ, I think that I still ought to say that it does not consist in delectation all by itself; for all grace of feeling is the grace of Jesus Christ. Now of this kind of grace there are several species, and of each species there is an infinity of degrees. God sometimes diffuses distaste and bitterness over the objects of our passions; he weakens their sensible attractions, or gives us a horror of them. And this species of the grace of feeling produces the same effect as preventive delectation. It re-establishes and fortifies our liberty: it puts us back nearly in equilibrium, and by this means we are in a condition to follow our light in the movement of our love. For to restore a balance to perfect equilibrium, or to change the way it inclines, it is not necessary to augment the weights which are too weak—it suffices to take away those which weigh too much. Thus there are graces of feeling of several species; and even each species is capable of an infinity of degrees, for there are greater and smaller pleasures, horrors, distastes to the point of infinity. What I have said up till now about delectation is easily applied to the other species of the grace of feeling. I have merely taken pleasure or delectation as a particular example in order to explain myself clearly and without equivocation.

If there is some other principle of our self-determination towards the good, except the grace of feeling and that of enlightenment, I grant that it is entirely unknown to me, and it is for that reason that I have not wished to explain the effects of grace which are necessary to the conversion of the heart except by these two principles, for fear that I be accused of speaking in general terms which in themselves awaken only confused ideas—something I avoid with all possible care. But, although I have explained myself in terms that everyone understands well, since there is no one who does not know that knowledge and a feeling of the good are the principles of our self-determination, I do not claim, however, to combat those who, not arriving at these clear ideas, say in general that God brings about conversion in souls through a particular action, different perhaps from everything I have said here and elsewhere concerning what God does in us. Since I experience in myself only movement towards the good in general, and the light or feeling which determine this movement, I must not suppose anything else—if by this alone I can give an account of all that Scripture and the Councils have defined on the subject which I treat. In a word I can strongly assume that light and feeling are the principles of our self-determination. But I declare that I do not know if there is any other whatsoever, of which I have not the slightest knowledge.

XXXV

Besides the grace which is efficacious by itself, and the grace whose effect depends entirely on the good dispositions of the mind, besides the grace of feeling and the grace of light, the just also have the habitual grace which makes them pleasing to God, and puts them in a condition to perform actions which merit salvation. This grace is charity, the love of God, or the love of order—a love which is never truly charity at all if it is not stronger and greater than all other loves. Since it is ordinarily pleasure which produces love of the object which causes it or which seems to cause it, it is the delectation of grace which produces the love of God. It is the enjoyment of sensible pleasures which augments concupiscence; it is also the grace of feeling which augments charity. Concupiscence diminishes through the privation of sensible pleasures, and thus charity preserves and augments itself easily. Charity diminishes also through the privation of the actual grace of Jesus Christ; and concupiscence increases and strengthens itself promptly. For these two loves, charity and cupidity, ceaselessly fight with one another, and grow stronger through the weakness of their enemy.

XXXVI

Whatever partakes of charity is pleasing to God, but charity does not always operate in the just themselves. In order that it act it must at least be enlightened; for light is necessary to determine the movement of love. Thus the grace necessary to every good work which has a relation to salvation, is the grace of feeling in those who are beginning their conversion; it is at least the grace of light, it is some movement of faith or of hope in those who are animated by charity. For though the just may do good works without the grace of delectation, they always have need of some actual help in order to determine the movement of their charity. But although charity without delectation suffices to vanquish many temptations, none the less the grace of feeling is necessary on many occasions. For men cannot, without the continual help of the Second Adam, resist the continual action of the first one; they cannot persevere in justice, if they are not often aided by the particular grace of Jesus Christ, which produces, augments, and sustains charity against the continual effects of concupiscence.

XXXVII

The effects of pleasure and of all the feelings of the soul depend in a thousand ways on the actual dispositions of the mind. The same weight does not always produce the same effects: it depends, in its action, on the construction of the machine by which it is applied to the contrary weight. If a balance is unequally suspended, the force of the weights being unequally applied, the lighter ones may overweigh the heavier. It is the same with the weights of pleasure; they act upon each other, and determine the movement of the soul according as they are differently applied. Pleasure must have more of an effect in a person who already feels love for the object which causes this pleasure, than in a person who will feel aversion to it, or who loves opposing goods. Pleasure strongly determines a person who knows clearly or who vividly imagines the advantages of the good which seems to produce it; and it acts weakly on the mind of him who knows this good only confusedly, and is distrustful of it. Finally pleasure acts with full force in him who blindly follows everything that flatters concupiscence; and it will perhaps produce no effect in him who has formed the habit of suspending the judgement of his love.

Now these different degrees of enlightenment, of charity, of concupiscence, the different degrees of liberty combine at every moment in an infinity of ways with the different degrees of actual pleasures; and these pleasures not having their effect except through the relation that they have with the disposition of the mind and of the heart, it is obvious that no finite mind can judge with any certainty concerning the effect which a particular grace must produce in us. For besides the fact that the combination of all that which combines to make it efficacious or to produce its effect involves something infinite, this combination is not like that of moving springs and forces, whose effects are always infallible and necessary. Thus no mind can uncover what happens in the heart of men.

XXXVIII

But since God has an infinite wisdom, it is evident that he knows clearly all the effects which can result from the mixture and the combination of all these things; and that, penetrating the heart of man, he infallibly uncovers even the effects which depend upon an act or rather upon a free consent of our wills. I grant none the less that I cannot conceive at all how God can uncover the consequences of actions which do not draw their infallibility from his absolute decrees; but I cannot resolve to put forward metaphysics at the expense of morality, or to offer as incontestable truths those opinions which are contrary to the inner feeling which I have of myself, or finally to speak to the ears a certain language which, it seems to me, says nothing clear to the mind. I know well that one can raise objections against me to which I cannot give clear and evident solutions. But it may well be that these objections themselves are full of obscurities and shadows. That is because they are based on our ignorance of the properties of the soul. Thus, as I have proved elsewhere, we have no clear idea of what we are; and what is in us, which gives way to be conquered by a determination which is not invincible, is entirely unknown to us. For the rest, if I cannot respond clearly to these objections, I can respond through others which seem even more difficult to resolve; I can, from principles opposed to mine, draw conclusions which are much more bad and vexing than those which are claimed to follow from liberty, such as I suppose it to be in us. I do not enter into the detail of all this: because I take no pleasure in walking in darkness, nor in guiding others to the precipice.

Illustration

What It Is to Act by General Wills, and by Particular Wills

I

I say that God acts by general wills, when he acts in consequence of general laws which he has established. For example, I say that God acts in me by general wills when he makes me feel pain at the time I am pricked; because in consequence of the general and efficacious laws of the union of the soul and the body which he has established, he makes me feel pain when my body is ill-disposed.

In the same way, when a ball strikes a second one, I say that God moves the second by a general will, because he moves it in consequence of the general and efficacious laws of the communication of motion—God having generally established that at the moment that two bodies strike, the motion is divided between the two according to certain proportions; and it is through the efficacy of this general will that bodies have the power to move each other.

II

I say on the contrary that God acts by particular wills when the efficacy of his will is not determined at all by some general law to produce some effect. Thus, supposing that God makes me feel the pain of pinching without there happening in my body, or in any creature whatsoever, any changes which determine him to act in me according to general laws—I say then that God acts by particular wills.

In the same way, supposing that a body begins to move itself without being struck by another, or without any change in the will of minds, or in any other creature that determines the efficacy of some general laws, I say then that God moves this body by a particular will.

III

According to these definitions, one sees that, far from denying Providence, I suppose on the contrary that it is God who does all in all things; that the nature of the pagan philosophers is a chimera; and that, properly speaking, what is called *nature* is nothing other than the general laws which God has established to construct or to preserve his work by very simple means, by an action which is uniform, constant, perfectly worthy of an infinite wisdom and of a universal cause. But that which I suppose here, though certain for reasons which I have given elsewhere, is not absolutely necessary to what I plan to prove. For if one will have it that God has communicated his power to creatures, in such a way that the bodies which surround us have a real and veritable power by which they can act upon our soul and make it happy or unhappy through pleasure and pain, and that bodies, in moving, have in themselves a certain entity which is called *impressed quality* which they can diffuse in those that they meet with, and diffuse it with that promptitude and that uniformity which we observe—it will still be equally easy for me to prove what I claim. For then the efficacy of the action of the concourse of the general cause will be necessarily determined by the action of the particular cause. God, for example, will be obliged, according to these principles, to lend his concourse to a body at the moment that it strikes others, in orders that this body can communicate motion to them—which is always to act in virtue of a general law. I do not, none the less, reason according to this supposition, because I believe it false in every way, as I have made clear in the third chapter of the second part of the sixth book of *Recherche de la vérité*, in the illustration of this same chapter, and elsewhere. These truths supposed, here are the marks by which one can recognize whether an effect is produced by a general will, or by a particular will.

Illustration 197

Marks by Which One Can Judge Whether an Effect is Produced by a General Will, or by a Particular Will

IV

When one sees that an effect is produced immediately after the action of an *occasional* cause, one must judge that this effect is produced by the efficacy of a general will. A body moves immediately after having been struck: the collision of the bodies is the action of the *occasional* cause; thus this body moves by a general will. A stone falls on the head of a man and kills him; and this stone falls like all others, I mean that its movement continues nearly according to the arithmetical progression 1, 3, 5, 7, 9, etc. That supposed, I say that it moves by the efficacy of a general will, or according to the laws of the communication of motion, as it is easy to demonstrate.

V

When one sees that an effect is produced, and that the occasional cause, which is known to us, has no part therein, one has reason to think that this effect is produced by a particular will—supposing that this effect is not visibly unworthy of its cause, as I shall say in what follows. For example, when a body moves without having been struck by another, there is great probability that this body was removed by a particular will of God. None the less one is not entirely assured of it. For supposing that there is a general law, that bodies move according to the different wills of the angels, or the like, it is clear that this body will be able to receive motion without being struck—the particular will of some angel being able, on this supposition, to determine the will of the general cause to move it. Thus one can often be assured that God acts by general wills; but one cannot in the same way be assured that he acts by particular wills even in the most attested miracles.

VI

Since we do not sufficiently know the different combinations of occasional causes, in order to discover whether such-and-such effects come about in consequence of their action—since we are not, for example, wise enough to recognize whether such-and-such a rain is natural or miraculous, produced through a necessary consequence of the communication of motion, or by a particular will—we must judge that an effect is produced by a general will, when it is obvious that the cause has proposed no particular end to himself. For the wills of intelligent beings necessarily have an end: general wills a general end, and particular wills a particular plan; nothing is more evident.

For example, although I cannot discover whether the rain which falls in a meadow falls there in consequence of general laws, or by a particular will of God, I have reason to think that it falls by a general will, if I see that it falls on neighbouring lands, or in the stream which borders this meadow, as well as on the meadow itself. For if God made it rain on this meadow through a particular good will for him who is the owner of it, this rain would not fall in the stream where it is useless: since it cannot fall there without a cause, or a will of God which necessarily has some end.

VII

But it is still more reasonable to think that an effect is produced by a general will, when this effect is contrary or even useless to the plan which faith and reason teach us that the cause has proposed to himself.

Reason teaches us, for example, that the end which God proposes to himself in the different sensations that he gives to the soul, when one tastes different fruits, is that we eat those which are suitable to nourish the body, and that we reject the others; I suppose it thus. Thus when God gives us a pleasant feeling at the instant that we eat poisons, or poisoned fruits, he does not act in us by particular wills. One must judge in this way, for the pleasant feeling is the cause of our death; and God gives us different feelings in order that we may preserve our life through suitable nourishment. Again I suppose it thus: for I speak only with respect to the grace which God doubtless gives us to convert us; such that it is obvious that God does not diffuse it in men by particular wills, since it often makes them more guilty and more criminal, and that God cannot have so unhappy a plan. Thus God does not give us pleasant feelings by particular wills at all, when we eat poisoned fruits. But since a poisoned fruit excites

Illustration 199

in our brain motions like those which good fruits produce therein, God gives us the same feelings, because of the general laws which unify the soul and the body—in order that it be wakeful to its preservation.

In the same way God gives to those who have lost an arm feelings of pain with respect to this arm only by a general will; for it is useless to the body of this man that his soul suffer pain with respect to an arm which he no longer has. It is the same with the movements which are produced in the body of a man who commits some crime.

Finally, supposing that one is obliged to think that God diffuses rain on the earth in order to make it fruitful, one cannot believe that he distributes it by particular wills, since it rains on the sands and in the sea as well as on cultivated grounds, and since the rains are often so abundant on seeded grounds that they uproot the shoots, and make the work of men useless.

Thus it is certain that rains which are useless or harmful to the fruits of the earth are necessary consequences of the general laws of the communication of motion which God has established to produce the best effects in the world: supposing, I repeat, that God cannot will by a particular will that rain be the cause of the earth's sterility.

VIII

Finally, when some effect comes about which has something quite singular about it, one has reason to think that it is not produced at all by a general will. None the less it is impossible to be assured of it. For example, if in a procession of the Holy Sacrament it rains on those who are present, except on the priests and on those who are carrying it, one has reason to think that this happens through a particular will of the universal cause. None the less one cannot be certain of it, because an intelligent occasional cause can have this particular design, and thus determine the efficacy of the general law to execute it.

IX

When the preceding marks are not sufficient to enable us to judge whether a certain effect is or is not produced by a general will, we must believe that it is produced by a general will—if it is evident that there is an occasional cause established for similar effects.

For example, one sees that it rains quite appropriately in a field; one does not enquire whether the rain falls or does not fall in the great highways; one knows not at all whether it is harmful to neighbouring lands; one even supposes that it only does good, and that all the circumstances which accompany it are entirely conformed to the plan for which one must believe that God wills that it rain: I say none the less that one must judge that this rain is produced by a general will if one knows that God has established an occasional cause for like effects; for one must not, without necessity, have recourse to miracles. One must suppose that God acts in this, by the simplest means; and although the owner of a field must give thanks to God for this favour, he must not imagine that God does it for him in a miraculous way, by a particular will.

The owner of this field must give thanks to God for the good that he has received, since God has seen and willed the good effect of this rain, when he has established the general laws of which it is a necessary consequence; and it is for like effects that he has established these laws. By contrast if the rains are sometimes harmful to our lands, since it is not to render them barren that God has established the laws which make it rain, since drought suffices to make them sterile, it is clear that we must thank God, and adore the wisdom of his Providence, even at the time that we feel not at all the effects of the laws which he has established for our benefit.

X

Finally, if we are not assured by the circumstances which accompany certain effects that there is an occasional cause established to produce them, it suffices to know that they are common enough, and that they have a relation to the main plan of the general cause, in order to judge that they are not produced at all by a particular will.

For example, the springs which water the earth have a relation to the first of God's plans—which plan is that men do not lack the things necessary to life; I suppose it thus. Moreover, springs of water are quite common. Thus one must think that they are formed by some general laws. For, since there is much more wisdom in executing his plans by simple and general means than in complex and particular ways, as I think I have sufficiently proven elsewhere, one must do this honour to God, to believe that this way of acting is general, uniform, constant, and proportioned to the idea that we

Illustration 201

have of an infinite wisdom. These are the marks by which one must judge whether an effect is or is not produced by a general will. I now prove that God diffuses grace in men by general laws, and that Jesus Christ has been established as *occasional* cause to determine their efficacy. I begin with proofs drawn from Holy Scripture.

XI

St Paul teaches us that Jesus Christ is the head of the Church, that he ceaselessly diffuses in it the spirit which gives it life, that he forms the members of it, and animates them as the soul animates the body: or to speak even more clearly, Holy Scripture teaches us two things—the first that Jesus Christ prays without cease for his members; the second that his prayers or his desires are always heard. From which I conclude that he was established by God as occasional cause of grace, and even that grace is never given to sinners except by this means.

Occasional causes have their effect always, and very promptly. The prayers or the different desires of Jesus Christ, in relation to the formation of his body, also have their effect always and very promptly. God refuses nothing to his son, as Jesus Christ himself teaches us.

Occasional causes do not produce their effect by their own efficacy; it is through the efficacy of the general cause. It is also through the efficacy of the power of God that the soul of Jesus Christ operates in us; it is not at all through the efficacy of the human will [of Christ]. It is for this reason that St Paul represents Jesus Christ to us as praying ceaselessly to his Father, for he is obliged to pray in order to obtain.

Occasional causes have been established by God to determine the efficacy of his general wills; and Jesus Christ, according to Scripture, has been established by God, after his Resurrection, to govern the Church which he has purchased with his blood. For Jesus Christ was the *meritorious* cause of all the graces through his sacrifice; but after his Resurrection he entered into the Holy of Holies as *Sovereign Priest of future goods*, to appear in the presence of God, and to diffuse in us the graces which he had merited for us. Thus he himself applies and distributes his gifts, as *occasional* cause. He disposes of everything in the house of God, like a well-loved son in the house of his father.

I think that I have demonstrated in *Recherche de la vérité* that it is only God who is a *true* cause, or who acts by his own efficacy, and that he communicates his power to his creatures only by establishing them as *occasional* causes in order to produce certain effects. I have proven, for example, that men have the power to produce any movement in their body only because God has established their wills as occasional causes of these movements; for fire has the power to make one suffer pain only because God has made the collision of bodies the occasional cause of the communication of motion, and the violent vibration of the fibres of my flesh the occasional cause of my pain. I can suppose here a truth which I have proven at great length in the third chapter of the second part of the sixth book [of the *Recherche*] and in the illustration of that same chapter, and which those for whom I principally write do not contest at all. Now it is certain by faith that Jesus Christ as man is our mediator, *Mediator Dei & hominum homo Christus Jesus, that all power has been given him* to form his Church: *Data est mihi omnis potestas in coelo & in terra*: and that cannot be understood as applying to Jesus Christ in his divinity, since in that quality he never received anything—for one receives only when one does not have. Thus it is certain that Jesus Christ, in his humanity, is the *occasional* cause of grace, supposing that I have well proven that it is only God who acts upon minds, and that second causes have no efficacy of their own; this is something which must first be examined by those who would understand my ideas, and bring their judgement to bear on them.

XII

I say further that no one is sanctified save by the efficacy of the *power* which God has communicated to Jesus Christ, in establishing him as *occasional* cause of grace. For if some sinner were converted by a grace of which Jesus Christ was not the occasional cause, but only the *meritorious* cause, this sinner, not having received his new life through the influence of Jesus Christ, would not be a member of the body of which Jesus Christ is the head, in the way explained by St Paul through these words from the Epistle to the Ephesians: *Crescamus in illo per omnia, qui est caput Christus, ex quo totum corpus compactum & connexum per omnem juncturam subministrationis, secundam operationem, in mensuram uniuscujuque membri, augmentum*

Illustration 203

*corporis facit in aedificationem sui in charitate.*⁵ Which words do not say simply that Jesus Christ is the *meritorious* cause of all graces: they express even more distinctly the notion that Christians are members of the body of which Jesus Christ is the head; that it is in him that we believe and that we live a wholly new life; that it is through his internal working, κατ ἐγέργε αν, that his Church is formed, and that he has thus been established by God as the sole *occasional* cause who, by his different desires and different efforts, distributes the graces which God as true cause diffuses in men.

It is for this reason that St Paul says that Christians are attached to Jesus Christ as their root: *Radicati & superaedificati in ispo.* It is for this reason that Jesus Christ himself compares himself to a vine, and his disciples to the branches which draw their life therefrom: *Ego sum vitis, vos palmites.* It is for this reason that St Paul assures us that *Jesus Christ lives in us, and that we live in Jesus Christ: that we are raised up in our head; that our life is hidden with Jesus Christ in God*— in a word, *that we already have eternal life in Jesus Christ.* Do not all these expressions, and several others, show clearly enough that Jesus Christ is not only the *meritorious* cause, but also the physical or natural *occasional* cause of grace, and that, as the soul informs, animates, perfects the body, Jesus Christ diffuses in his members, as *occasional* cause, the graces which he has merited for his Church through his sacrifice?

As for me, I do not understand how one can doubt these reasonings, nor on what basis one can treat as dangerous novelty a truth which is quite edifying, and as old as the religion of Jesus Christ. I grant that my expressions are new; but that is because they seemed to me quite fitting to expound distinctly a truth which I can demonstrate only confusedly through terms which are too general. These words, *occasional causes* and *general laws*, seem to me necessary, to make philosophers—for whom I have written the treatise on *Nature et grâce*—understand distinctly that which the majority of men are content to know confusedly. Since new expressions are not dangerous, except when they conceal some equivocation, or when they cause some thought contrary to religion to spring up in the mind, I do not believe that equitable people, knowledgeable in the theology of St Paul, will find fault with the fact

⁵ Ephesians 4: 15–16.

that I explain myself in a particular way which tends only to make us adore the wisdom of God and to link us strictly to Jesus Christ.

First Objection

XIII

It is objected against that which I have just established, that neither the angels nor the saints of the Old Testament received the slightest grace in consequence of the desires of the soul of Jesus Christ, since this holy soul did not yet exist; and that thus, although Jesus Christ is the *meritorious* cause of all graces, he is not at all the *occasional* cause who distributes them to men.

Response

With respect to the angels, I answer that there is some probability that grace was given to them only once. Such that, if one considers things from that side, I grant that nothing obliges God's wisdom to establish an *occasional* cause for the sanctification of the angels. But if one considers these blessed spirits as members of the body of which Jesus Christ is the head, or if one supposes that they were unequally aided, I believe that one has reason to think that the diversity of their graces must come from him who is the head of the angels, as well as of men, and who in this quality not only merited by his sacrifice all the graces that God has given his creatures, but who applied these same graces differently to them through his different desires.

Since one cannot deny that Jesus Christ, long before having been born or having merited, was able to be the *meritorious* cause of the graces which were given to the angels and to the saints of the Old Testament, one must, it seems to me, remain in agreement that by his prayers he was able to be the *occasional* cause of the same graces, long before having been asked for them. For in the end there is no necessary relation between *occasional* causes, and the time in which their effects are produced; and while ordinarily these kinds of causes produce their effects at the same time as their action, none the less,

Illustration 205

since their action is not at all efficacious by itself—since its efficacy depends on the will of the universal cause— it is not at all necessary that they exist presently in order to produce their effects.

For example, supposing that Jesus Christ asks today of his Father, that such-and-such a one receive certain help at certain moments in his life, the prayer of Jesus Christ will infallibly determine the efficacy of the general will that God has to save all men through his Son. This person will receive this help, though the prayer of Jesus Christ be in the past, though his holy soul think presently of something else altogether, and though it may never again think of what it has asked for him. Now the past prayer of Jesus Christ is no more present to his Father, than a future prayer; for all that must happen in all times is equally present to God. Thus, since God loves his Son, and he knows that this Son will have such desires with respect to his ancestors and to those of his nation, and even with respect to the angels who must enter into the spiritual edifice of the Church, and comprise the body of which he is the head, it seems that he must fulfil the desires of his Son before they have been formed, in order that the elect who have preceded his birth and whom he has purchased by the merit of his sacrifice, will belong to him as particularly as the others, and in order that he be their head as truly as he is ours.

I grant that it would be appropriate that *meritorious* and *occasional* causes precede their effects rather than follow them, and that order itself seems to require that these causes and their effects exist at the same time. For it is clear that all merit ought to be instantly rewarded, and every occasional cause should presently produce its effect—provided that nothing hinders that it may or ought to be done, as happens in the rewarding of the just and in the punishment of sinners. For the simplicity of general Providence does not permit that God presently render to each according to his works. But since grace was absolutely necessary to the angels and to the patriarchs, it could not be deferred. As for the glory and the recompense of the saints of the Old Testament: since it could be put off, it was fitting that God suspend the accomplishing of it until Jesus Christ rose into heaven, was established High Priest over the House of God, and began to exercise the sovereign power of occasional cause of all the graces merited by his labours upon earth. Thus we believe that the patriarchs did not enter heaven until after Jesus Christ himself, their head, their mediator, and their precursor, entered it.

None the less, even if it should be agreed that God has not established any occasional cause of all the graces which were given to the angels and to the patriarchs, I do not see that one can conclude therefrom, that Jesus Christ now does not diffuse in the body of the Church the spirit which gives it growth and life, that he does not pray for it, or that his desires or his prayers do not infallibly have their effect—in a word, that he is not the *occasional* cause who now applies to men the graces which he merited for them on earth. God, before the birth of Jesus Christ, gave grace by particular wills. I grant it, if one wishes: the necessity of order demanded it; the occasional cause, according to order, could not be so soon established; the elect were very few in number. But now that the rain of grace is general over the whole earth—I mean that it does not fall as heretofore on a very small number of men of a chosen nation; now that Jesus Christ can or must be established as occasional cause of the goods he has merited for his Church, what reason has one to think that God still performs as many miracles as he gives us good sentiments? For finally all that God does by particular wills is certainly a miracle—since it does not happen through the general laws which he has established, and whose efficacy is determined by occasional causes. But how can one think that in order to save men he performs all these miracles which are useless to their salvation? I mean, that he gives them all these graces which they resist, since they are not proportioned to the actual power of their concupiscence?

St John teaches us that Christians receive graces in abundance from the bounty of Jesus Christ: because, he says, *the law was given by Moses, but true grace has been given by Jesus Christ.*[6] For indeed the graces which preceded Jesus Christ ought not to be compared to those he distributed after his triumph. If they were miraculous, one must think that they were extremely rare. Even the grace of the Apostles, before the Holy Spirit was given to them, could not come in comparison with those they received when the Sovereign Priest of future goods, having through his blood entered the Holy of Holies, obtained by the power of his prayers and sent by the dignity of his person, the Holy Spirit, to animate and sanctify his Church. The strange blindness of the Jews, their gross and carnal notions, their frequent relapses into idolatry after so many miracles, make it clear that they scarcely had any love for true goods; and the timidity of the

[6] John 7: 39.

Illustration 207

Apostles before they had received the Holy Spirit is a sensible mark of their weakness. Thus grace in those times was extremely rare, because our nature in Jesus Christ was not yet established as the occasional cause of graces: Jesus Christ was not yet fully consecrated priest, after the order of Melchisedech: and his Father had not yet given him that immortal and glorious life which is the particular character of his priesthood. For it was necessary that Jesus Christ should enter the heavens and receive the glory and the power of occasional cause of true goods before sending the Holy Spirit, according to these words of St John: *Nondum erat Spiritus datus, quia Jesus nondum erat glorificatus:*[7] and according to these others of Jesus Christ himself: *Expedit vobis ut ego vadam. Si enim non abiero, Paraclitus non veniet ad vos. Si autem abiero, mittam eum ad vos.*[8] Now one must not imagine that Jesus Christ, considered as God, is the head of the Church. It is as man that he gained that quality; the head and the members of a body must be of the same nature. It is as man that Jesus Christ intercedes for men; it is as man that he received from God a sovereign power over his Church. For as God he does not intercede at all; he has not received, as God, a name which is above every name; he is equal to the Father, and the absolute master of all things by the right of his birth. These truths are certain through faith, and Jesus Christ himself assures us of them, since he has said that his Father has given him the power to judge men, because he is the son of man. Thus one must not think that the expressions in Scripture which teach us that Jesus Christ is the author of grace, should be understood of Jesus Christ considered according to his divine person. For if that were so, I grant that I would not have demonstrated that he is the *occasional* cause of it; he would only be the *true* cause of it. But since it is certain that the three persons of the Trinity are equally *true* causes of grace, because all the external operations of God are common to the three persons, one cannot contest my proofs—since Holy Scripture says of the Son, and not at all of the Father or of the Holy Spirit, that he is the head of the Church, and that in this quality he communicates life to all the members who compose it.

[7] John 1: 17.   [8] John 16: 7.

Second Objection

XIV

It is God who gives to the soul of Jesus Christ all the thoughts and all the movements which relate to the formation of his mystical body. So that if on one side the wills of Jesus Christ determine, as occasional or natural causes, the efficacy of the general wills of God, on the other side it is God himself who determines the different wills of Jesus Christ. Thus it comes down to the same thing: for in the end the wills of Jesus Christ are always conformed to those of his Father.

Response

I grant that the particular wills of the soul of Jesus Christ are always conformed to those of his Father: but it is not the case that the Father has particular wills which answer to those of the Son, and which determine them; it is only that the wills of the Son are always conformed to order in general, which is necessarily the rule of divine wills and of all those who love God. For to love order is to love God, it is to will what God wills, it is to be just, wise, governed in one's love. The soul of Jesus Christ wills to form, for the glory of his Father, the greatest, the most magnificent, the most finished Temple that can be. Order will have it so; for one can do nothing which is too great for God. All the different thoughts of this soul, always given over to the execution of his plan, also come to him from God, or from the Word to which it is united. But all these different thoughts certainly have his different desires for occasional causes; for he thinks of what he wants.

Now these different desires are sometimes entirely free: apparently the thoughts which excite these desires do not always invincibly bring the soul of Jesus Christ to form them and to will to execute them. It is equally advantageous to the plan of Jesus Christ that it be Peter or John who brings about the effect that the regularity of his work demands. It is true that the soul of Jesus is not at all indifferent in anything which concerns the glory of his Father, or in that which order necessarily demands, but he is entirely free in the rest; there is

Illustration 209

nothing outside God which invincibly determines his love. Thus one need not be astonished if the soul of Jesus has particular wills, although there are not similar wills in God [the Father] which determine him.

But I grant that the wills of Jesus Christ are not free: I grant that his enlightenment brings him, even invincibly, to will, and to will always in a determinate way in the construction of his Church. But it will be Eternal Wisdom, to which his soul is united, which will determine his wills; for this effect one need not suppose particular wills in God at all.

It must be remarked that the wills of the soul of Jesus Christ are particular, or have no occasional cause that determines their efficacy, like that of God. For the soul of Jesus Christ not having an infinite capacity of thinking, his knowledge, and in consequence his wills, are limited. Thus it is necessary that his wills be particular, since they change according to his different thoughts or his different applications. For apparently the soul of Jesus Christ, otherwise occupied in contemplating the beauties and in tasting the infinite sweetnesses of the true good must not, it seems to me, according to order, will to think at the same time of all the ornaments that it wants to give to its Church, and of the different means of executing each of its plans. Jesus Christ willing to make the Church worthy of the infinite majesty of his Father, he wants to place in it an infinity of beauties, and by the means most in conformity to order. Thus it is necessary that he incessantly change his desires—it being only an infinite wisdom which can prescribe general laws to itself in order to execute its plans.

Now since the future world must subsist eternally, and be infinitely more perfect than the present world, it was suitable that God establish an intelligent occasional cause, enlightened by eternal wisdom, in order that he might remedy the defects which are met with necessarily in works formed by general laws. The collision of bodies, which determines the efficacy of the general laws of nature, is an occasional cause without intelligence and without freedom. Thus it cannot bring it about that there be no defects in the world, and that monsters not be produced—defects which it would be unworthy of God to remedy by particular wills. But Jesus Christ being an intelligent occasional cause, enlightened by eternal wisdom, and capable of having particular wills, according to the particular needs demanded by the work which he forms, it is clear that the future world will be infinitely more perfect than the present world, that the Church will be without deformity, as Scripture teaches us, and that this work will be quite worthy of the indulgence of God himself.

It is in this way that eternal wisdom returns, so to speak, to its Father that which it had taken away from him—for, not permitting him to act by particular wills, it seemed to make him impotent. But being incarnate it so brings it to pass that God, acting in a way worthy of him by quite simple and quite general means, produces a work in which the most enlightened intelligences will never be able to observe the slightest defect.

XV

After having proven by the authority of Scripture that the different movements of the soul of Jesus Christ are *occasional* causes which determine the efficacy of the general law of grace, by which God wills to save all men through his Son, one must also prove in general through reason, that one ought not to believe that God acts in the order of grace by particular wills. For, although by reason independently of faith one cannot demonstrate that God has established the wills of a man-God as occasional cause of his gifts, one can none the less, without faith, make it known that he does not distribute them at all to men by particular wills—and this in two ways, a priori and a posteriori, that is to say through the idea we have of God, and through the effects of grace: for there is nothing which does not serve to prove this truth. Here is a proof a priori.

A wise being must act wisely; God cannot deny himself; his ways of acting must bear the character of his attributes. Now God knows all, and foresees all; his intelligence has no limits. Thus his way of acting must bear the character of an infinite intelligence. Now to choose occasional causes, and to establish general laws to execute some work, indicates a knowledge infinitely more extensive, than to change his wills at every moment, or to act by particular wills. Thus God executes his plans by general laws, whose efficacy is determined by occasional causes. Certainly it requires a greater breadth of mind to create a watch which, according to the laws of mechanism, goes by itself and regularly—whether one carries it on oneself, whether one holds it suspended, whether one shakes it as one pleases—than to make one which cannot run correctly if he who has made it does not

Illustration 211

change something in it at every moment according to the situations it is placed in. For finally, when there is a greater number of relations to compare and to combine with each other, a greater intelligence is needed. To foresee all the effects which must come about in consequence of a general law, an infinite foresight is needed; and there is nothing to foresee in all of this, when one changes one's wills at every moment. Thus to establish general laws, and to choose the simplest ones, which are at the same time the most fruitful, is a way of acting worthy of him whose wisdom has no bounds; and by contrast to act by particular wills indicates a limited intelligence which cannot compare the consequences or the effects of the last fruitful causes. One can even demonstrate a priori the same truth through several other attributes of God, such as his immutability; for it is evident that the conduct of God must bear the character of his attributes, since he acts only through his will, only through the love he bears them. But these proofs a priori are too abstract to convince the majority of men of the truth which I expound. It is more suitable to prove it through the marks which I have given beforehand, in order to distinguish the effects which are produced by particular wills from those which are necessary consequences of general law.

XVI

God, being infinitely wise, wills or does nothing without a plan or without an end. Now grace often falls on hearts so disposed that it is fruitless. Thus it does not fall on these hearts by a particular will, but only through a necessary consequence of general laws—for the same reason that rain falls on the sands and in the sea, as well as on seeded grounds.

Although God may punish sinners, or make them more unhappy than they are, he cannot will to make them more guilty or more criminal. Now grace sometimes makes certain people more guilty and more criminal, and God actually knows, always and quite certainly, that according to their present dispositions the graces which he distinguishes to them will have this unhappy effect. Thus these graces do not fall on these corrupted hearts by a particular will of God, but by a necessary consequences of the general laws which he has established in order to produce the best effects—for the same reason that in certain situations rain which is too abundant corrupts and spoils the fruits of the earth, though God by his general will makes it rain in order to make them grow.

XVII

If God willed that certain lands remain sterile, he would only have to cease to will that rain water them. Just as, if God wills that the hearts of certain sinners remain hardened, since it is sufficient that the rain of grace not water them, he has only to leave them to themselves, and they will be corrupted. Why attribute to God a particular will to make so hard and unfortunate a use of the price of his Son's blood? But, some people will say, God never has this plan when he gives his grace to sinners. That no doubt seems more reasonable.

But if God gives his grace by a particular will, he has some particular plan. Now since his grace has this unhappy effect, God is frustrated in his attempt, since he has given it with a particular aim of doing good to this sinner. For I do not speak here of the graces, or rather of the gifts which St Paul explains in the twelfth chapter of his first Epistle to the Corinthians; I speak of the grace which God gives for the conversion of him to whom he gives it, and not at all of those gifts which God gives to some for the benefit of others—such as the gift of prophecy, of discernment of spirits, that of speaking different tongues, of curing the sick, and the like.

XVIII

When a rain falls in such abundance that the streams deracinate the fruits of the earth, one must judge that this rain comes on through a necessary consequence of the general laws which God has established for the best effects. However, it is certain that God may have ordained it by a particular will. For God, to punish men, can will that the rains, established to make lands fruitful, make them sterile in some situations. But the cause is not the same with the rain of grace, since God cannot diffuse it with the plan of punishing men, or still less to make them more guilty and more criminal. Thus it is much more certain that the rain of grace is diffused by general wills than ordinary rains. Howsoever the majority of men have no difficulty in believing that rains are necessary consequences of general laws of the communication of motion, there are but few who

Illustration 213

do not feel some repugnance in believing that God gives us, by general wills, all those movements of grace whose effects we hinder.

It is quite probable that this disposition of mind comes from the fact that naturally one thinks that God acts very nearly in the same way that we act, and that at every moment he has particular wills for men—more or less like those which we have with respect to our friends. For while with the mouth one admits that there are infinite differences between God's way of acting and ours, none the less, since one ordinarily judges of others with respect to oneself, without reflecting thereon, few persons seriously consult the idea of the infinitely perfect Being when they want to speak of God. And since there is some air of novelty in what I say, that causes some kind of pain to the mind, which is reasonably mistrustful of what is not ordinary.

I particularly honour and esteem all those who, in matters of religion, have a secret aversion to all novelties. I do not take offence, when they oppose my notions, when it is this motive which makes them act; and since their prejudices are quite legitimate, even when they gravely offend me, I do not lack respect for them. For their disposition of mind is infinitely more reasonable than that of certain people who seize upon all that bears the character of novelty. None the less, since I think that one must love and seek after the truth with all one's power, and communicate it to others, when one thinks one has recognized it; I think that, after having assumed as incontestable all that faith teaches us, one can, and one even must, strive to reveal that which is capable of confirming it, and of making all men embrace it. I can justify this feeling through the conduct of the Fathers, and even by the authority of St Augustine—who often exhorts us to seek after an understanding of truths which one already believes through the obscurity of faith. But I do not think that there are persons unreasonable enough to find anything objectionable in my conduct, however prejudiced they may be against my ideas. Thus I pray those who are willing to take the trouble to read what I have written, not to assume that I am mistaken, to suspend their judgement until they have well understood my thought, not to condemn me in general terms, and not to draw unfortunate conclusions too quickly from my principles.

In matters as obscure as those which concern grace, the advantage is always on the side of him who attacks: it is not just to make use of it. One must act with equity, and compare without prejudice all the consequences that can be drawn from different sentiments, in order finally to embrace that which seems most in conformity to the goodness and to the wisdom of God. For it is not being equitable to condemn an opinion without examination, because of some unfortunate consequences which men never fail to draw from it when the imagination is frightened, and when one is prejudiced by contrary notions.

XIX

I know, for example, that some people have said that I make all prayers useless, and that I take from men the confidence they ought to have in God: because, God always acting by general wills, one should not (according to them) hope for particular helps from heaven. I grant that if this single consequence were involved in my principles, they would be false, heretical, impious. For one overturns religion, if one takes away hope and the confidence one ought to have in God; and it is partly for that reason that I cannot share the feeling of those who are the most opposed to my way of harmonizing grace and liberty. But so far from my principles bringing people to despair, they teach on the contrary—to the just, and even to sinners, in a way that seems to me quite consoling—the means of obtaining from God the things that one needs.

For if we are just, our prayers are meritorious; and if they are meritorious, order requires that they be fulfilled. And since order is, with respect to God himself, a law infinitely more inviolable than the laws he has established for the preservation of his work, he never fails to do that which order prescribes to him. Thus the prayers of the just are never useless. It is this that I have established in article XIX of the Second Discourse [in *Nature et grâce*].

But if we are sinners, it is certain that our prayers by themselves are useless. For God does not listen to sinners at all; order will not have it so. None the less we must not be desperate: *We have an advocate with the Father, Jesus Christ the righteous. He came into the world to save sinners.*[9] His prayers are always and very promptly fulfilled; let us pray in his name, or let us address ourselves to him. Our prayers prompt him to form certain desires with respect to us; and his desires are the occasional causes which infallibly determine

---

[9] I John 2: I.

Illustration 215

the efficacy of the general law of grace by which God wills to save all men through his son. This is what I establish at great length in the Second Discourse. Thus, so far am I from taking away the confidence that one ought to have in God, that on the contrary I indicate precisely, through the authority of Scripture, the way we ought to take in order to obtain from God the graces which are necessary to us. For just as one does not deprive men of the confidence they have in God, when one tells them that if they do not work their lands they will get nothing from them, and that they must approach the fire when the cold bothers them—in a word when one instructs them concerning the effects of second causes, which are always the same in the same circumstances, and which are such only because God acts in consequence of some general law—in the same way, I say, that one does not deprive men of their confidence in God when one teaches them natural science [*la physique*], one is quite far from depriving them of it when one teaches them, with Scripture, that it is through the influence of the head of the Church that the members who compose it receive the spirit that sanctifies them, that Jesus Christ is always living to intercede for us, and that his prayers are always answered: in a word that no one goes to the Father except through him, and that he is thus the occasional cause of grace, according to the idea attached to this word by those for whom I have written my treatise. I pray, then, that readers do me the justice of examining my notions without prejudice; and I am content that they judge them afterwards according to their lights. For I submit all my thoughts not only to the censure of the Church, which has the right to make me give them up through an authority to which I shall always be ready to defer, but also to the enlightened judgement of all individuals, from whose opinion I shall strive to profit.

Select Critical Bibliography

Editions of the Treatise

Traité de la nature et de la grâce (Amsterdam: Chez Daniel Elsevier, 1680). The first edition, without 'additions' or 'illustrations'.

Traité de la nature et de la grâce (Strasbourg [Lyons]: Chez George André d'Olhopff, 1681). This edition, designated IIS by the editors of the Librairie Vrin *Œuvres complètes de Malebranche* (see below), includes the first 'illustration' (but not the last three, and none of the disfiguring 'additions'). Since this is philosophically the best edition, it has been used as the basis of the present Oxford edition.

Traité de la nature et de la grâce (Rotterdam: Chez Reinier Leers, 1684). The 'scripturalized' version, with additions and four 'illustrations'.

Traité de la nature et de la grâce (Rotterdam: Chez Reinier Leers, 1712). The final edition supervised by Malebranche during his lifetime.

Traité de la nature et de la grâce, 1680 original text, ed. with introductory monograph by Ginette Dreyfus (Paris: Librairie Vrin, 1958). The monograph gives an excellent account of the 'doctrinal antecedents' of Malebranchism, and of the reception of *Nature et grâce* at the hands of Leibniz, Bayle, Bossuet, Fénelon, Arnauld, and Fontenelle.

Traité de la nature et de la grâce, final 1712 text, ed. with an introduction by Ginette Dreyfus (Paris: Librairie Vrin, 1958), as part of the *Œuvres complètes de Malebranche*, general editor André Robinet, vol. V (2nd corrected edn., 1976).

English Translations

Father Malebranche's Treatise concerning the Search after Truth. To which is added the Author's Treatise of Nature and Grace, trans. Thomas Taylor (London: for Thomas Bennet *et al.*, 1694).

A Treatise of Nature and Grace, trans. Richard Sault (London: 1695).

General Studies of Malebranche and Malebranchism

ALQUIÉ, FERDINAND, *Le Cartésianisme de Malebranche* (Paris: Librairie Vrin, 1974). A brilliant account of Malebranche's demi-Cartesianism and (sometimes) anti-Cartesianism.

DREYFUS, GINETTE, *La Volonté selon Malebranche* (Paris: Librairie Vrin, 1958). The most learned and intelligent study of the moral consequences of Malebranchism, by the editor of the critical edition of *Nature et grâce*.

GOUHIER, HENRI, *La Philosophie de Malebranche et son expérience réligieuse* (Paris: Librairie Vrin, 1926). The first important work by the founding father of modern Malebranche studies.

GUÉROULT, MARTIAL, *Malebranche: Les cinq abîmes de la Providence* (Paris: Aubier, 1959), esp. vol. iii (a fine account of Malebranche's views on grace).

MCCRACKEN, C. J., *Malebranche and British Philosophy* (Oxford: Clarendon Press, 1983). An excellent brief account of Malebranchism, followed by a study of the relation of that doctrine to the thought of Locke, Berkeley, Hume, Norris, and others.

ROBINET, ANDRÉ, *Malebranche et Leibniz: Relations personnelles* (Paris: Librairie Vrin, 1955). A splendid edition of the complete correspondence between the two philosophers, together with all of Leibniz's writings (published and unpublished) on Malebranche and Malebranchism.

—— *Système et existence dans l'œuvre de Malebranche* (Paris: Librairie Vrin, 1965). The most comprehensive modern study of Malebranche's entire philosophical system.

RODIS-LEWIS, GENEVIÈVE, *Nicolas Malebranche* (Paris: Presses Universitaires de France, 1963). A study of every aspect of Malebranchism by the best editor and interpreter of *De la recherche de la vérité*.

SAINTE-BEUVE, C. A., *Port-Royal* (Paris, 1908). Book VI of this classic work contains the best 19th-century account of Malebranche's thought.

Studies of Malebranche Which Stress Nature and Grace

BRÉHIER, ÉMILE, 'Les Lectures malebranchistes de J.-J. Rousseau', *Revue internationale de philosophie*, 1 (1938–9), 113 ff.

LAPORTE, JEAN, *La Doctrine de Port-Royal: Les Vérités sur la grâce* (Paris: Librairie Vrin, 1923). A remarkable study by a modern 'Jansenist'.

POSTIGLIOLA, ALBERTO, 'De Malebranche à Rousseau: Les Apories de la volonté générale', *Annales de la Société Jean-Jacques Rousseau*, 39 (Geneva: Chez A. Jullien, 1980), 134 ff. Extraordinary on the Malebranche–Rousseau rapport.

SHKLAR, JUDITH N., 'General Will', in *Dictionary of the History of Ideas*, ed. P. Wiener (New York: Charles Scribner's Sons, 1973), ii. 275 ff. A dazzling account of the later career of Malebranche's most famous term in *Nature et grâce*.

Treatments of Nature et grâce by Malebranche's Contemporaries

ARNAULD, ANTOINE, *Des vrais et des fausses idées* (1685).

BAYLE, PIERRE, *Pensées diverses sur la comète* (1682).

BOSSUET, JACQUES-BÉNIGNE, *Oraison funèbre de Marie-Thérèse d'Autriche* (1683).

BOURSIER, LAURENT, *De l'action de Dieu sur les créatures* (1713).

FÉNELON, FRANÇOIS DE, *Réfutation du système du Père Malebranche sur la nature et la grâce* (*c.* 1688).

FONTENELLE, BERNARD, *Doutes sur le système physique des causes occasionnelles* (1686).

LEIBNIZ, G. W., *Essais de Theodicée* (1710).

LOCKE, JOHN, 'An Examination of P. Malebranche's Opinion of Seeing All Things in God' (*c.*1694).

ROUSSEAU, J.-J., *Lettre à Voltaire sur la Providence* (1756).

TERTRE, RODOLPHE DU, *Réfutation d'un nouveau système de métaphysique proposé par le Père Malebranche* (1715).

Note. The sole known existing manuscript of *Nature et grâce*—not, apparently, in Malebranche's hand—is in the collection of documents relating to Port-Royal at Amersfoort, Holland, under the number 1084. Details of this manuscript are given in *Œuvres complètes de Malebranche*, ed. André Robinet, vol. v, p. xx n. 31. (The editor has examined this manuscript—now transferred to the Royal Library at The Hague—and the handwriting bears no resemblance to that seen in the one substantial manuscript known to be in Malebranche's hand: the original draft of *Réflexions sur la prémotion physique*, which the editor has reviewed at the Bibliothèque d'Honfleur, Calvados, France.)

Index

Abel (Old Testament) 123, 166
Abercrombie, Nigel: *The Origins of
Jansenism* 4 n. 16
Abimelech (Old Testament) 31–2
Adam (Old Testament): as cause of
'disorder' in Malebranche's *Nature et
grâce* 150; Fall of, as cause of God's
abandoning a general will to save all
men: in Arnauld 4; in Pascal 11–12;
God expresses his self-sufficiency by
not stopping Fall (in Malebranche)
24–5; treated by Bayle as objection to
God's justice 89–90
Adam and Eve: as 'representation' of
Christ and the Church in
Malebranche's *Nature et grâce* 165
Alexander the Great: treated by
Fénelon 79
Allemans, Armand Joubert de Lau,
Marquis de 2 n. 5, 72 ff.
Alquié, Ferdinand: on Malebranche 57
n. 215, 72 n. 261
André, le Père Y. M. xi
Aquinas, St Thomas: on antecedent and
consequent will in *De Veritate* 9; on
grace in *Summa Theologica* 2 and n. 4;
treated by Bossuet 71
Aristotle: criticized by Malebranche 53;
Ethics, Book X 66; God as self-
contemplative 66; *Metaphysics* 1 n. 3;
Physics 1 n. 3
Arnauld, Antoine: attacks
Malebranche's *Nature et grâce* 1, 13,
30–1, 66; defends Jansenius and
Jansenism 7 and nn. 30–3, 8 n. 34;
effort to minimize God's general will
to save all men 7–10; first to use term
'general will' of God 5 and n. 21; has
Malebranche's *Nature et grâce* placed
on Index 67; influence on Bayle 85;
originally favourable to Malebranche
xi; Scripture as final authority 30–1;
translation of Augustine's *De
Correptione et Gratia* 9–10, 21; use of
Aquinas's *De Veritate* 9; use of

Augustinianism 8–9
Augustine, St: Arnauld's admiration for
De Correptione et Gratia 9–10;
Augustinianism: Bossuet's treatment
of 75 ff.; Bayle's criticism of
Augustine's defence of Abraham 87;
De Natura et Gratia 1–2; *De Spiritu et
Littera* 77; *Enchiridion* 8; God wills to
save all kinds of men 8 and n. 36;
interpretation of Paul's 'God wills that
all men be saved' 6; Jansenius'
interpretation of 8–9; Malebranche's
interpretation of xiv, 53, 65–6;
Pascal's reading of 10–12; struggle
with Pelagians 4
Augustinus, see Jansenius, Cornelius
Averroës 56

Barbeyrac, Jean (translator of Leibniz's
*Opinion on the Principles of
Pufendorf*) 43
Bauni (Bauny), Étienne 87
Bayle, Pierre: critique of Jaquelot's
Malebranchism in *Entretiens* 88–91;
defends Malebranche's *Nature et
grâce* xii, 1, 13, 81 ff.; doubts about
general will of God to save all (in
Réponse aux questions) 85–6; fideism
of 86; general will as good, particular
will as bad in *Commentaire
philosophique* 84–5; influence of
Arnauld 85; *La France toute
catholique* 83–5; his Malebranchism in
Pensées diverses 81–3; rejection of
Malebranchian general will in
Entretiens 88–91; on revocation of
Edict of Nantes 83–4; treatment of
Abraham, Sarah, and King David in
Dictionnaire 86–8
Bentham, Jeremy 44 and n. 170
Berkeley, George 57
Bossuet, Jacques Bénigne: accuses
Malebranche of misusing
Cartesianism 73–4; accuses
Malebranche of 'naturalizing'

Bossuet, Jacques Bénigne (*cont.*):
grace 72–3; commissions Fénelon to
write against Malebranche's *Nature et
grâce* 67; compared to Pascal 69;
criticizes Malebranche's *Nature et
grâce* 1, 26, 38–9, 70 ff.; critique of
Calvinism 71; critique of
Jansenism 69–70, 77; critique of
Richard Simon 75; on Descartes's
Principia 73–4; *Histoire universelle*
favours idea of *Providence
particulière* 32, 74–5; *Histoire
universelle* praised by Arnauld 32;
hostility to particularism in 'Sermon
sur la providence' 68; on
interpretation of Augustine 75 ff.;
interprets 'God wills that all men be
saved' 75–6; letter to Marquis
d'Allemans 72–4; *Oraison funèbre de
Cornet* 69; *Oraison funèbre de Marie-
Thérèse d'Autriche* xii, 13, 67, 70, 72;
*Politique tirée . . . . de l'écriture
sainte* 67–8; his preface to Benedictine
edition of Augustine 76–7 and n. 276;
rejects Malebranche's *généralité* 38–
9; *Traité du libre arbitre* 70–2; use of
Scripture 73–4
Boursier, Laurent: attack on
Malebranche from demi-Jansenist
standpoint in *De l'action de Dieu* 32–3
and nn. 126–31
Bréhier, Émile, 'Les lectures
malebranchistes de Rousseau' 15 n.
64, 93 n. 335
Brunschvicg, Léon 10 n. 45
Brush, Craig 83 n. 299

Calvinism: Bayle's reading of 87;
Bossuet's critique of 71–2; Jansenius
accused of 7–8; Malebranche's
critique of 65; Pascal's critique of
10–12
Cana, wedding-feast of 98
Ceyssens, Lucien 6 n. 28
charity: Leibniz on justice as charity of
the wise 49; in Malebranche's *Nature
et grâce* 126, 191; as 'order' in
Malebranche's *Traité de Morale* 45–6
Chomsky, Noam: on *Port-Royal
Logic* 10 n. 44
Christ, Jesus 12, 48, 50, 62 ff., 110,
112–13, 120 ff.
Connell, Desmond: *The Vision of God*

(on Malebranche) 46 n. 175
Cornet, Nicolas: identifies 'five
propositions' in Jansenism 6; *Oraison
funèbre* preached by Bossuet 69
Costabel, Pierre 52 n. 195
Council of Trent 94
Cum Occasione (papal bull against 'five
propositions' in Jansenism) 6

David, King 88, 148, 159
de Mairan, Dortous: letter from
Malebranche 55
Delmont, Théodore, *Bossuet et les Saints
Pères* 13 n. 55
Descartes, René: Cartesian constancy in
nature (for Malebranche) 1, 14, 28;
Cartesianism xi, 37–9; his *De l'homme*
inspires Malebranche xi; letter to
Mersenne on grace and Pelagianism
54 n. 205; occasionalism in Cartesianism
52–4; his *Reply to the Six Objections*
criticized by Malebranche and
Leibniz 3 and n. 8, 38; treated by
Leibniz 37–8; treated by Rousseau in
Institutions chymiques 102
Dreyfus, Ginette: on Malebranche 1 n.
1, 39 n. 155, 64 n. 238; on original
edition of *Nature et grâce* xv; on
philosophical importance of *Nature et
grâce* 13; *Volonté selon Malebranche*
51 n. 192, 52 n. 195, 60 n. 225
Du Tertre, Rodolphe 25–6

Edict of Nantes 83–4
Escobar y Mendoza, Antonio 87

Faydit, Pierre-Valentine 39 and n. 153
Fénelon, François de Salignac de la
Mothe: critic of Malebranche as
destroyer of *Providence
particulière* 78–9; critic of
Malebranche's theory of general will
of God 1, 64, 77 ff.; on defects of
Malebranche's theory of grace 50 and
n. 189; Malebranche's letter to
(1713) 56; *Réfutation du . . . Père
Malebranche* 13 and n. 56, 50, 64,
77 ff.; treatment of Bossuet's *Histoire
universelle* 78–9; treatment of grace
and predestination in letters to
Lami 79–80

'five propositions', *see* Jansenius, Cornelius

Fontenelle, Bernard de: critique of Malebranche 13

Gaberel, Jean Pierre 95 n. 346

general will: 'always right' in Rousseau's *Du contrat social* 28; 'antecedent' will in Scholastic theology as ancestor of general will 4 and n. 18; Bossuet's hostility to 70–1; Fénelon's treatment of in letters to Lami 13, 79–80; first used by Arnauld in defence of Jansenius 5 ff.; general will of citizen in Rousseau 28; general will of God to save all men: in Arnauld 5 ff.; in Augustine 3–4, 8–9; in Bossuet 79–80; in Malebranche 3, 128; in 1 Timothy 3; God governs nature and grace by general wills and general laws (in Malebranche) 1–2, 46, 51, 126 ff., 195 ff.; Shklar's treatment of 1 n. 1

Genesis, Book of: Malebranche's 'Cartesian' rejection of 28

Geneva 94–5

Gouhier, Henri xv, 2 and n. 7, 13 n. 56, 45, 48 n. 182, 54 n. 202, 77 n. 278

grace: in Arnauld 9–10; Christ as distributor of, in Malebranche's *Nature et grâce* 39, 62 ff., 132 ff.; Pascal on sufficient and efficient grace in *Écrits sur la grâce* 11–12; Rousseau's view that 'all' receive the same grace 93 ff.

Grotius, Hugo: on 'eternal verities' 38 and n. 151

Grua, Gaston 14 n. 58, 37 n. 145

Guérolt, Martial: on Malebranche 39 n. 155

Habert, Isaac 5–6

Herod 167

Hobbes, Thomas: correspondence with Mersenne 5 n. 24; criticized by Leibniz 34 and n. 137; criticized by Malebranche 34; on God's irresistible power in *Leviathan* 34 and n. 136; linked with Spinoza by Locke 61 and n. 228; on perception 52 and n. 196

Jansenism 2, 6 ff., 26, 65, 107–8

Jansenius (Jansen), Cornelius: Arnauld's defence of 5 ff.; author of

Augustinus 4; Bossuet's critique of 69–70; general will of God not in *Augustinus* 4 and n. 17; Malebranche's critique of xii, 2, 10, 14, 21, 32 ff., 65, 107–8; orthodox use of Augustine 8–9; Pascal's defence of 10–13; on Paul's 'God wills that all men be saved' 8–9; Rousseau's treatment of in *Lettres écrites de la montagne* 94–5 and n. 345; use of term 'particular will' of God 14 n. 17

Jaquelot, Isaac: his Malebranchism attacked by Bayle 88–91

Jews 19, 159–60, 165 ff.

John, Gospel according to: treated by Malebranche in *Nature et grâce* 206–7, 214

Julie de Wolmar: character in Rousseau's *La Nouvelle Héloïse* 92–3; defends *Providence particulière* and questions Malebranchian *généralité* 92–3; letter-exchange with St Preux 15, 92–3

Jurieu, Pierre xii, xviii, 22 and n. 94, 39 and n. 152

justice: as 'charity of the wise' in Leibniz 49–50 and n. 187; as general law with no particular exceptions in Bayle's *Pensées diverses* 82; in Malebranche's *Nature et grâce* 17 ff.; in Pascal's *Écrits sur la grâce* 11–12

Kant, Immanuel: doubts about mechanism in biology (*Critique of Judgement*) 102; on Malebranche as a 'father' of modern philosophy xii–xiii; on moral necessity in *Critique of Pure Reason* 57 and n. 214

Labrousse, Elizabeth 81 n. 290, 83 n. 298

Lami, François, Fénelon's letters to 79 ff.

Leibniz, G. W.: on best of all possible worlds 49–50; compared to Malebranche 35 ff., 66; criticizes Descartes 37–8; critique of Hobbes 35 ff.; defends Malebranche in *Theodicée* xii, 1, 13–14; on justice as 'charity of the wise' 49–50 and n. 187; letter to Malebranche 25; on Malebranche's 'relations of perfection' 43–4; *Meditation on*

Leibniz, G. W. (*cont.*):
Common Concept of Justice 38; notion
of general will of God in *Theodicée* 5
n. 20; *Opinion on the Principles of
Pufendorf* 4 n. 13, 34 and n.
158, 43–
4; shares Platonic anti-Hobbes-ism
with Malebranche 37–8; 'universal
jurisprudence 4; on will of God in
Conversation sur la liberté 37
Locke, John: criticism of Malebranche's
occasionalism 45, 56–7; criticism of
Malebranche's theory of will xii, 61–
2; on laws as moral 'relations' in
Essay 60–1; Malebranche's criticism
of Locke's theory of perception 56–7;
Spinoza and Hobbes as determinists
61
Louis XIV, King of France: Bayle's
criticism of Louis' revocation of Edict
of Nantes 84–5; and Malebranche xi
Lovejoy, A. O.: *The Great Chain of
Being* 44 n. 172
Luther, Martin: criticized by Bossuet
71–2

McCracken, Charles J.: *Malebranche and
British Philosophy* 218
MALEBRANCHE, NICOLAS: accused of
ruining Providence by Jurieu 22
on charity as love of 'order' 45–6
on Christ: as occasional cause of
distribution of grace 39, 62 ff., 80,
180 ff.; as 'saviour' of
Malebranche's philosophy 50
compared to: Aristotle 56, 66;
Kant 57; Leibniz 25, 37 ff., 44–5;
Rousseau 91 ff.
on consent as suspension of motives in
Prémotion physique 59
correspondence: with de Mairan 55;
with Fénelon on *pyrrhonisme* 56 and
n. 210
Creation as particular will of God 22
criticized by: Arnauld 30–1;
Bayle 83 ff.; Bossuet 27 and n.
210, 70 ff.; Boursier 32–4; Du
Tertre 25–6; Fénelon 77 ff.;
Leibniz 35 ff., 43–4; Locke 56–7;
Régis 29–30; Sainte-Beuve xv, 64
n. 238
deism as outgrowth of Malebranchism
50
devotion to St Augustine 43, 55,

107–8
early use of general will in *Recherche*
14–15
editions of *Nature et grâce* between
1680 and 1712 xiv–xvi
Entretiens sur la métaphysique 40, 44,
48, 75
on free will 58 ff., 169 ff.
his fusing of Cartesianism and
Christianity xi
general will and general law express
God's wisdom 15, 128 ff.
God acts by general wills xii, 15, 40,
116–18, 158
God should avoid particular wills as
'lawless' 6, 118–19, 129
God should not deviate from
Providence générale to prevent Fall
of Adam 24–5
God's omnipotence exaggerated by
some theologians 35
on Hobbes 34, 56
influence of Cartesianism xii, 27–8
on Jansenism xii, 2, 10, 14, 21, 32 ff.,
65, 107–8
laws of motion 117, 140
legalizes general will in *Recherche* and
Nature et grâce 17–18, 40
life of xi–xiii
on love of general order in *Traité de
morale* 18, 41–5
Méditations chrétiennes 19, 29, 41, 47,
51, 97 n. 354
his *Nature et grâce* popularizes idea of
divine general will 6–7, 15 ff.
Nature et grâce written in response to
Arnauld 6–7, 14, 23–4
nature as model for grace 16, 27, 65–6
occasionalism 22, 51 ff., 139 ff.,
201 ff.
particular will as sterile and
unintelligent 16, 118
particularism as morally defective 15,
17, 20, 22–3
Recherche de la vérité xi, xv, 14, 41,
53–4, 59, 196, 202
Réflexions sur la prémotion physique xii,
24–5, 32 ff., 40, 59 ff.
rejection of scriptural 'anthropologies'
20 ff., 32, 50, 66
relations of perfection and
suitability 41 ff.
Traité de l'amour de Dieu 68

'we see all things in God' 54 and n.
202, 55
Malesherbes, Chrétien Guillaume de
Lamoignon de 96
Marie-Thérèse d'Autriche, Queen of
France: treated by Bossuet 70
Matthew, gospel according to 4; treated
by Fénelon 80 and n. 289
Mersenne, Marin: defends general
salvation in correspondence with
Rivet 5 and n. 22; Descartes's letter
to 54 n. 205
Miel, Jan: on Pascal 12 n. 49
Molina, Luis de 4
Molyneux, William 61
Montaigne, Michel de: called one of
'four great poets' by Montesquieu xii;
treated by Oakeshott viii
Montesquieu, Charles Secondat, Baron
de: calls Malebranche a great poet xii
Moses (Old Testament) 28, 123

Newton, Isaac 100
Nicole, Pierre 6 n. 25

Oakeshott, Michael: dedication to v;
interpreter of Augustine and
Montaigne viii

Paquier, J.: *Le Jansénisme* 65 n. 241
particular will: God acts rarely by
particular wills in Malebranche's
Nature et grâce 16 ff., 128 ff.; God
must act by particular wills to realize
justice in Arnauld 30 ff.; God should
have willed particularly to prevent Fall
of Adam in Bayle 89–90; successor to
'consequent' will in Scholastic
theology 4
Pascal, Blaise: Christ's death redeems
only the elect 11–13; critique of
Pelagianism 11–12; *Écrits sur la
grâce* 10–12; follows Augustine's
Enchiridion 12; God's pre-lapsarian
general will to save all replaced by pity
for elect 10–13; grace, sufficient and
efficient 11–12; justice of God's
abandoning general will to save all
men 11–12; *Lettres provinciales* 87;
presentation of Jansenism as orthodox
Augustinianism 10–12
Paul, St: Ephesians, letter to, cited by
Malebranche 202–3; Romans, letter

to ('hath not the potter power over the
clay'), Jansenist reading of 69–70; 1
Timothy 2: 4 ('God wills that all men
be saved') xvii, 3, 6, 69–70;
interpreted by Arnauld 6–9;
interpreted by Augustine 8;
interpreted by Bossuet 69–70;
interpreted by Malebranche 21, 35,
63–4, 149
Pelagius (and Pelagianism) 1, 4, 7, 64
Plato: compared to Rousseau 100;
eternal verities of mathematics and
morals (*Euthyphro* and *Phaedo*) taken
up by Leibniz and Malebranche 1, 3,
34–5, 38; treated by Malebranche as
basis of Augustinianism 37
Porte, Jean la 6 and n. 25
Postigliola, Alberto 8 and n. 35
Prosper, St 9
Pyrrhonism: feared by Malebranche 56

Quesnel, Pasquier 14
quietism: and Fénelon 68

Régis, Pierre-Sylvain 29–30 and n. 115
relations (*rapports*): Malebranche on
morality as 'relations of perfection' in
Morale 40 ff.
Revelation, Book of: treated by
Malebranche 166
Richelieu, Cardinal 5–6
Rivet, André (Calvinist theologian) 5–6
Robinet, André 26 n. 105, 36 n. 142
Rodis-Lewis, Geneviève: on Descartes
29 n. 115; on Malebranche as 'greatest
French metaphysician' xvi and n. 3
Roman emperors: treated by
Malebranche 159–60
Rousseau, Jean-Jacques: against
Fénelon's theory of particular
grace 93; agrees with Malebranche in
rejecting scriptural 'anthropology' 96;
appeals to Vauvenargues's
authority 94; Bréhier's reading of 93;
Christ not miracle-worker 96–8; as
citoyen de Genève 92; compared to
Arnauld 97–8; compared to
Kant 102; compared to Locke 100;
Confessions describe knowledge of
17th-century theology 99–100;
correspondence with Malesherbes on
grace in *La Nouvelle Héloïse* 96;

Rousseau, Jean-Jacques (*cont.*):
denounces particular grace in *La Nouvelle Héloïse* 95–6; distribution of grace must be general 95–6; *Émile* 91; general laws of nature in *Institutions chymiques* 100–2; general will 'always right' 28; as heir of 17th-century theology 91–2; on Jansenism and 'five propositions' 94–5, 98; *Lettre à Christophe de Beaumont*, Archbishop of Paris 99; *Lettres écrites de la montagne* show hostility to miracles 73, 94–5; particular grace as unjust 93–4; poem, 'Le Verger des Charmettes' 100; *Profession de foi* 98–9; ranks Malebranche with Plato and Locke 100; relation to Malebranche 91, 98 ff., 102; St Preux's Malebranchian *généralité* in *La Nouvelle Héloïse* 15, 92–3; St Preux's rejection of miracles and prayer 96–7; on Savoyard Vicar's love of order 98–9; theological controversies in Geneva, 94–5; Vauvenargues as link between Pascal and Rousseau 95

St Cyran, Duvergier de Hauranne, Abbé de 4 and n. 17
St Preux (character in Rousseau's *La Nouvelle Héloïse*) 15, 92–6, 100
Sainte-Beuve, Charles Augustin: *Port-Royal* xv, 39 and n. 154, 64 n. 238
Scotus, Duns 38
Scripture: viewed by Malebranche as

'full of anthropologies' xv, 20 ff., 32, 50, 66, 136 ff.; viewed sceptically: by Bayle 84–5, by Rousseau 93–4
Sedgwick, Alexander: *Jansenism in Seventeenth-Century France* 6 nn. 26–8
Sellier, Philippe: on Augustine and Pascal 12 n. 49
Shklar, Judith: article 'the general will' 1 n. 1
Simon, Richard 75
Spink, J. S. 95 n. 345
Spinoza, Baruch 61
Suarez, Francesco 5 n. 19

Taylor, Thomas (translator of Malebranche's *Nature et grâce*) 102
Timothy, letter to, *see* Paul, St
Tronchin, R. 94

Unigenitus (papal bull): condemns Jansenism 14

Vassor, Michel de: and Malebranche's *Nature et grâce* 14
Vauvenargues, Luc de Clapiers, Marquis de 95
Voltaire, François-Marie Arouet de: defends Malebranche's theology of divine general will 35; on 'naturalization' of grace 72 and n. 261

Walton, Craig 40 n. 156
Warens, Mme de 99